W9-BAX-697

Rule by Incarnation

Also of Interest

Mongolia's Culture and Society, Sechin Jagchid and Paul Hyer

Nepal: Profile of a Himalayan Kingdom, Leo E. Rose and John T. Scholz

The People's Republic of China: A Handbook, edited by Harold C. Hinton

Patterns of Change in the Nepal Himalaya, Mark Poffenberger

† *China: A Political History, 1917–1980*, Revised Edition, Richard C. Thornton

† *Pakistan: The Enigma of Political Development*, Lawrence Ziring

† *Japan: Profile of a Postindustrial Power*, Ardath W. Burks

† *A Theory of Japanese Democracy*, Nobutaka Ike

† *Religion and Politics in the Middle East*, edited by Michael Curtis

† Available in hardcover and paperback.

A Westview Special Study

Rule by Incarnation:
Tibetan Buddhism and Its Role in Society and State

Franz Michael
(in collaboration with Eugene Knez;
assisted by Lobsang Lhalungpa and Tashi Densapa)

The 1959 Chinese military takeover of Tibet brought an end to a unique way of life in which Buddhism provided legitimacy to political and social authority in Tibet and served as value system, cultural bond, philosophy of life, and framework for a complex political and social order. The religious-political system of Tibet now exists only in the memories of those who experienced it. This book documents the human heritage and cultural traditions of Tibet's singular society as they developed and existed during a period of several hundred years.

Using Max Weber's framework of the interrelationship between religious ideologies and the emergence of social, economic, and political systems, Franz Michael and his colleagues analyze the concepts that are central to Tibetan Buddhism and apply them to the Tibetan people, their social and political order, and their way of life. Much of the study is based on interviews with Tibetans in exile—from incarnations and highly placed ecclesiastical and secular government leaders to farmers, herdsmen, and housewives. The result is important not only as the record of a culture, but also as it is related by the authors to the broader issue of the modernization of non-Western traditional societies.

Franz Michael is professor emeritus at George Washington University, where he was associate director and director of the Institute for Sino-Soviet Studies from 1964 to 1972. Earlier he served in academic and administrative positions on the faculties of Johns Hopkins University and the Far Eastern Department and the Far Eastern and Russian Institute of the University of Washington. Born in Germany, Dr. Michael resigned from the German diplomatic service in 1933 and taught at a National University in China, prior to and during World War II, before coming to the United States.

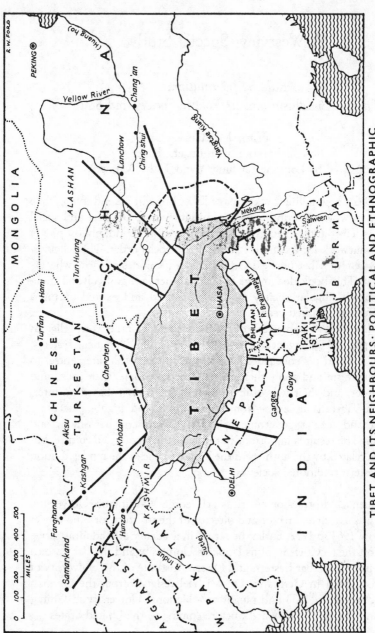

TIBET AND ITS NEIGHBOURS: POLITICAL AND ETHNOGRAPHIC

Shaded area: Political Tibet
Broken line: Limits of Ethnographic Tibet
Radiating lines: Extent of Tibetan influence in 6th to 10th centuries

Source: A Short History of Tibet by H. E. Richardson. Copyright © by H. E. Richardson.

Rule by Incarnation

Tibetan Buddhism and
Its Role in Society and State

Franz Michael

Westview Press / Boulder, Colorado

A Westview Special Study

Published in 1982 in the United States of America by
Westview Press, Inc.
5500 Central Avenue
Boulder, Colorado 80301
Frederick A. Praeger, Publisher

Library of Congress Cataloging in Publication Data
Michael, Franz H.
  Rule by incarnation.
  (A Westview special study)
  Includes index.
  1. Buddhism and state—China—Tibet. 2. Tibet (China)—Politics and government.
3. Tibet (China)—Social conditions. I. Title.
BQ7576.M52   322'.1'09515   81-16130
ISBN 0-86531-226-5   AACR2

Printed and bound in the United States of America

Contents

Illustrations

Preface

The mystique of Tibet—land of snowy peaks, of lamas, and of outgoing and cheerful mountain people—has always attracted students of human history, but it is the uniqueness of the Tibetan story that gives it its special place in the course of great human cultural traditions. Tibetan Buddhism created a state that was sui generis in its system as well as its goals, and that state must be analytically explored not only for its own sake but also for the sake of a comparative grasp of the broader intellectual problems in our fast-moving world.

Western scholarship has been slow in adjusting its conceptual and analytical frameworks to the great non-Western societies, particularly to the relationship between ideologies and the political, social, and economic systems. Max Weber has been the pioneer, and his studies of Confucianism, Hinduism, and Buddhism and their impact on the life of the societies in which they flourished have, together with Weber's other famous works, provided a new approach to the analysis of the non-Western world. Following Weber's approach, we venture in this study to describe and analyze the Tibetan religiopolitical order by tracing the particular concepts Tibetan Buddhism provided and applied to the Tibetan people—to their social and political order—and the way of life that resulted.

The timing of the study was dictated by political events. The Chinese Communist takeover of Tibet in 1959 ended the Tibetan polity in its homeland, and the large number of Tibetan refugees in India and elsewhere means that a new source of information is available. But those who have firsthand experience of the past are advancing in age, and their valuable knowledge has to be gained while they are alive and their memories are clear. Together with documentary library sources, secondary studies by leading Tibetologists, and other reports, interviews with those Tibetans in exile were a major source for this study.

My collaborator, Dr. Eugene Knez, formerly of the Smithsonian and an anthropologist with a special interest in the Himalayan border areas, helped in planning the project and editing the manuscript. He also traveled with me to Dharamsala, Mussoorie, Sikkim, and Ladakh, where we conducted a great number of interviews with Tibetans from all levels of life—from incarnations and ecclesiastical and secular officials of all ranks to ordinary farmers, herdsmen, and housewives—and all readily told us their stories. To them we want to express our deep gratitude and sympathy. Neither of us speaks Tibetan, and we were ably assisted in the interviews by a young Tibetan scholar, Tashi Tsering, presently at the Library of Tibetan Works and Archives in Dharamsala. The director of that institution, Gyatso Tsering, has most generously assisted us.

The major work in Washington was done with the assistance of two Tibetan scholar-informants, Lobsang Lhalungpa and Tashi Densapa (Barmiok Rinpoche). Lobsang Lhalungpa, who has done much scholarly work of his own and has worked with leading Tibetologists, has had extensive experience in many branches of the Tibetan government and is blessed with an encyclopedic memory. His far-reaching knowledge of the intricacies of Tibetan Buddhism, of the practice of ecclesiastical and secular administration, and of Tibetan life in general has been a rich source of information for this work. We are deeply grateful for his constant willingness to contribute from the great store of his learning and for his patience. Tashi Densapa, deputy director of Cultural Affairs, government of Sikkim, has been a solicitous helper in our work. Both he and Lobsang Lhalungpa have shared our personal commitment to this record of Tibetan culture.

At the final stage, we had the most generous and invaluable help of E. Gene Smith, presently field director of the U.S. Library of Congress office in New Delhi and a foremost student of Tibet. He read the whole manuscript and contributed important corrections and additions. Gisela Minke, a world traveler who is keenly interested in the Tibetan people, the Himalayan borderlands, and especially Ladakh, has done a judicious job of typing. I admit my responsibility for the conceptual framework, the analysis, and the writing of this study—and any mistakes.

To make it all possible, we had a one-year grant from the National Endowment for the Humanities and a second small grant from the Earhart Foundation. We are beholden to them for their confidence and understanding. Our special thanks are due to the Library of Congress for providing space for our work and generous assistance in the use of its Tibetan material.

Franz Michael
Washington, D.C.

1
Introduction

The Tibetan Polity: Rule by Incarnation

Over the last centuries of its history, the Tibetan polity and its culture have been decisively shaped by Buddhism, which, having originated in India, assumed particular characteristics in the Tibetan setting, both in its doctrine and in its practice. It was thus possible for Buddhism to provide not only a religious system for the Tibetan people but, combined and integrated with it, political, social, and economic structures that set Tibet apart from all other great cultural traditions as a unique human order in which all leadership was in religious hands and the ultimate purpose of all human action was believed to be the liberation of all sentient beings. This sociopolitical system was sanctioned by the general acceptance of particular Buddhist teachings that became an unquestioned and self-contained force of tradition on which all authority was based.

Because of the dominance of religion over the Tibetan polity, this system has often been called a theocracy, but the term is not really appropriate, because Buddhism does not recognize a divinity (*theos*) but rather a spiritual essence in which all beings partake. According to this belief, the degree of enlightenment reached by each being in its present existence determines its future existence in a chain of rebirth. The final goal is liberation, which is attained by breaking the chain of rebirth and physical existence and entering into Nirvana, a state of undefinable bliss.

Religious teachers provide not only spiritual but also political and social leadership for all who move toward the goal of liberation. The general Tibetan term for these teachers is *lama*, a direct translation of the Sanskrit word *guru*. In the Tibetan system, however, the status of lama came to denote much more than the original master-disciple relationship that characterized the guru. There were, in fact, three types of sanctions for the immense authority and charisma that the lama enjoyed. They depended on three different kinds of lineage through which the authority and the charisma were transmitted from a former to the present holder. Traditionally the lineage was based on transmittance of the pedigree of teaching from the recognized master to the selected student, whom the master initiated

1

into his own metaphysical insight and state of enlightenment. This transmittance led the recipients to paramount positions in the monastic hierarchy, those of the abbots of the great monasteries or famous scholars who in turn selected favorite disciples to carry on their roles. To this intellectual lineage was later added a biological one; it was believed that the charisma could be passed from generation to generation in a meritorious family whose members had obtained, through special sutras or texts, a unique link to enlightenment.

The last and most important lineage was derived from the basic Buddhist idea of rebirth—the concept of the reimbodiment of a saintly predecessor's existence in a reincarnation of the same being in a new appearance, discovered anywhere in a child born at the right time and recognized by the leading monks and lamas. The belief in living reincarnations, so-called Living Buddhas, was made possible by the emphasis in Tibetan Buddhism on the concept of *bodhisattvas*, beings who have reached a state of enlightenment that would enable them to enter Nirvana but who are voluntarily being reborn in order to assist (out of compassion) in the liberation of all fellow beings. A bodhisattva was believed to be able to manifest himself in innumerable embodiments or incarnations. On the basis of this belief, there were in Tibet numerous lineages of incarnations, which formed the apex of the spiritual, social, and political leadership in a hierocracy headed by the Dalai Lama, the religious and temporal head of the Tibetan polity and nation. This system may well be called "rule by incarnation."

To describe this system as it existed before the Chinese invasion of Tibet in 1959 (and as it is still reflected in the refugee communities in India) and to describe the continued charismatic role of the Dalai Lama, it will be necessary to draw on the past for a short analytical examination of the stages of religiopolitical development as they evolved after Buddhism first reached Tibet. The focus of this study, however, is on the fully matured religiopolitical order of the last four centuries. We begin this introductory chapter with a description of the physical and human setting of Tibet, then turn to a discussion of the main tenets of the Buddhist faith as it was practiced in Tibet, and conclude with a short analysis of Max Weber's theoretical concepts as they bear on this study of Tibetan polity.

Land and People

Tibet, popularly known as "the roof of the world," is in the center of Asia; it is a land of high plateaus and river valleys surrounded by snowy mountain ranges, and—because of its altitude—it geographically dominates the surrounding Asian scene. The altitude and the problem of access through the high mountain barriers made communication with the rest of the world dif-

View from Phiang monastery in Ladakh toward the Indus River valley and snow mountains (photo by Franz Michael and Eugene Knez).

ficult and contributed to a degree of isolation that favored a unique form of human intellectual and social development. The isolation, in turn, contributed to a lack of knowledge and understanding of Tibet by the outside world and to the creation of a mystique that often clouded the Tibetan reality. Although the geographical setting was a factor in shaping the emerging Tibetan culture, it should not overshadow the intellectual, social, and political aspects of Tibetan life—our main theme.

The geographical setting of Tibet is much more varied than is often assumed. The central Tibetan river valleys of the Brahmaputra River (Tsangpo)* and its tributaries, at an altitude of 11,000 feet and above, provide the basis for an irrigated agriculture that colors the landscape with the lush green of cultivated fields and a variety of crops. The surrounding mountains are barren—violet and brown up to the snow level on their southern slopes—because of the impact of the sun and the scarcity of rainfall. The more protected northern slopes often have some sparse forests and some grass cover and can thus serve as pastureland.

In the western region of Tibet, the upper courses of the Indus (Sengye Khabab), the Sutlej (Langchen Khabab), and the Ganges (Macha Khabab) rivers provide a similar setting for irrigated agricultural cultivation at a level of 12,000 feet and above, and the mountains form the same stark background for the western Tibetan landscape as they do in central Tibet. Those three western rivers and the Brahmaputra, which from its origin runs through the whole of central Tibet, all originate in western Tibet near the large and famous Turquoise Lake (Mapham Yutsho; Indian, Manasarovar). Near the lake stands Mount Tise (Indian, Mount Kailash). The lake and mountain are sacred to both Hindus and Buddhists.

In contrast to the central and western landscape, which may be regarded as the most typical Tibetan scenery, the much more extensive northern steppe country is largely dry and provides limited pastureland for nomad life. This stretch of windy desert and steppe plateau is crisscrossed by mountain ranges and is frequently dotted by salt lakes. Because of its geographical inhospitality to human life, it is the least populated region of Tibet.

The eastern and southeastern regions of Tibet are much more suited to both agricultural life and animal husbandry and are therefore as densely populated as the central part of the country. The lowest areas of habitation are 4,000 to 7,000 feet, but people also live at the 12,000-foot level. Because the rainfall is greater here than in the central and western regions, the mountains are covered with evergreens and in the southeast, with subtropical forests. The amount of rainfall also means that agricultural cultivation is possible without extensive irrigation. In Tibetan folklore eastern

---

*All names and words in parentheses are Tibetan or Sanskrit unless otherwise indicated.

Tibet is the land of four rivers and six mountain ranges. The rivers are the upper courses of the Yellow River (Machu; in Chinese, Hwang Ho), the Yangtse (Drichu, with its tributary the Yarlung [Nyagchu]), the Mekong (Zachu), and the Salween (Nagchu). In Tibet they flow in a general northwest-southeast direction, cutting deep valleys and gorges into the mountain ranges of eastern Tibet before descending into western China and/or southeastern Asia. Between the four rivers and their tributaries, the mountainous highlands of eastern Tibet form the six mountain ranges of Tibetan folklore. Tibet is therefore the land of the origin of the four great rivers of East Asia as well as those of the Indian subcontinent. The whole of the Tibetan highlands generally slopes from west to east.

Tibet, located approximately between the 27th and 38th parallels of northern latitude and the 78th and 101st of eastern longitude, is demarcated in the south by the high mountain ranges of the Himalayas and in the north by those of the Kunlun (or Kuen Lun) and Altyn Tagh. The western and eastern borders of Tibet are composed of river gorges and high mountain ranges. Although these also present natural obstacles to the traveler or the invader, they have permitted somewhat easier access.

The mountainous area of Ladakh, to the west, is Tibetan in its location and features and largely peopled by Tibetans with a Tibetan culture and lifestyle. It has at times been incorporated into the Tibetan polity; however, the rugged passageways through the narrow gorges of the upper Indus River enabled Ladakh to maintain its political independence under a local dynasty until the nineteenth century, when it was conquered by the Dogra raja of Jammu.[1] Ultimately Ladakh became a part of the Union of India, along with Jammu and Kashmir, of which it is a part.

In eastern Tibet, the Chinese governments of Imperial China, the Republic of China, and the People's Republic of China have each sliced off areas of Tibetan territory and incorporated them into their adjacent provinces, until finally all of Tibet was invaded by and merged into the People's Republic of China as the Tibet Region of China. In speaking of Tibet, it is therefore necessary to distinguish the geographic and ethnic entity from the political unit.[2] This distinction explains the differences often encountered in the data given by various authors concerning the size of the population and the square mileage of the country. At its largest extent, Tibet covered an area of an estimated 850,000 to 900,000 square miles, and before the Chinese occupation, the political boundaries of Tibet encompassed 500,000 square miles. What is left of the area within the Chinese system as the Tibet Region of China, which includes only central and western Tibet, covers approximately 300,000 square miles according to Chinese claims.[3]

The same uncertainty exists in regard to the Tibetan population, and the figures vary from two million to eight million. These figures not only reflect

View from the road to Phiang monastery in Ladakh (photo by Eugene Knez).

a difference between ethnic and political criteria, but in the absence of any census, they are clearly vague estimates. Richardson, perhaps the best foreign authority, has given a figure of two million to three million for political Tibet before the Chinese occupation.[4] The official ethnic figure given by the Dalai Lama in exile is six million.[5]

Before the Chinese takeover, the large majority of the Tibetan people lived in villages or in monasteries; a much smaller number lived in nomadic camps. However, in the centers of administration and of trade and craft a distinctly urban life had emerged. As was the case in other non-European areas, the towns of Tibet did not flourish outside the established political order or in contrast to it. The three major urban centers—Lhasa, Shigatse, and Gyantse—were all seats of central or provincial administrations and grew in part because of that administrative role. They became centers for religious life, as important temples and monasteries were situated around or near them. They also became centers of trade and crafts, and because of the entrepreneurial spirit that pervaded in those trades, and because of the lack of government control and interference, each became a locale for the formation of an urban and a "middle-class" society.

The old castle at Leh in Ladakh (photo by Franz Michael and Eugene Knez).

The Potala Palace (photo by David T. Parry).

Lhasa, the seat of the Dalai Lama's government and dominated in the background by the magnificent Potala Palace, was the unquestioned religious, political, economic, and social center of the country. Shigatse, the seat of a governor and of the monastic establishment of the Panchen Lama at Tashilhunpo, was similarly of great importance. Gyantse, on the trade route from India and at the fork in the road that led to Lhasa and Shigatse, was also the seat of a governor. All three towns were famous not only for their temples and monasteries, but also for their craftsmen, and all were important centers of trade. Each of them, especially Lhasa, contained a considerable number of foreign traders and professionals—chiefly Indian, Nepalese, and Chinese—and some Muslim inhabitants.

The racial origin of the Tibetan people is still a matter of uncertainty. Even today physical anthropologists have not conducted systematic observations and measurements, either in Tibet proper or among the Tibetan refugees in Indian territories. From what has been done, it appears that at least two main racial strains contributed to the makeup of the Tibetan population. Part of the population is long-headed and tall, often with aquiline noses and sharp facial features; the other is round-headed and shorter in stature, with higher cheekbones and less pronounced nose-bridges. Speculation has it that the round-headed, shorter type, which predominates in the agricultural valleys of central and western Tibet, may be

Great Chorten in Gyantse, with Tibetan cart and family in foreground (photo by Betty Goff C. Cartwright).

the stock of the earliest settlers. The long-headed type is chiefly found among the nomads in the North and East and in the Kham and Amdo regions among agricultural as well as nomad sections of the population. This type is also characteristic of the aristocratic families throughout Tibet. One theory proposes that this type came from the north, imposed its power, and came to dominate the original inhabitants of the valleys. All we know for sure is that the Tibetans appear to be a racial mixture of these and possibly other strains—and indeed every great human civilization has been based on such biological intermixtures.

As in other cultural traditions, Tibetan legend has its own account of the origin of the Tibetan race. According to the myth, Tibetans descend from the union of a mountain monkey and a female demon. They were said to have lived together at Tsetang in the Yarlung River valley, the region of Tsang that was the first political center of ancient Tibet, and pilgrims have been shown caves near Tsetang, in the mountain of Gongpori, where these legendary ancestors allegedly lived.[6] In later representations, the monkey was identified with an incarnation of Chenrezi or Avalokitesvara, representing the compassionate aspect of the Buddha. The female ogre became a tara in later legend.[7]

According to some tales, six children were the offspring of the couple, divided in their personalities according to the characteristics of their parents. Those taking after the father were mild and compassionate, intelligent, and sensitive, and those taking after the mother were fierce and wrathful and fond of sinful pursuits. In this way Tibetans have liked to explain their own natural inclinations. Less fantastic is another Tibetan legend that explains the origins of the Tibetan royal dynasty. According to the Blue Annal, the dynasty descended from a group of Indians who—under their chief or military commander, King Rupati of the Kaurava tribe—fled to Tibet during a war with the Pandava.[8]

Whoever the ancestors of the Tibetans—eastern or northern Mongoloids or Caucasoids from the Indian sub-continent[9]—they developed their own uniform Tibetan language, albeit with a number of dialectic versions. Tibetan is regarded by most Western comparative linguists as belonging to the Tibeto-Burman language group, which used to be tabulated as a subgroup of a Sino-Tibetan language family—the other major subgroup being Sino-Thai.[10] But the broader classification of a Sino-Tibetan language family has become more questioned of late, while the Tibeto-Burman connection is firmly established. Like Chinese, Tibetan is classified as a monosyllabic language. But the syntactic order of words in a sentence in Tibetan is subject, object, verb, which is similar to the order of Ural-Altaic—and, for that matter, Indian and Japanese languages—but contrary to the order of Chinese and Indo-Germanic languages.[11]

The distinctiveness of the Tibetan language finds its parallel in the Tibetan script, which was introduced at the time of political unification. According to Tibetan histories, the Tibetan script was created in the seventh century, during the reign of King Songtsen Gampo. According to tradition, the author of the script, Thonmi Sambhota, was the sole survivor of a mission that King Songtsen Gampo sent to India for the express purpose of bringing back knowledge about Indian writing that could be introduced into Tibet. It was indeed at that time that the Tibetan script appeared in Tibet in an alphabet closely linked to the Indian Gupta script. It is obviously most significant that as a result, Tibetan writing—indeed, the whole of Tibetan literature—is linked in this way to India because this major cultural factor was a chief tool of the general religious, philosophical, and artistic impact India had on Tibet.

The historicity of Thonmi Sambhota, who, according to Tibetan tradition, became Songtsen Gampo's minister, has been questioned because of the lack of contemporary documents. All we have today are fragments of grammatical writings that date back to that period but were seemingly edited at a later time. The sophistication of these fragments show the influence of the Indian grammarians on the Tibetan author or authors. It may never be possible to say whether the author was the traditionally renowned Thonmi Sambhota or another man, but it seems somewhat tortuous to construct a different authorship if legend—which, in the absence of other data, is a historical source—provides us with this story.[12] The important point is that Tibetan writing came from India and not from China, became sophisticated early, and enabled the development of a rich Tibetan literary tradition that followed its own course. In their language and writing, as well as in their ethnic composition, the Tibetans established their own distinct linguistic and cultural identity.

Tibetan Buddhism

Buddhism was introduced into Tibet in the seventh century A.D., 1,200 years after the life of its founder, the historical Gautama Buddha. Before the introduction of Buddhism, there apparently was no organized religion in Tibet. The early Tibetan religious specialists were magicians and sorcerers who served the needs of individuals and families and protected them against assumed evil spirits that caused disease and misfortune by using incantations, charms, and sacrifices to conjure up and exorcise local spirits. These Tibetan practitioners of the magic arts were probably similar to the shamans of several other Asian preliterate societies, including that in Siberia. The practitioners were believed to have control over forces in nature, communicating with them and gaining from the spirits the power to deal with human problems. They were individual practitioners with essentially no religious organization and no organized system of religious belief. Their practices were referred to as Bon.

In recent research, it has been pointed out that in early times, the word Bon did not refer to any organized religion but simply to the practice of magicians serving local needs, a quasi-religious service that was totally inadequate as the basis of a state organization. The earliest Tibetan kings appear to have established a royal cult, Tsug, to sanction their rule. The cult was linked to a claim of divine origin and to their presumed descent from a heaven that was supported by the high mountains, from which some of the kings were believed to have come. The religion of the mountain gods (*kulha*) was fused with the concept of the magic power of the kings, who were placed between heaven and earth and possessed superhuman force. To maintain their position, the early kings employed a group of diviners and attached them to their courts.[13] In an age that believed in magic, this cult may have sufficed to establish a royal authority above that of the clan chieftains, but it would not suffice as a rational state structure.[14] When Tibetan kings introduced a larger political and social order in the seventh century A.D., they were obviously in need of a broader value system and ideology than what was provided by the earlier religious practices, and they welcomed Buddhism, which gave them such an ideology and, with it—eventually—literacy.

The Buddhism that entered Tibet was already established in the countries and areas surrounding Tibet—northern India, central Asia, and China. At the time, one major branch of Buddhism, Mahayana Buddhism, was one of the leading religious ideologies of much of India and central Asia; it also had a tremendous impact on China and through China, on Korea and Japan. Theravada Buddhism, the other major Buddhist tradition, provided the religion and culture for much of Southeast Asia. A few centuries later, however, after Mahayana Buddhism had reached the height of its intellectual, political, and social role in Tibet, Buddhism in northern India and central Asia was routed by Islam and almost disappeared; in China, Korea, and Japan its power also waned. Although Mahayana Buddhism still remained an important religious force, its challenge to the existing philosophical, religious, political, and social systems in those countries had failed. Tibet, then, became the chief receptacle and sanctuary of this major Buddhist tradition, which remained in force in Tibet until the onslaught of the Chinese Communists in 1959. The faith in and commitment to this Tibetan Buddhist cultural tradition is carried on by the Tibetan refugees in India under the leadership of the Dalai Lama, and many accounts indicate that it has continued under the surface in the Chinese-dominated Tibet Region of China.

This is not the place for a detailed exegesis of the complexity of the Buddhist concepts. For this study of the role of Buddhism in the Tibetan polity it must suffice to recall the basic precepts of the faith and to provide a short account of the schools of Buddhism that contributed to the religious beliefs and practices in Tibet.

The essence of the teachings of Buddha is stated in the Four Noble Truths and the Eightfold Path.[15] The Four Noble Truths are (1) life is sorrow—birth, age, disease, and death are all unavoidable, and the quest is to find liberation from the suffering of this existence; (2) sorrow arises from the sensual craving that binds man to this existence and to the chain of rebirth; (3) liberation lies in ending this craving; and (4) the way to gain liberation is to follow the Eightfold Path.

To follow the Eightfold Path is to gain (1) the right view and understanding of the concepts of the Four Noble Truths; (2) the right aspiration and thought, renouncing the craving for existence and seeking an attitude of equanimity toward life; (3) the right speech, avoiding lying and slander; (4) the right conduct and action, no stealing or appropriating anything to which one is not entitled; (5) the right mode of life, avoiding violence and drunkenness; (6) the right endeavor, not to think evil but to correct and control one's mental state; (7) the right mindfulness to control one's body and feelings; and (8) the right concentration to meditate and awaken one's mind.

What the Buddha taught was the "middle path," a course between ascetic self-castigation and indulgence in sensual delights. The human craving for clinging to the chain of existence (samsara) is due to a cosmic ignorance that includes a delusion of selfhood. The phenomenal universe is impermanent and transient (*anicca*); full of fear, suffering, and pain (*dukkha*); and soulless (*anatta*). Everything perceived through the senses is impermanent. In contrast to the delusion of the empirical world, true freedom from the entanglements of the world can be gained through enlightenment—a state of mind reached through meditation, a freedom that places a being outside the world of phenomena, a state that leads to undefinable bliss, Nirvana. The teachings of the Buddha are the *dharma* (the "wheel of law" that the Buddha set in motion), and the Buddha, the dharma, and the *sangha* ("community of the faithful") are the Three Jewels of the Buddhist faith.

During the centuries after the life of the Buddha and before Buddhism entered Tibet, Buddha's teachings were explored and interpreted by a number of schools and monastic systems that stressed and developed different aspects of the doctrine. Tibetan Buddhism, profiting from this development, consists of a body of thought and practice that combines and fuses the three major schools—Theravada (Hinayana), Mahayana, and Vajrayana. The practical doctrines derived from these three modes of the Buddhist tradition are called the *domsum* (the "three vows" and their concomitant precepts). Every Tibetan order has a domsum of its own that explains the moral codes.

Theravada, the school of the elders and the oldest tradition, stresses the community of Buddha's disciples, the sangha of the *arhats* ("perfected men," united by their knowledge and right conduct). The arhats seek liberation by following the Buddhist law through a monasticism that stresses the rules of monastic discipline (*vinaya*).[16]

Mahayana, meaning "large vehicle," is the chief component of Tibetan Buddhism. The Mahayana followers contrast it to the older school of thought—Theravada—which they call Hinayana, the "small vehicle," a designation the followers of the older tradition do not accept. As the term implies, Mahayana incorporates the fundamental views, techniques of practice, and discipline of the Hinayana school. Indeed all Tibetan monks of the Gelukpa and other sects accept the fundamental precepts of the Theravada tradition.

In that tradition, Buddha's doctrine of the impermanence and flux of mind and matter and Buddha's teaching that all things have no self-entity are understood by the concept that all beings and indeed all things, spiritual and material, are a conglomeration that is reducible to a combination of physical atomic particles and psychic unreducible moments (*skanda*, "five aggregates"), which shape and reshape all temporary reality. These five aggregates are material properties, feelings or sensations, perception of sense-objects, fifty types of mental formations (including tendencies), and consciousness, and they combine to form a given being at the time of its existence. The potential of each human being is to gain insight into this impermanence and nonselfhood to gain a state of liberation that will bring freedom from the chain of rebirth. The way to this state is the path (*lam*) of meditation and of moral conduct, following the rules laid down by the Buddha.

Including these concepts but going beyond them, Mahayana Buddhism follows ontologically the teachings of the great Indian philosopher Nagarjuna of the Madhyamika school (the "school of the middle way") in exploring and interpreting Buddha's message. Nagarjuna postulated that not only the empirical world is unreal, but so are dharma and samsara, which are all part of the cosmic flux. Beyond them is emptiness or the void (*sunyata*), which is the essence of all and incorporates everything. This elaboration of the doctrine of emptiness is one of the major philosophical contributions of the Mahayana school. Its other major tenet, the heart of Mahayana philosophy, is its stress on the concept of bodhisattva.[17] A bodhisattva is an awakened being who, having reached the state of enlightenment, chooses to be reborn, instead of entering Nirvana, out of compassion for all sentient beings and in order to assume the burden of saving them all. In the words of the bodhisattva: "I must bear the burden of all beings, for I have vowed to save all things living. . . . I give myself in exchange. . . . for I have resolved to gain supreme wisdom for the sake of all lives, to save the world."[18]

The concept of bodhisattva—*bodhi* meaning "enlightenment" and *sattva*, "being or essence"—is of tremendous appeal and greatly contributed to the spread of Mahayana Buddhism in central and northeastern Asia. The two chief qualities a bodhisattva is believed to possess are wisdom and compassion. Compassion is the boundless feeling of mercy for all beings, the deepest concern for their lives and dignity and for their liberation from suffering. This compassion is entirely self-effacing, as is stressed in countless stories and parables. Those who believe and, under the bodhisattvas' guidance, strive for liberation have to maintain the same selfless attitude toward all living beings. Only striving for the liberation of all others can lead to one's own enlightenment and liberation. All beings are on the same path, and there is the potential for Buddhahood in everyone.

In following Buddha's teaching that there is no selfhood, no concept of soul in the Western religious sense, Mahayana Buddhists understand rebirth as the continuance of a stream of spiritual energy (*gyü*). The image is that of a river, which continuously discharges and takes on water without losing its identity. What remains of an existence is a bundle of impressions, habits, unfulfilled desires, or accomplishments and merits; realization; and insight. In the case of the incarnation of a bodhisattva, what moves on is the ultimate, the omniscience that results from wisdom, and the all-encompassing compassion that is linked to it. This wisdom means insight into the nature and meaning of life, the causes and effects of events, and the conceived deeper meaning behind the unreality of the phenomenal world.

This concept of the bodhisattva as a redeemer was perhaps a chief reason for the far-flung response to Mahayana Buddhism throughout Asia. The image of an ideal being that personified the noblest concepts of thought and behavior and that was acting, indeed living, for all beings moved the deepest human emotions and adoration of people, regardless of social level, in many countries. In Tibet, however—and later under Tibetan influence in Mongolia—the role of the bodhisattva took on a special significance. In Tibetan Buddhism, these "Buddhas to be" are not only religious concepts but actual living and identifiable beings, the so-called Living Buddhas, incarnations of various bodhisattvas who appear in human form, are discovered as such, and are believed to have been reincarnated time and again in human form to continue their mission of mercy. These incarnations represent both an emanation of a bodhisattva and an earthly lineage of continued existence of human predecessors. The emphasis on and the development of the concept of bodhisattvas, which is a great contribution and a distinctive characteristic of Mahayana Buddhism, thus reached its culmination in Tibet. There the incarnations were not only the apex of the religious conceptual system, but they also provided the political and social leadership for a religiously dominated society.

As there are infinite aspects of Buddha, there are countless bodhisattvas. Among the most revered is Avalokitesvara (Chenrezi), the bodhisattva of action and compassion, who became the chief deity of Tibet and whose emanations are believed to be incarnated as the lineage of the Dalai Lama. Of similar importance are Manjusri, the bodhisattva of transcendental wisdom, and Vajrapani, the bodhisattva whose chief characteristic was power. It was this ability to see Buddha's emanations in many forms that made it possible for Tibetan Buddhism to incorporate and redefine many of the deities and spirits of pre-Buddhist beliefs and to develop a vast Buddhist pantheon that personifies the great multitude of spirits and conceptual beings who are believed to fill the realms of existence and emotions.

The third major strand of Tibetan Buddhism is Vajrayana, a term that has been given a wide range of definitions. In the application of the school's tradition its meaning is that of the indestructible essence of things—hence the symbol of the diamond—and Vajrayana can therefore be rendered as the "adamantine vehicle."[19] The "indestructible essence" refers to the indivisible unity of the external and internal worlds, the inseparability of the form and nature of all things, the nonduality of the self and the phenomenal world, and the contemplative bliss and the transcending insight into its essenceless character experienced by practitioners of Vajrayana.

Organized in East India in the eighth century A.D., the Vajrayana school adds another dimension to the practice and beliefs of Mahayana Buddhism. The new factor is the use of tantric practices—magical, supernatural powers obtained by religious practitioners through their initiations and meditative attainments. The search for magic power has a long history among Indian ascetics—and among magico-religious practitioners the world over—but what distinguishes Vajrayana from this general human history is that in India it became organized into a school of Buddhism, which took its name from Vajra as a symbol of magic power. The sect flourished, established its own monasteries and schools, and extended its influence into Tibet. This is the tradition that gave Tibetan Mahayana Buddhism an extensive body of tantric beliefs, practices, rituals, and texts.

The traditional sources hold that Vajrayana recognizes the hidden higher potential in man's physical aggregates and neuropsychic system and energies, thus widening the scope of human possibilities. Vajrayana propounds many different methods of using those physical and neuropsychic attributes for an immediate awakening through initiations followed by teachings, including secret oral instructions. Considered as being a living and functioning tradition through an ever-expanding awakening and through compassionate deeds, this whole process of higher self-transformation is contingent upon the strict observance of esoteric moral precepts and adequate preparation. Like other aspects of Buddhist philosophy, Vajrayana Buddhism holds that there is no real evil in human consciousness, only a transient defilement, which temporarily obscures the potential for supreme perfection in man's stream of consciousness. The transient defilement takes the forms of passion, prejudice, and delusion, but these can be transformed into spiritual purity.

The role of teachers with knowledge, experience, and compassion is considered as essential as the spiritual devotion of the disciples. The teachers' role is based on and represents the accumulated insight of their lineage predecessors. Both teachers and disciples are required to live scrupulously by what the esoteric tradition describes as the "sacred bond" (*damtsik*). This means that disciples must place their full trust in their teachers, with a pure spiritual attitude and reverence, while each teacher must treat his disciples as his spiritual responsibility. This relationship and its obligations became an intrinsic feature of the system. Indeed, one might state that the fundamental discipline of Tibetan Buddhism is the *guruyana* ("way of the guru").

The Vajrayana tradition is immensely rich in symbolism, much of which can be understood and is meaningful only to trained initiates. The diverse forms of mystical Buddhas, peaceful and wrathful male and female deities, are, in the ultimate sense, symbolic visual representations of aspects of enlightenment already achieved or to be achieved. The entire pantheon falls into five genres of supreme manifestations, the five Buddha families. Each family of deities symbolizes one of the psychophysical aggregates, and five basic aspects of enlightened awareness represent the five purified states of the human emotive defilements—delusion, jealousy, conceit, lust, and hate. Diverse forms of ritual—music, art, dance, etc.—are not only essential aspects of the symbolism and practical aids to meditation, but they are essentially the active process of the awakening itself. The use of ritual mask dances and community recitations of verbal formulas, mantras,[20] are communal rites designed to aid in the practice of the realization of the nonduality of the self and the phenomenal world. They are to be performed at regular intervals to guarantee the physical and spiritual well-being of the community that performs them.

The reason for the great influence on Buddhism of this system of belief in supernatural powers may perhaps be seen in its relationship to the pre-Buddhist indigenous beliefs in Tibet, the magic practices of a former day. As stated earlier, the teachings subsumed by later historians under the term *Bon*—literally, "incantations"—were essentially a belief in the forces of good and evil in nature and in the existence of supernatural forces in the universe that could be dealt with by magic. The goal was to nurture the good forces and control or exorcise the evil ones.[21]

When Buddhism was being introduced into Tibet in the seventh century, Bon was used by people who wanted to resist the new faith. A pro-Buddhist king was forced to yield, foreign priests were temporarily driven off, and a political struggle, complete with assassinations, was fought over the old versus the new religion.

The conflict between Buddhism and Bon was obviously linked to the political strife between the kings, who were attempting to introduce an ideology that could serve their new central authority, and the aristocracy, which was fighting to maintain its power by supporting the faith that believed in the clan deities of old and the magic practices of its sorcerers.[22] In relying on the traditional Tibetan shamanism, the aristocrats could also appeal to Tibetan ethnic pride against the foreign religion and the foreign monks who brought it. But even those opponents of a centralized rule by the kings had to realize the inadequacy of shamanist practices for any emerging political system. So there was an attempt to organize the Bon practices into a religion with its own literature, and this was done largely by copying texts and institutions from the superior Buddhist rival, making the necessary changes in names and conceptual terms. It seems that as a result of the Buddhist competition, Bon became an organized religion,[23] and later records list Bon titles and ranks for officials, presumably to make the case that the Bon religion could have served as the basis for an organized state.

The political struggle led to the fall of the royal house and a period of prolonged disunity. But the attempt to create a synthetic ideology for Bon, so that it might serve a larger political unity, failed—as it had to. The failure is an indication of the obvious limitations of practices of diviners and magicians as the foundation for any centralized government organization that might be needed to handle more than a primitive clan structure. Bon—though transformed by the influence of Buddhism—could not play the larger part assigned to it by the aristocrats. Under the tolerance of the victorious Buddhist system, however, Bon has survived into modern times, with monasteries of its own and localized traditional magic practices.

Buddhism, the newly accepted ideology, had to become assimilated to the Tibetan setting and to come to terms with it. The services that the folk religion had provided were therefore included in Tibetan Mahayana Buddhism for the benefit of the lay population, to replace and give a deeper meaning to Bon shamanist practices. This inclusion in turn strengthened the influence of the Vajrayana school in Tibetan Buddhism. That school's emphasis on tantric practices and forms of magic enabled it to replace the native shamanism and its practices with rituals that related "Buddhist magic" to the philosophy and metaphysics of a doctrine that was much more profound than anything Bon had to offer. Similarly, an Indian philosopher, invited to Tibet to proselyte on a much larger scale than had been attempted before, was chosen for his ability to present the philosophical, metaphysical, and mysterious elements of the faith and because he could combine that ability with a great reputation of magic power, through which, according to legend, he could defeat the native spirits and force them into the service of the Buddhist faith.

The Indian scholar was Padmasambhava, who arrived in Tibet in A.D. 747, and his life history tells of many conversions of Bon and other native spirits and their incorporation as "protectors of religion" into the Buddhist pantheon.[24] Padmasambhava was steeped in the Vajrayana tantric wisdom. It was he who started the practice of leaving "hidden texts" under rocks, in caves, in lakes, or in other out-of-the-ordinary places, texts that were believed to contain spiritual wisdom and revelations and were treasured by contemporary and later finders (*terton*) for their contribution to religious wisdom. Padmasambhava traveled widely in Tibet, and—by himself and together with his much more austere Indian colleague, Santaraksita—he founded temples and the first monasteries and trained disciples in the doctrines and practices of Mahayana Buddhism, thereby becoming one of the most influential and revered Indian masters in Tibet.

Before the eleventh century, there were no broad sectarian divisions in Tibet. Rather the pattern was one in which families and their lineages preserved tantric teachings through texts that were acquired through perilous journeys and the expenditure of a great deal of gold and many presents. Rival families based their religious authority and the political power derived from it on the texts and teachings they possessed and functioned much as religious corporations. When Buddhism was destroyed in the latter part of the twelfth century in Bengal and other parts of India by the onslaught of the fanatical and intolerant Islam, there was a new reason for Indian masters to take refuge in Tibet, and at the same time, Tibetans continued to go to India and Nepal to obtain their teachings and texts from the surviving holy places. By this time religious establishments had been founded in Tibet, and henceforth they were to follow their own traditions.

Once introduced and entrenched in Tibet, the complex Buddhist faith generated, in due course, a number of sects that shared all the basic elements of doctrine and practice but differed in their interpretation of and emphasis on specific aspects of rituals and in the choice of some of the texts on which they concentrated their studies. The Buddhism spread in Tibet by Padmasambhava later became known as Nyingmapa. It was at first the only tradition of Buddhism in Tibet, though it had little in the way of a centralized organization. It included the traditions and teachings of all the schools that had been brought to Tibet by Indian scholars, and it had been conceptually broadened to incorporate local beliefs and deities into its pantheon and doctrinal framework. Nyingmapa was a manifold system that ranged from philosophical, metaphysical, and psychological studies and practices of meditation to the elaborate magic, rites, spells, and mantras. The latter were practiced by religious specialists to serve the laity and also to provide a mystical experience for the practitioners, who, through magic, dealt with the forces in nature and in themselves. Some of these practitioners disregarded the disciplinary vows; their practices included the use of sex between religious teachers and consecrated women, the use of alcoholic beverages, and a disregard of other prohibitions—all justified in the framework of religious practices. In fact, a number of Nyingmapa scholars and followers did not accept the rule of celibacy, were married, and led a family life.

The destructive magic and the excesses of some tantric practitioners brought about a reaction among the laity and the Buddhist teachers themselves and became the chief causes for the founding of new sects and for the reform of religious life and discipline. With the exception of the Indian monk Atisha (Dipankara Atisha, A.D. 980-1052), the leading advocates for reform and the founders of the new sects were no longer Indian but Tibetan scholars, so the foreign religion was transformed into a truly Tibetan cultural tradition.

Three major paths of reform and new doctrinal development were entered upon, all in the eleventh century. The first and most important was introduced by Atisha, who went to Tibet in A.D. 1038 and died there in 1052. Trained by Mahayana masters in India, Atisha promoted reforms of religious life; a formalized structuring of Buddhism, including the three vows (i.e., Theravada, Mahayana, and Vajrayana); and a reform of relationships, which emphasized celibacy and high morality. However he maintained tantric practices and meditation in his curriculum. Through his teachings and writings and the propagation of his ideas by his disciples, Atisha initiated what became a most important reform movement in Tibetan Buddhism. The best known among Atisha's Tibetan disciples was Dromton, who founded the first monastery of the new school at Rading, near Lhasa, in 1058 and became the formal head of the Kadampa sect, the forerunner of the famous Yellow Hats, which eventually became the ruling order of Tibet. In its monastic discipline and return to the teachings of the original Mahayana concepts, the Kadampa sect already included the basic ideas of the later founder of the Yellow Hat order, the Tibetan monk and scholar, Tsongkapa.

Two other schools originated in the same century. The Kagyupa sect (kagyu meaning "oral transmission of secret teachings") is to be traced to the Tibetan yogi Marpa (1012-1096), who had traveled to India and been a student of great Indian masters. Marpa and his student Milarepa (1040-1123) led, for the most part, hermit lives, and their legendary histories characterized them as great magicians who conquered many demons. Marpa was a mystic, famous for his magic powers and translations of tantric texts, and Milarepa was a romantic and a poet. His poetry and the lengendary adventures of his ascetic wanderings make him a widely known and beloved figure in Tibetan folklore.

It was a student of Milarepa, Gampopa,[25] who founded the Kagyupa order, which later divided into four major and eight lesser sects, each organized by a religious family. The Karmapa sect became the most important, and it was to play a major part in Tibetan politics. The head of the Karmapa sect was the first to establish the concept of reincarnation for the head of the sect, and the Gyalwa Karmapa is believed to have been continuously reincarnated up to the present (sixteenth) incarnation. It was this concept, followed soon by all other sects, that transferred the power from the religious families or outside aristocrats to the leading body of monks, who played their part in the discovery of the incarnations and helped to guide them. Like the Dalai Lama of the Gelukpa sect, the Gyalwa Karmapa is believed to be an incarnation of Avalokitesvara, and the two rival cults eventually engaged in a political rivalry, in which the Gelukpa sect prevailed.[26]

The original founder of the Sakya sect was Konchog Gyalpo, who established the Sakya monastery on his ancestral land in 1073. Located on

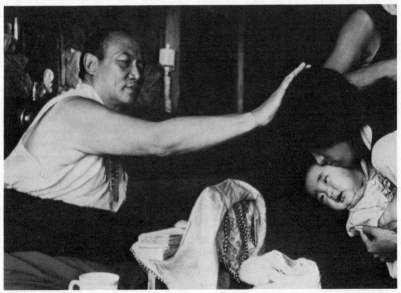

H.H. the Gyalwa Karmapa, blessing a mother and child (photo by Franz Michael and Eugene Knez).

the trade route between Nepal, Lhasa, and other inland centers, and at the point of contact of nomadic and agricultural ways of life, the monastic center flourished and soon became politically powerful. Its best known scholarly head, the Sakya Pandita (1182–1251), together with his nephew Phagpa (1235–1280), was invited by the Mongol Godan Khan to his camp in the Koko Nor (now Tsinghai), in 1244, and the Khan appointed the Sakya Pandita the temporal ruler of Tibet. The nephew, Phagpa, received the same authorization in 1253 from Kublai Khan, who later became emperor of China. These appointments began the so-called client-patron relationship of Tibetan ecclesiastical leaders to Mongol and later Manchu rulers of China. This relationship, by means of which the foreign ruler indirectly extended influence over Tibet, gave the Tibetan religious organization the power to shake off the authority of the Tibetan rulers and the power of the Tibetan aristocracy and enabled it to assume control of the temporal government of the country.

The sects and subsects thus became involved in politics. At first they served the interests of powerful secular families, who would use a sect against family rivals and rival sects. Later a sect itself became the power base of a family that joined the sect and controlled it, proclaiming that the religious complex of teachings of its own sect was superior to that of other sects, though in reality there was no doctrinal division between sects, which emphasized only their specially selected sutras and tantras. With such a claim, the Sakya family and sect gained control over all of Tibet for seventy-five years, until it was replaced by the Phamo Drukpa family and sect for a short period. Finally, however, the concept of incarnation, of a leader selected by the monks, took authority away from the leading families and turned it over to the monks of the various sects, who thus acquired the power that had been denied to them as servants of the ruling houses. It was this very development that created the unique religiopolitical order of Tibet, rule by incarnation.

The most important religious organization in Tibet was that of the Gelukpa sect, known popularly as the Yellow Hat sect, in contrast to the Red Hat sects, a term usually and not quite correctly applied to all other sects. The Gelukpa was founded by the great scholar and reformer Tsongkapa (1357–1419). Tsongkapa entered monastic life in his youth and studied with teachers and texts of all existing schools of religious instruction. His subsequent teaching and writings therefore are a synthesis of many theoretical concepts and ritualistic traditions. Tsongkapa did not introduce any basic innovation of doctrine or ritual, studying and accepting many varying texts, including tantras, and using them for meditation and rituals. But he did change the freewheeling interpretation of texts and the looseness of practices, indeed of monastic life, that had affected the Buddhist monastic sects of his time. In this respect, he followed the Kadampa tradition of the Indian monk Atisha, and it was in the Kadampa monastery at Rading that he retired and wrote his great works of philosophy and meditation (*Lamrim* and *Ngagrim*).

What Tsongkapa stressed was, in essence, a return to strict monastic discipline, requiring celibacy and a moral life, and instead of the practices of instant revelations, he advocated a gradual path to enlightenment for all. To introduce this new, disciplined religious life, Tsongkapa decided to found a new monastic order, which eventually received the name of Gelukpa ("those who follow virtue"). The appeal of the disciplined life was great, and the number of monks in the order grew rapidly. Tsongkapa and his disciples founded a number of important monasteries: Ganden in 1409, Drepung in 1416, and Sera in 1419—all near Lhasa, which became the center of the new faith. These three became the leading monasteries of the country, and they were also large academic institutions divided into colleges, including tantric colleges for advanced work. Other Gelukpa monasteries eventually were founded in all parts of the country, and some monasteries were taken over from other sects.

The success of the new monastic order created some hostility. Tsongkapa—in contrast to some of the other. sects' leaders at the time—refused to take part in the political power game, an abstention that was intended to keep the religious purpose free from such involvement and may have contributed to the attractiveness of the new order. But under Tsongkapa's successors, that policy could not be maintained, and actual hostilities began with the Gelukpa sect's rivals, especially the Karmapa, who had become dominant after the decline of the Sakya and had the military support of the king of Tsang. The Gelukpa turned to the Mongols for help, and they defeated and killed the king of Tsang and established the head of the Gelukpa order as the ruler of Tibet, as the Sakya had previously been given control of the central government by the Mongol khans. With the help of the Mongols—and later the Manchu emperors of China—the Gelukpa leader thus became the temporal ruler of Tibet. Following the example of the Karmapa, he was regarded as an incarnation of Avalokitesvara, the bodhisattva of compassion, and he became known by the title given him by the Mongol ruler, the Dalai Lama ("ocean of wisdom").

Evolving from an ideology for the kings or ruling houses, Buddhism thus became the ruling force of Tibet. A unique form of hierocratic government emerged, which combined a rich religious practice with the highly complex institutional form of political and social life that characterized the Tibetan cultural tradition.

Max Weber's Approach

To fit the Tibetan Buddhist polity into the typological approach of Max Weber, let us first outline Weber's relevant concepts. Weber was concerned with the rationalization of government, which, according to him, led to a bureaucratization of political as well as economic, social and religious institutions in modern times. According to Weber, bureaucracy, not any dictatorship of the proletariat, is on the march, and the extreme bureaucratization of totalitarian regimes appears to have confirmed his thesis. Weber's important contribution to political theory was his stress on the importance of a uniform system of values and knowledge for the education and cooperation of an intellectual elite, so that its members could work together as part of a bureaucracy.[27] Weber's definition of bureaucracy is as follows:

1. an organization serving functional goals through specialized functionaries;
2. a hierarchical structure with a clear chain of command;
3. a division of labor among officials;
4. detailed rules understood and applied by all members of the bureaucracy and the public;
5. the selection of personnel on the basis of competence;
6. service by official functionaries as a life-long vocation.[28]

We shall see that all of these stipulations clearly applied to the Tibetan traditional system. So did Weber's definition of a state as a "human community that successfully claims the monopoly of the legitimate use of force (*Gewalt*) within a given territory"[29]—a definition that is not limited to Weber but widely accepted by political scientists.

However Weber's highly suggestive typology deals with ideal types and has often led to abstractions that hardly meet the realities of any given historical order. Beyond Weber's famous dictum of the relationship of the protestant ethic to the development of capitalism in the Western world, his ideas cover the whole area of the relationship of state and society and can be used as guidelines to test historical realities rather than as given patterns into which to place different political, social, and economic systems. When Weber dealt with non-Western religious or philosophical orders—such as Confucianism, Hinduism, or Buddhism—he demonstrated a remarkable insight into the value systems of those faiths and the management of affairs by the respective elites educated in them. However he did not provide definite conclusions about the scope and potential of those ideologies in relation to the actual working of the systems and in relation to problems caused by changes in the modern world.

Weber distinguished three types of sanction for authority—traditional, constitutional/legal, and charismatic—and at times he added a fourth type, a rational belief in an absolute value of natural law. According to Weber, constitutional/legal authority replaced traditional authority when the modern concepts of laws emerged. Charismatic authority arises with the personalities of extraordinary leaders, whose ideological claims are generally accepted, but after their dynamism ends, rationalization returns and, with it, the constitutional/legal order. In Weber's view, the dialectic interplay between the constitutional/legal order and the appearance of charismatic leaders prevents the ossification of bureaucratic systems. Actually no system exists in pure form; traditional, constitutional/legal, and charismatic elements can be found in every order, but the emphasis varies and is decisive.

Max Weber believed that the Western Judaeo-Christian ideology retains the potential of the dynamic evolution derived from the prophetic traditions, and therefore an openness to dynamic change, which Oriental religions or ideologies lack. In the East, religious institutions are not differentiated from the total social structure as in the West, where the man of religion has been replaced by the man of science and the trained expert. Therefore Weber spoke of the Orient as ossified by the monks' bureaucracies of Buddhism and Hinduism, and similarly by the Confucian literati. In the West, recurring charismatic leadership combined with the technical proficiency of a rational bureaucracy was to keep society from ossification and to maintain the dynamism of power.

The key question is whether a separation of state and religion alone can guarantee the acceptance of science, and therefore of modernization, or whether a particular religious system other than Christianity—in this case Tibetan Buddhism—could, without difficulty, come to terms with modern science and technology not only by tolerating science but by incorporating it into the system's body of wisdom without a separation of state and religion. In other words, Can a church state be modernized? That was and perhaps still is a most intriguing question, not only for Tibetan Buddhism, with its impact on Tibetan society, but also for other societies of the developing world.

2

Religion and Government in Tibet

The Making of a Religious Government

Let us now examine the story in some more detail. In the early centuries of the Christian era, Tibet consisted of numerous groups of clans under the leadership of local chieftains. Beginning in the seventh century, the most powerful of the leaders made attempts to gain control of larger areas, first in southern Tibet, and eventually to unify the whole country under the central rule of a king. Namri Songtsen is the first historically documented king to establish his control over southern and central Tibet in the late sixth and early seventh centuries.[1] His son, Songtsen Gampo (617–647), extended his power over eastern and western Tibet and founded a powerful state, which even became a menace to neighboring countries.[2] At the time, Tibet's power extended beyond its own borders to Ladakh, Nepal, Bhutan, and the north-western Chinese corridor.[3]

Up to that period, the religious beliefs in Tibet were mostly based on the practices called Bon, and shamanist practitioners who were believed to be possessed by spirits would assist in curing ills and could control demons and hostile spirits with magical formulas. The Bon magic, like shamanism elsewhere, had served to satisfy the needs of clan and tribal life, but it could not provide an educational or ideological basis for a larger social and political order.[4] Because of his political ambition to extend his power over all of Tibet and beyond, Songtsen Gampo clearly needed a broader ideological basis and educational system than could be provided by the magic and curing practices of the Bon magicians and diviners. One might interpret his problem as that of a king in search of an ideology.

At the time, the Buddhist faith was spreading rapidly over central Asia, China, Korea, Japan, and Southeast Asia, serving religious as well as political purposes. Buddhism almost replaced the Confucian order in China during the Sui and Tang dynasties, and it left a lasting imprint on the politics, art, architecture, and intellectual traditions of Korea and Japan. Along the caravan routes through central Asia, from Bamiyan through Tunhuang and the Chinese corridor, Buddhist sculptures and texts found

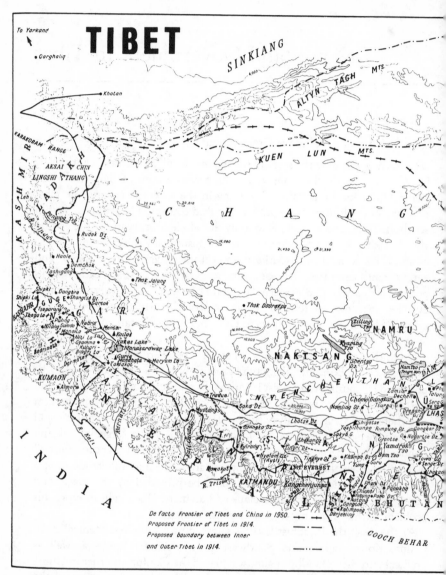

Source: *A Short History of Tibet* by H. E. Richardson. Copyright © by H. E. Richard-

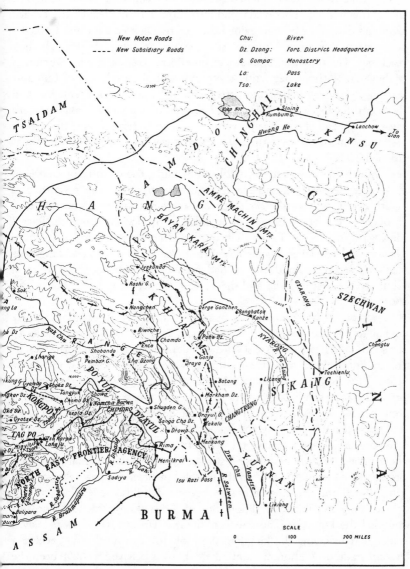

son. Reprinted by permission of the publisher, E. P. Dutton.

by historians still testify to the momentous role this religion played as well as to its linkages with trade and politics.

In its expansion, Buddhism had already divided into two major traditions. In Southeast Asia, Theravada Buddhism stressed the ideal of the arhats, Buddha's disciples who had gained their own enlightenment and formed a community of followers (*sangha*) that carried on the faith through their teachings. The northern branches of Buddhism accepted the appellation of Mahayana. Without neglecting the philosophical foundation of Buddhist learning, they placed greater stress on faith and enlightenment and developed the belief in bodhisattvas, beings who have gained enlightenment but who, instead of entering Nirvana, choose to be reincarnated in order to assist all sentient beings in their liberation. It was Mahayana Buddhism that reached Tibet.[5]

Although the influence of Buddhism in India, the country of its origin, eventually became negligible and almost disappeared, the seventh and eighth centuries were the high tide of Buddhist expansion and influence throughout the whole East Asian world. Clearly Buddhism was the logical ideological foundation for the Tibetan kingdom emerging under Songtsen Gampo. Indeed, Tibet was already surrounded by countries and kingdoms that had accepted Buddhism or had been deeply influenced by it—from China to the east to India and the Tibetan border states to the south and southwest.

In accepting the teachings of Buddhism, the Tibetan king apparently sought to balance the respective influences of China and the countries to the south, and he made his first official Buddhist contacts with both sides. In the tradition of the time, these contacts were accomplished through marriage. The king's wives included a Chinese princess[6] and a Nepalese princess,[7] and each brought with her dowry an image of Gautama Buddha from her home country. Each built a temple in Lhasa to house the image, and those temples, Jokhang and Ramoche, are the oldest Buddhist religious structures in Tibet to survive into modern times.[8] Three Tibetan wives of the king also each built a Buddhist temple, presumably to maintain their prestige by contributing toward the establishment of the new religion. The king himself and the king's ministers became Buddhists.

According to Tibetan tradition, one of the Buddhist teachers who surrounded the king was Thonmi Sambhota, a Tibetan who was to play a major part in giving the kingdom the tool that was needed to develop a literary tradition.[9] Thonmi Sambhota, who was believed to have been the king's chief minister and teacher of Buddhism, was responsible for inventing the Tibetan script by adapting the Indian Gupta system of writing[10] to the Tibetan language. It is perhaps significant that this introduction of a script, combined with the development of a grammar on which all later Tibetan

Jokhang temple details, with Potala in the background (photo by Betty Goff C. Cartwright).

literature was based, came from the south and not from China. This turning away from China, in spite of a linguistic relationship—though distant and questioned[11]—is in marked contrast to the acceptance of a Chinese or Chinese-derived system of writing by the non-Sino-Tibetan languages of Korea and Japan. Thonmi Sambhota is also said to have translated Buddhist sutras from Sanskrit into Tibetan, recording them in the new script and inventing new Tibetan terms for Sanskrit concepts. This new script, in fact, provided the foundation for the Tibetan Buddhist culture; its coming from India was an assertion of Tibet's cultural as well as political independence from the great Chinese Tang Empire.[12]

The first acceptance of Buddhism in Tibet was enhanced three generations later when King Trisong Detsen (ca. 740–798)[13] extended an invitation to the famous Indian Buddhist scholar Santaraksita[14] to come to Tibet to teach Buddhism. When strongly opposed by the Bon practitioners, backed by "evil omens," Santaraksita advised the king to invite the great Indian tantric master Padmasambhava[15] to visit Tibet. In order to overcome the obstacles caused by the indigenous belief in mountain spirits, Santaraksita's moral and rational teachings had to be complemented by the tantric ritualistic mysticism that eventually flourished in Tibet. Together the two Indian teachers, Padmasambhava and Santaraksita, founded the first Buddhist monastery in Tibet in 779, Samye, about fifty miles southeast of Lhasa. Beginning with seven young Tibetan monks, they established there the first organized Buddhist academic institution, which changed the casual form of study of kings, princes, princesses, ministers, and other ruling figures into an institutionalized, religious educational system.

At this point, the dominant Indian influence was challenged by Chinese Buddhist monks, a confrontation that was said to have led to the Great Debate (792–794) between a Chinese monk, Makotse,[16] popularly known as Mahayana, and an Indian pandit, Kamalashila,[17] a disciple of Santaraksita. The debate has since become known as the Council of Tibet.

According to a Tibetan record, the Chinese monk advocated that Nirvana was to be obtained through a state of quiescence alone, rather than combined with religious devotion and works, and the Indian debater propounded the "middle doctrine," which rejected holding extreme views between nihilistic and phenomenological philosophies and advocated a medium between meditation and action.[18] The substance of the debate has come to us in an official Tibetan version and, for the statements of the Chinese monk, in documents found at Tungkuang.[19] The Tibetan version ascribes a more realistic and balanced view to the Indian scholar than to his Chinese opponent, which explains why the Indian was regarded as the winner. According to the Tibetan account, even the Chinese opponent agreed with that outcome, allegedly joining in the honors given the Indian champion.[20]

Tibetan tradition has it that the debate was carried on in the presence of the king, but this appears to be unlikely, particularly since the debate was carried on over a period of up to two years and seems to have been conducted in writing. Recent studies[21] have raised questions about the outcome as well as about the form of the debate, and there is disagreement between the earlier Chinese sources from Tunhuang, which ascribe victory to the Chinese contender, and the later Tibetan account, which glorifies the Indian's success in the debate. The two-year duration of the debate and its disputed outcome seem to preclude any personal confrontation (let alone in the royal presence) and may indicate that neither side would change its position.

Whatever the form and outcome of the actual debate, the king accepted the Indian Buddhist system as the state religion as a result of it. Since the doctrine of contemplative techniques, which spontaneously lead to enlightenment, was not alien to Indian Mahayana and Vajrayana teachings, the outcome of the confrontation—the choice of India over China as Tibet's cultural link with Buddhist religion—may have been determined as much by political as by religious considerations.[22] The Indian view, which expressed the need for learning as a part of religious training, may also have served better the purpose of the Tibetan ruler. According to the Tibetan story, the debate ended with great official festivities, during which the proclamation of Buddhism as the religion of the land and the successful training of the first monks were celebrated.

Under King Ralpachen (reigned 815–836),[23] a number of Indian Buddhist teachers were again invited to Tibet, and architects—this time from India, Nepal, and China—were brought to build a temple near Lhasa. Monastic life was placed on a financially sound basis by the decree that seven households would support one monk in each of the monasteries.[24]

King Ralpachen was assassinated by his older halfbrother Lang Darma, who used traditionalist opposition to the increasing influence of Buddhism to establish a government that purged his predecessor's Buddhist officials, expelled many monks, and burned Buddhist scriptures. Eventually Lang Darma was in turn assassinated by a Buddhist monk, and Buddhism, which had never been fully eliminated, was revived.[25]

The period that followed was one of political power struggles and decentralization. The king's natural son was driven from power by an adopted son who took control of central Tibet, and the legitimate son escaped to western Tibet where he established a kingdom over the Guge region, including portions of Ladakh. Buddhism flourished in both parts of Tibet. In the West, the king's son and his successors sent groups of students to India to study Buddhism at Nalanda University and invited the famous Indian Buddhist teacher Atisha[26] to western Tibet where he played an important role in the revival of Buddhist teaching and the establishment of monasteries. In central Tibet, regional conflicts resulted in the dissolution of central political unity. In the absence of any outstanding ruler, the principalities claimed full jurisdiction over their territories and formed their own armies. Without any political restraint, Buddhist monasteries were established in many places under their own authority. They, in turn, were used by some of the secular principalities in their search for greater prestige and power. The Indian teacher Atisha also entered central Tibet to assist in the founding of such monasteries. This period of political division and the spread of Buddhism lasted over two hundred years, from the ninth to the eleventh centuries.[27]

During the eleventh century, the loose tantric practices of erotic rites and the profanation of religious dances into forms of public entertainment (practiced by an increasing number of individual magicians of the early Buddhist tradition) provoked a reform movement initiated by the Nyingmapa monk Konchog Gyalpo from the aristocratic Khon clan. This movement led to the establishment of the new Sakyapa order, named after the place in which the first and chief monastery of the sect was built.[28] Konchog Gyalpo's new order separated monks from the lay public, established monastic discipline, and made dances and rituals part of the monastic religious actions and experience. His son, Sachen Kunga Nyingpo, introduced the tradition of *lamdre* (literally, "the path and its fruits"), a comprehensive program and curriculum of tantric teachings and practices. It was this new system of education and monastic discipline that became the chief reason for the Sakya's success. The discipline and educational uniformity introduced into the heretofore detached system of Buddhist practices provided the basis for a monk bureaucracy. Indeed the Sakya established ranks and positions, incorporated families other than their own into the system, and gave them such administrative ranks and titles as *tishih* or *kuoshih* ("chief") under a *panchen* ("commander").[29]

It was the success of the Sakya educational system and monastic bureaucracy that impressed the Mongols, who were then in the process of conquest and empire building. When the founder's grandson, Sakya Pandita,[30] and his nephew Phagpa visited the Mongol ruler Godan Khan at the latter's request in 1244, Sakya Pandita was appointed vice-regent of Tibet by the Mongol ruler. In 1253, his nephew Phagpa visited the court of Kublai Khan and was appointed by him as his vice-regent over all Tibet with the title of tishih, which gave him control over the revenue and judicial authority.[31] As the great military power of the time, the Mongols thus used what must have appeared to them as the most promising new Buddhist order to incorporate Tibet, which they could militarily dominate, into their political domain. The Sakya leader became the first religious head of the Tibetan government under Mongol control and with Mongol military backing.

But the rule of the Sakya was constantly challenged, perhaps because it lacked the religious authority that was only later provided by the concept of incarnation. Other sects and the secular principalities grudgingly accepted the authority of the Sakya only as long as the Mongols had to be feared and respected. By 1350, after one hundred years of rule and weakened by internal struggles, a military rebellion ended the Sakya rule even before the Mongol dynasty in China collapsed.

What the Sakya had accomplished was to create a bureaucracy out of the monastic system, systematically training monks, not only of their own clan but of other clans as well, for the administration of the thirteen administrative districts or myriarchies (*trikor*) into which they had organized their domain.[32] The training and education of the administrators were provided by the Sakya. One of these myriarchies derived its origin from a Kagyu monk, Phamo Drukpa, who had built a hermitage and gathered many disciples.[33] This group had been placed in charge of the Nedong estate, which became the Phamo Dru myriarchy. To keep the rule of the governorship of this territory in the hands of the family (the Lang family), it followed the practice of having one son become a monk, so that he could head the monastery and be the governor of the myriarchy, while another or others married to perpetuate the line—a practice followed also by other religio-aristocratic houses.

One of the gifted sons of the Phamo Drukpa family, Changchub Gyaltsen (b. 1302), was sent as a monk to Sakya for training under the famous Sakya scholars. The story has it that his Sakya teacher advised Changchub Gyaltsen not to pursue a scholastic vocation but to become an administrator, since that was the career for which he was especially gifted. Consequently he was trained in military strategy, political affairs, public speaking and group leadership. Then he was sent back as the tishih of Nedong, and he gained a great reputation by building forts, a fortified palace, roads, and bridges; planting trees; and providing relief from taxes for the farming population. He soon got into conflict with a neighboring province over territory and became involved in a lengthy conflict among various provincial alliances. Surviving many setbacks, he finally conquered the Sakya sect itself and established a new government in 1358.

Changchub set himself up as a lama king and was recognized by the other religiosecular families. He reorganized the government along the lines he had used in his former domain, but went a step further. He replaced the thirteen myriarchies, which had been based on family rule, with numerous *dzongs* ("districts") commanded from a fortified headquarters (*dzong* also means "castle" or "fort"), and appointed district officials (*dzongpon*) from among his followers. He divided the land equally among the farmers and reduced the tax to one-sixth of the crop. He built roads, bridges (establishing ferries at important river crossings), and rest houses on the pilgrim routes. Military posts were established in strategic places to protect the local population and travelers from bandits. He promulgated a criminal code, making use of a contemporary compilation of earlier codes ascribed to King Songtsen Gampo, to give his code a historical and an ideological justification.[34] Changchub Gyaltsen's code, later expanded, was the basis of Tibetan criminal law. Changchub remained a Buddhist monk, keeping his vows, and when he died in 1364, he was succeeded by his nephew who was also a monk.

Like the Sakya, the Phamo Drukpa family rule collapsed in 1434 because of internal strife caused by rivalries among competing nephews and because of outside competition from other clans. By this time, the system of Tibetan bureaucracy was established, but the leadership of the system was in doubt. The political claims of the competing families were all based on religious status. Any Tibetan prince or local ruler based his claim to authority on this reputation as a patron of religious learning. To increase prestige and political authority, the practice was to send monks to India or invite Indian scholars to Tibet and to collect texts and have them translated. Each competing family produced scholar-monks but continued its line through biological inheritance.

The Phamo Drukpa and the other most important and powerful

Gangon Tashi Choe Zong monastery near Leh, Ladakh (known as Phiang monastery), of the Drigung Kagyupa sect. Location of the eight-hundred-year anniversary celebration of the founding of Drigung monastery in Tibet, July 1979. (Photo by Franz Michael and Eugene Knez.)

religiopolitical families of the time, the Drigung and Taglung monasteries and families, were branches of the growing Kagyupa order. It was in that order that a new concept of highest religious leadership, as well as of political authority, was introduced: the concept of the reincarnation of a religious leader as a living bodhisattva. That institution was started when the founder of the Karmapa sect, before his death, indicated his reincarnation as a newly born child at a specific place and in a specific family. The tradition of predicting incarnation has been carried on ever since in the case of the Gyalwa Karmapa.[35] This newly introduced institution, the belief in a living incarnation of a bodhisattva, proved to be not only of revolutionary religious consequence, but also of decisive institutional importance for the Tibetan polity.

The ideological confrontation between Buddhism, introduced by the kings to support a centralized government system, and the Bon practices, backed by the aristocratic families who saw in an expanded Bon religion an ideological instrument that would help them maintain their power, clearly ended in the victory of Buddhism but not in the victory of the monarchy, which was destroyed in the power struggle. The attempts of large aristocratic

The crowd of faithful at the ceremonies celebrating the eight-hundredth anniversary of the founding of Drigung monastery (photo by Franz Michael).

families to use different Buddhist sects as ideological props for their claims to central authority, and to strengthen their authority by becoming religious leaders themselves and bequeathing their religiopolitical authority to their heirs, were to be equally unsuccessful. In a Buddhist environment, rule by biological inheritance has no religious sanction. Eventually the lineages that mattered were those based on spiritual continuity, which was provided by reincarnations of saintly beings. These reincarnations were carefully selected by the leading monks, who thus became the kingmakers and indeed the managers of the emerging hierocratic system, the unique form of government of Tibet. The Sakya still tried religious leadership by heredity, and so did their first successors, but the system of rule by incarnation waited in the wings.

There followed a period of political infighting during which the secular heads of government were strongly backed by the Karmapa incarnations, who did not assume open power but were deeply involved in politics. The new political role of the incarnations marked a decisive shift of power away from the ruling houses, and from now on, the incarnations were installed by the monks of a sect and monastery, who assumed the authority to determine

Mr. and Mrs. G. N. Tsarong and the sister of the Dalai Lama at the eight-hundred-year celebration of the founding of Drigung monastery (photo by Franz Michael).

the succession of the new religious leadership and who found the candidates in families of humble, common background. Unable to vitiate this new procedure and the resulting authority of the monastic hierocracy, the aristocratic families attempted at first to join with the sects and their incarnations in the continuing power struggle. It was only a matter of time, however, before the incarnations and the monk bureaucracy established themselves and their new authority. Eventually the kings of Tsang, the chief and ruling aristocratic family of the time, whose seat of government was then at Shigatse, lost their power to the incarnation of a new sect, the Gelukpa, which was backed by a superior Mongol military force.

The example of the Karmapa incarnations was soon followed by other sects, and the fourteenth century was a major turning point in the development of Tibetan Buddhism and its role in society and government. At the time of the lama king, a famous teacher and learned scholar concerned himself with purifying the Buddhist monastic system and its discipline. Following the teaching of the Kadampa sect, Lozang Dragpa, generally known as Tsongkapa, advocated an interpretation of Buddhist doctrine that stressed the "middle path" between the concepts of nihilism and the ab-

Tibetan dignitaries at the eight-hundred-year celebration of the founding of Drigung monastery (photo by Franz Michael).

solute reality of phenomena, which teaches that reality is relative or the nonduality of the appearance of phenomena and their intrinsic emptiness. Tsongkapa claimed that this middle path had been the Buddha's original approach, and, without attacking other sects, he demanded from his followers a new devotion to a strict life within the discipline of monastic vows. Using this new approach, he founded a new sect, the Gelukpa sect ("those who follow virtue"), and through his followers established monasteries in many parts of the country. Of the three main Gelukpa monasteries near Lhasa (popularly known as the *serdegasum*, the "big three"), Ganden was founded by Tsongkapa himself, and Drepung and Sera were founded by his disciples. These monasteries became the most powerful religious and political institutions in the country. The monastery of Tashilhunpo near Shigatse was founded by Tsongkapa's nephew and disciple, Gedun Drubpa, later regarded as the first Dalai Lama. When the king of Tsang attacked the Gelukpa monasteries, the monks fought back with Mongol support and established their own political power over Tibet. Once again it was the outside power of the Mongols, who used the religious structure to assert their own political influence, that reinstated religious leadership in Tibet.[36] This form of religious leadership differed, however, from any previous one by the fact that the religious ruler was no longer a simple lama king but claimed to be, and was believed to be, an incarnation of a previous saint, a living bodhisattva.

Tsongkapa's nephew and disciple, Gedun Drubpa, who at the time of his death was the Grand Lama or chief abbot of Drepung monastery, was, like the Gyalwa Karmapa before him, declared to have been reincarnated. In this case the Grand Lama did not predict his reincarnation, but the community of monks of Drepung monastery found his successor. The third incarnation of this line was Sonam Gyatso (1543-1588). As a well-known and distinguished scholar he visited the Mongol court of Altan Khan at Chahar in 1578 and established a relationship similar to that of the Sakya Pandita to Godan Khan. He converted the Mongols to Buddhism and received gifts and the title of Dalai Lama (*dalai* meaning "ocean," indicating the depth of learning).[37] This title was later applied retroactively to the first and second incarnations, who became the first and second in the line of incarnations of the Dalai Lama.

The Politico-Religious System

The foundation for the Tibetan religiopolitical system was laid in the fourteenth century, but it came to full fruition in the seventeenth century under the fifth Dalai Lama. To secure Mongol support, the reincarnation of Sonam Gyatso had been found in the person of a Mongol prince who became the fourth Dalai Lama. And when pressed by the troops of the king of Tsang, who supported the Gyalwa Karmapa, the fifth Dalai Lama sought the help of the Mongols under their chieftain Gushri Khan, whose troops defeated the forces of the king of Tsang and established the rule of the Dalai Lama over Tibet. With this assumption of authority by the fifth Dalai Lama, rule by incarnation by the successive lineage of Dalai Lamas was instituted in Tibet.

This system remained in force from the seventeenth century until the Chinese takeover in 1959 ended the government of the Dalai Lama, and it is this system that is the topic of this and the following chapters. During those centuries, the system of government was sanctioned by the religious authority of the Dalai Lama, which was absolute and based on his unique position as the highest incarnation, a position that could not be challenged from outside or within. However during many periods of the reigns of the Dalai Lamas, the actual power was in the hands of regents because of the minority of the Dalai Lama, an important limitation since many of the Dalai Lamas did not reach an advanced age.[38] Under the regencies, the government often declined, and intrigues and corruption became rampant. A regent's authority was derived entirely from the authority of the Dalai Lama, but the regents, who were elected by the Tsongdu (Assembly), could be—and were—replaced by decision of that body, so they never enjoyed the same authority the Dalai Lama did. The strength and continuity of the system still depended on the unchallengeable concept of the sanctity of the incarnate ruler.

The politico-religious order of Tibet would, however, have been unthinkable without the monastic establishments. Their main purpose was religious, but they also provided the basic education and religious concepts on which the whole Tibetan political and social order was founded. As indicated earlier, the Tibetan monastic system evolved historically through four major sects.[39] A short reassessment of the contribution of each of these sects to the monastic-bureaucratic order of the last four centuries may help to clarify their respective importance.

The oldest of the sects, the Nyingmapa, which was founded in the eighth century by the Indian teacher Padmasambhava, was divided from the outset into two separate wings. One was made up of monk communities that, among other vows, required celibacy, and the other consisted of secular, "white-clad" yogi communities that permitted their members to marry. From the beginning the Nyingmapa teachings placed a heavy emphasis on tantric writings and practices.[40] As stated earlier, it seems likely that at first this tantric emphasis was related to the task that the new Buddhist religion faced in its confrontation with Bon magic, and some of the ritualistic practices of this sect appear to have been initially introduced to facilitate acceptance by Bon believers. But the tantric emphasis became and has remained a major part of the Tibetan Buddhist tradition. The Nyingmapa sect is still reckoned as one of the four major Buddhist sects, flourishing all over Tibet and since 1959, in the Indian Himalayan areas. The important role of this tradition, in tandem with the Gelukpa sect, is attested to by the fact that the fifth Dalai Lama studied Nyingmapa teachings intensely. Among his teachers were Nyingmapa monks, and he was proclaimed as having been the finder (*terton*) of hidden Nyingmapa scriptures.[41] It was believed that he revealed from his transmigrating consciousness teachings from his previous embodiment as King Trisong Detsen.[42]

The importance of the second of the major sects, the Sakyapa, was that it not only established the first religious government over all Tibet but it also laid the foundation for the formation of a monastic bureaucracy. Its headquarters, some fifty miles west of Shigatse, and its estates, especially those in eastern Tibet, formed one of the major religious units of the Tibetan system.[43]

The Kagyupa sect, founded in the eleventh century almost contemporaneously with the Sakyapa order, emphasized from the outset the meditational training of monks. The foundation of this sect and its several major branches demonstrates more than anything else the growing religious fervor of the time. Many monasteries and meditation centers sprang up in the valleys and on the mountainsides of the Tibetan landscape. Four major and eight minor sects, differing only in minor ritualistic practices, branched out of the main Kagyupa order as a result of the division of lineages among its ecclesiastical leadership.[44] The Karmapa sect was the most important of these branches, because the concept and realization of the institution of incarnation emerged through its leadership.

The last and most important sect, the Gelukpa, provided not only the leadership of Tibet, in the person of the Dalai Lama, but Tibet's three leading monasteries near Lhasa. Those monasteries, the serdegasum, dominated the scene within the government institutions, and the "five ling" monasteries traditionally provided the regents during the minority of the Dalai Lamas.[45] Not only in Lhasa but also in Kham the largest monasteries, such as Kumbum[46] and Tashikhil, were Gelukpa monasteries, and the large majority of the monk population was of the Gelukpa order. Even more important, most of the monk officials came from the Gelukpa order—indeed, many families who were members of other sects sent their sons to Gelukpa monasteries because of the greater prestige of those monasteries, which gave their children a greater chance in a government career.

No monastery of any sect paid any attention to the original affiliation of any of the monks or laymen,[47] which demonstrates the eventual close cooperation among the sects in Tibet. Each followed its own specialization and training without interfering with the others' interests, but all contributed to the common religious effort. Added to that spirit of cooperation, the function and economic status of each sect was guaranteed and supported by the Lhasa government, so the strong cohesion of the system on the basis of a common Buddhist belief becomes apparent.

From the twelfth century on, all four of the major sects followed the example of the Karmapa sect and recognized the institution of incarnations, which led to the emergence of numerous incarnations in almost all monasteries. At the peak of this development, at the turn of the twentieth century, there were believed to have been well over ten thousand such incarnations in Tibet. These incarnations could roughly be grouped into three categories, not counting the Dalai Lama, who—because of his highest authority—belonged in a category by himself. The first and highest group consisted of the ranking incarnations who headed the major sects and some of the leading monasteries. To this group belonged the Panchen Lama (the second-highest incarnation of the Gelukpa sect),[48] the Gyalwa Karmapa, and some of the other leading Gelukpa incarnates, such as the Trulku (incarnations) of Kundeling, Tshemönling, Tengyeling, Zhide, and Dedruk.[49] The candidates for these incarnations were found by the monks of their respective orders and were usually confirmed by the Dalai Lama, who also made the decision of selection if there was more than one candidate. That

Drukpa Thuksae Rinpoche, incarnation at Hemis monastery in Ladakh (photo by Franz Michael).

the unity of the religious establishment transcended the distinction of the sects can be recognized also by the fact that an incarnation could be found in a family that belonged to a sect other than the one in which the incarnation was established.

The second level consisted of lesser though still important incarnations, including the heads of other important monasteries of all sects, who were found by the monks of their monasteries and also usually confirmed by the Dalai Lama. The third group consisted of a very large number of incarnations who were proposed by their monasteries and confirmed by the head or another one of the leading lamas of their respective sect.[50]

The institution of incarnations became a part of all sects. Even those sects that still determined succession by biological lineage, such as the Sakya, introduced incarnations and placed them over the existing inheritance system. Even though each sect had its own incarnations, the system of confirmation, the mutual acceptance of each other's incarnations, and the common hierarchical order under the Dalai Lama bound the sects together in a common belief in and practice of a unique type of Buddhism that gave Tibet its extraordinary cultural, social, and political unity.

On the basis of the priority of the Buddhist religion, the government formed under the Dalai Lama divided its performance between religious and secular affairs. The religious and the secular sectors both believed that the primary purpose of all endeavor was religious liberation, not only for all Tibetans but for all sentient beings. As a result, the religious and the secular aspects of the Tibetan politico-religious structure were so closely linked that it is difficult to draw a distinct line between them.[51] In the monasteries of all sects, the monks were trained for the management of human affairs as well as for religious service.

Trained monk bureaucrats formed the link between religious and secular affairs as the secular administration organized by the Dalai Lamas was, to a large degree, staffed by monk officials. These monks, though still belonging to their respective monasteries, worked full time at their administrative duties and no longer played any part in the affairs of their respective monasteries. Their religious character was, however, maintained by the fact that they had to uphold their religious vows.[52] By working on all levels of government, they provided the cohesion for the political structure. Monks worked in the offices of the central government at Lhasa, together with their secular colleagues, and they held regional and local positions for the central government as governors of the seven provinces. They also served as *dzongpon* ("district magistrates") in the more than two hundred districts into which Tibetan local government was divided.[53] They shared all these positions with secular colleagues, in some cases by joint appointment. Monks also served the central government in special assignments at home and abroad. The body of about three hundred to four hundred monk officials was the core of the administrative system and supplied the religious quality and purpose to the government.[54] They were expected to apply ethics and religious principles to the mundane affairs they had to handle.

Their partners, the secular officials, were from the aristocracy. When the religious order of the Gelukpa assumed governmental power in the person of the Dalai Lama and all authority was vested in him, the role of the aristocratic families changed fundamentally. Their previous power, based on their territorial authority and their own military forces, was ended and transferred to the religious state. Indeed the aristocrats became the servants of the state. Each family's chief obligation was to provide one son for secular official service; in exchange, the family was permitted to retain the income from its estates. That privilege was linked, however, to the service their sons provided for the state. If no such service was forthcoming, because there were no sons or adopted sons or there was an unwillingness to serve, a family would lose its estates.[55] The income from the estates provided the aristocratic families' livelihood, as well as that of the sons who were officials during times when they were not assigned to a specific office. Since the secular officials' private income was constantly at their disposal, their living standard was on the whole significantly higher than that of their monastic colleagues. There were about two hundred secular officials, so the ratio of secular to monk officials was about two to three or four. But it was the monk officials who gave the ethical and religious quality to the administrative order.[56]

The incorporation of the aristocratic families into the religiopolitical order has been called a "feudal factor" in the Tibetan state. The use of the term *feudalism* in characterizing this aspect of the Tibetan system is, however, a misnomer and very misleading. The services the aristocratic families provided to the government of Tibet under the Dalai Lama were no more feudal than, for instance, the services the Prussian aristocrats rendered to the Prussian state under Frederick the Great—the king of so-called benevolent absolutism, who called himself the "first servant of the state" and who engaged the services of the sons of his aristocracy to build the strength of his army and his administration. The creation of a secular component of the government from representatives of these Tibetan families transformed feudal aristocrats into servants of the state. There were no longer any feudal territories, feudal loyalties, feudal armies, or feudal territorial jurisdiction.[57] The term *feudal* is often used loosely today, mainly with a derogatory implication, but it is clearly wrong to use it in connection with Tibet under the Dalai Lama.[58] What the Tibetan religious government accomplished was to transform territorial aristocratic rule into a bureaucratic segment of a centralized religious state. The aristocratic families became incorporated into the bureaucratic structure as a secondary source of administrative talent, and their sons were especially trained for this purpose in government schools.

Another frequent misinterpretation of the Tibetan social and political order is to describe the ordinary Tibetan people by translating the Tibetan term *mi-ser* into the Western term *serf*. Except for the substantial number of monks and nuns, the small number of aristocrats, and a small number of outcasts (*yawa*) or professional beggars, the majority of the Tibetan people were called mi-ser, a term that is best rendered in English as "subject" or "commoner." The misinterpretation of that word and the status it signified is based on the fact that some mi-ser were obligated to cultivate the land or tend the herds of government, monastic, or aristocratic estates, an obligation that was inherited from father to son. This obligation was, however, combined with a hereditary and contractually documented right to one's own land, and it was entirely an economic obligation. It did not carry the meaning of being physically "subject to the will of the owner"—as is indicated by the term *serf* or the German term *Leibeigener*—the position of the peasantry in medieval Europe. Also, only a minority of the mi-ser were obligated to cultivate government or private land in exchange for their property rights.

A more detailed description of the status of mi-ser will follow in a later chapter;[59] here it will suffice to outline the chief divisions of the mi-ser according to their status and economic activity.[60] The mi-ser who had service obligations to government or private estates and, in exchange, owned their own hereditary land were the *tral-pa* ("taxpayers"), a prosperous upper group of farmers who formed the most influential families in the villages. A larger group were the *dü-chung* ("landless laborers"), who hired themselves out as laborers or worked as sharecroppers for the well-to-do tral-pa or for aristocratic or monastic estates. They were free to sell their labor and although generally not as well off as most of the tral-pa, they had no corresponding obligations and were therefore unrestrained in their movement. Both groups were free to engage in other enterprises, particularly trade, a major source of income on which there was no taxation to speak of. As a result, a substantial proportion of the mi-ser were traders (*tsong-pa*), a well-to-do group, which, together with the dü-chung, made up the largest proportion of the town dwellers. All mi-ser were thus much better off and economically far more independent than the term *serf* implies. The term *mi-ser* was therefore a genus term that described a variety of social groups whose status, economic pursuits, and level of income varied greatly.

Most of all, the estates had only very limited, delegated juridical authority to carry out minor legal duties and to settle local quarrels. The state alone—through the district magistrate and, in the final instance, the Dalai Lama's government—had full juridical authority. What is more, if a mi-ser complained to the Lhasa government about any act of oppression by his estate owner, the Lhasa government would investigate, and its decision was binding on the estate owner. In essence, therefore, the mi-ser of the state or the estates as a whole shared similar rights and obligations, and the Dalai Lama was the final authority over all of them.[61] Neither in the status of Tibet's subject population nor in the role of its secular officials of aristocratic origin can one discern any element of what in Western constitutional parlance could be called feudalism.

The term best suited to describe the Tibetan polity is *bureaucracy*, a term that may be used for the political and religious system as well as for the social order. Indeed, the government of Tibet was managed by a religiously organized and motivated bureaucracy under an absolute ruler whose authority was based on the religious concept of incarnation. The constitutional link between the religious and the secular human order was the Dalai Lama, who fulfilled a double role that in constitutional terminology can be defined by the German concept of *Personal-Union*, two authorities combined in one person. The extraordinary strength and success of this institutional form of the religiopolitical order can perhaps best be attributed to four major factors.

1. At the time of the establishment of this political order, the Gelukpa sect had entered the Tibetan religious scene as a new moral force, one that was bent on cleansing religious practices of the corruption and misuse of the time and establishing a new monastic discipline and organization that, emerging in the religious world, could easily be transferred to the social and political scene. The Gelukpa's new dynamism, so much stronger at the time than that of the older orders, gave that sect a moral superiority and motivation, which was expressed by the rapid spread of Gelukpa monasteries in Tibet and Mongolia. The danger that this new religious powerhouse posed to the political authority was obviously recognized by the king of Tsang, as he sent his troops against the chief Gelukpa monasteries of Sera, Drepung, and Ganden and forced those monks to flee several times. This harassment led the Gelukpa leaders to ask the Khoshot Mongols to come to their rescue, and the Mongols defeated the king's troops and killed him. In turn the Mongols, presumably recognizing the political potential of this new religious force and its disciplined organization, entrusted the head of the Gelukpa sect with the government of Tibet under Mongol protection. The new monastic discipline proved an ideal training ground for a political bureaucracy.

2. The principal strength of the system, however, was derived from the particular and unique system of its leadership, rule by incarnation. The religious concept of incarnation asserted the incarnate's absolute authority, based on the status of enlightenment and the purpose of compassionate care that was believed to have been reached by him. This authority and purpose could easily be transferred to the mundane world of social and political af-

fairs. Moreover, the selection of the incarnation was itself religiously sanctioned and therefore could not be challenged.

In practical terms, rule by incarnation had a great advantage over other
available forms of succession—monarchical heredity or selection by
aristocratic oligarchy. The careful search for the incarnation by especially
selected monk commissions, with or without advice of the previous incarnation or other spiritual guidance by the faithful, proved to be a very effective
way of continuing the system without incurring the dangers of incapable
heirs or intrigues or nepotism on the part of powerful families or aristocratic
usurpers. Since the selection of the incarnations was in the hands of the
monastic leadership, the actual power to determine succession remained in
the hands of the monastic order—the ecclesiastical segment of the Tibetan
people and the segment that had the fullest social mobility. It is particularly
significant that with the exceptions of the fourth Dalai Lama (who was
found in the Mongol royal family) and the fifth Dalai Lama (who came from
a Tibetan aristocratic family), all Dalai Lamas were found in commoner
families, which kept the institution of the Dalai Lama free of politically
powerful connections. It is no wonder that the selection process itself was
open to attempts of outside influence, particularly from the Chinese, but the
system survived and maintained its independence. Even in modern times,
the concept of succession by incarnation has retained its powerful sanction,
and so has the belief in the qualifications of the incarnation for leadership in
political and social affairs.

3. Both the Gelukpa and the Karmapa sects instituted the system of
leadership by incarnation. In fact, not only did the Karmapa sect precede
the Gelukpa in the establishment of the new system of rule by incarnation,
but it also proclaimed that the Gyalwa Karmapa was the incarnation of a
manifestation of the bodhisattva Avalokitesvara, so that the Gelukpa and
the Karmapa became political rivals within the Avalokitesvara cult. Yet, the
Gelukpa sect had an organizational advantage because it established its base
in firm monastic settlements. The sect's three great monasteries ringed
Lhasa, the center where the kings had reigned and where the faithful now
had to come on their pilgrimages to offer gifts for the blessings they received.
The Gyalwa Karmapa focused on his great mobile encampment. Although
he established his chief monastery at Tsurphu, he moved with his
bureaucracy from camp to camp to hold the rituals of *gar* ("encampment"),
depending on the princes to support him.

4. The disciplined religiobureaucratic structure of the Gelukpa sect and its
incarnated leadership could, however, be accepted only on the basis of a
strong and dynamic faith of the majority of the Tibetan people. Buddhism
had provided this faith since the seventh century, but the new zeal of the
Gelukpa order revived and stimulated a religious fervor among the Tibetan

people, and the Gelukpa influence extended beyond the religious domain to all political and social life.

The political link between the religious and the social order had its parallel in the economic field in the institution of the labrang. Once the institution of the incarnation was recognized, it had to be financially supported, and the labrang, an economic enterprise, served that purpose. When the first monastic orders had been established, income had been assigned to them for their support, and the same was done for the incarnations. The word *labrang—la* ("the lama"); *brang* or *drang* ("home")—originated from the word for a camp of the nomad, and it was first used for the physical residence of the incarnation, in the sense of the camping place for that spirit on its present sojourn in the mundane world. As such the incarnation's residence was separate, at least conceptually, from the monastic establishment, and it became the private property of the incarnation. To this residence of the incarnation were added sources of income, such as landed property or animal herds or the proceeds of trade and business.

Administered by a manager who might or might not be a monk, the labrang became a private, profit-making "capitalist" enterprise. It was capitalist in the sense that the manager's aim was clearly and admittedly to make the greatest possible profit for its owner, the incarnation. This profit was primarily used to support the incarnation, his activities, and his establishment. Since the incarnation was regarded as a precious person, it was important to protect him from hardship and illness and to facilitate a long life and freedom of action. However the profit from the labrangs was also used by the incarnations to support their monasteries and for other religious purposes.[62] The labrang was therefore a capitalist enterprise in the service of religion. Although all incarnations can be assumed to have had labrangs as residences, not all of those labrangs had a profit-making enterprise connected with them. On the other hand, some abbots who were not incarnations also had labrangs.[63]

The profit-making purpose of the labrangs was similar to the economic management of the monasteries themselves. The monastic business managers were monks, but their assistants, who managed properties or businesses outside the monasteries, may or may not have been monks. The income from the economic activities served to support the monasteries, the monks, and their religious activities. The monasteries, too, carried on profit-making capitalist activities to serve the overall religious purpose.

What is important for an assessment of the economic activities of both the labrangs and the monastic enterprises is the relative importance of the sources of income. Usually more than half the income came from land or, in the case of monasteries in nomadic areas, from animal husbandry, but a substantial part—estimated by some informants as 30 percent or more—came from trade, business, and banking activities, such as money lending and investment.[64] This openness of the religious economic enterprises to commercial and financial activities demonstrates that this type of Buddhist religious system might have been quite capable of serving a modern economy, in contrast to some medieval European or Asian religious or philosophical ideologies.

3

The Ecclesiastical and Secular Arms of Government

The Ecclesiastical Government and Bureaucracy

In accordance with the double function of the Dalai Lama's rule, the government administrative structure was divided into a religious and a secular segment. However the religious segment of the administration also dealt with the appointments of monk officials who had to handle secular matters, so the religious component of the Dalai Lama's government overlapped the secular. Throughout the complex government structure, religious and secular affairs were thus intricately intertwined.

At the head of the structure was the Dalai Lama himself, and all powers converged in his hands. He was an absolute ruler of unchallengeable authority. During a Dalai Lama's minority, this power was exercised by a regent, always a high lama,[1] who had almost the same power as that of the Dalai Lama himself. However, because a regent lacked the Dalai Lama's ultimate authority and the highest prestige connected with it, he had to be more cautious and circumspect in his actions, aware of the fact that his peers could vote him out of office and replace him, as indeed happened in more than one case. As a result, no regent could be as active or innovative as a Dalai Lama, and consequently the rule of the regents was sometimes characterized by political stagnancy and also by corruption. Indeed the fact that the rule by Dalai Lamas was interspersed by so many, often long, periods of regencies has been regarded as a distinct weakness of the Tibetan sociopolitical system.

Under the Dalai Lama, there were the two administrative structures, one secular and one religious. The personal staff of the Dalai Lama was headed by the *chikhyab kenpo* (literally, "chief abbot"), a lord chamberlain who served as the Dalai Lama's link with both the religious and the secular administrative staffs. The chikhyab kenpo took part in their sessions and lent his voice to the decision-making process in the highest religious and secular councils. He was selected by the Dalai Lama himself from the monk civil service as a personal secretary and counselor.

Under the Dalai Lama level, the two administrative structures remained divided,[2] and the religious administration was handled by the Tseyigtsang, the peak ecclesiastical secretariat. It consisted of four grand secretaries, high monk officials who held the fourth rank in the bureaucracy.[3]

The four grand secretaries (*drunyik chemo*) made their decisions jointly. The daily agenda for their sessions was prepared by a monk official who was the superintendent of the Tseyigtsang, which moved with the Dalai Lama from the Potala Palace in winter to the Norbu Linka Palace in summer. The office dealt with religious and particularly monastic affairs on its own authority under the Dalai Lama, with occasional consultations with the political branch of government, the Cabinet, when joint action was required. The importance of the Grand Secretariat was indicated by the popular name for the grand secretaries: the "four inner pillars" (*nangi kawazhi*).

The four grand secretaries handled the affairs of all monk officials – their appointments, transferals, or dismissals – as decided by the Dalai Lama. They dealt with monastic quarrels and subsidies to the monasteries, and in general they handled all monastic affairs. They also dispatched all orders of the Dalai Lama throughout the country. They were thus the chief executives of the Dalai Lama in the religious sector but also, as far as ecclesiastical authority affected and dominated the secular sector, of the Dalai Lama's government. The monk Cabinet minister and the lord chamberlain were usually chosen from the ranks of the grand secretaries. It is for this reason that we list the Grand Secretariat and its "four inner pillars" first in the institutional structure, even though the Cabinet ministers had a higher official rank, the third rank, than the grand secretaries, who held the fourth rank in Tibetan officialdom.

The grand secretaries also enjoyed a judicial authority as they adjudicated all civil suits between and within the monastic establishments. This adjudication included the disposal of property of deceased monks and cases of litigation between monastic institutions and secular people. In the latter case, the litigants had the freedom to submit their case to either the ecclesiastical or the secular authority, the Kashag, but submission to the grand secretaries had the advantage that the case could reach the Dalai Lama himself or the regent.

The authority of the grand secretaries extended in another crucial way into the area of secular affairs. Together with the four chiefs of the revenue department, they served as the joint chairmen of the General Assembly, the highest joint deliberative body of the Tibetan state, which was called only during times of special emergency or when major decisions were needed. They also served as joint chairmen of the assembly's smaller Working Committee, which met more frequently than the General Assembly. Both of these bodies were composed of religious as well as of secular leaders, but the religious leaders clearly had a major voice in the discussions as well as through the joint chairmanship of the grand secretaries.

For all these duties, each grand secretary maintained a personal staff of two or three aides—either monks or laymen—a manager, a secretary, and other assistants. The Grand Secretariat itself had a chief administrator, one assistant, twenty or more secretaries, about five trainees, one record keeper, and an indefinite number of messengers and servants. These were all nonofficial positions filled by monks or laymen.

The grand secretaries thus dealt not only with the specifically religious affairs of the Dalai Lama's government but also with the secular affairs. That fact demonstrates again the superior importance attached to the religious sector of the administration.

An essential responsibility of the grand secretaries was the selection and supervision of the education of future monk officials. For this purpose a special school was established at the Potala, the Peak School (Tselabdra). Its students, about thirty of them, were monks who were especially selected by the grand secretaries from a list submittd by the Gelukpa monasteries. The students entered the school when they were about fourteen to—at the most—nineteen or twenty for three years or more of study. The role of the grand secretaries was to decide on the qualifications of the students, who had to pass an examination, given twice a year, and to satisfy the secretaries in personal interviews as to their capabilities. The candidates were also interviewed by the Dalai Lama or the regent for final selection. This was the formal road to becoming a monk official.

Much larger numbers of future monk officials, however, did not attend the Peak School but accomplished the same preparation through private tutoring. These monk students came mostly from middle-class families of some wealth (and in a few cases, aristocratic families), which enabled them to maintain a certain expected standard of living and to wait for an appointment. These private students had to pass the same type of examination as the Peak School students, have personal interviews with the grand secretaries, and be approved by them. They were then introduced to the Dalai Lama or the regent for final selection.

All candidates thus selected, whether trained in the Peak School or through private studies, entered the ranks of the monk officials (*tsedrung*), the ecclesiastical bureaucracy that managed Tibet's secular as well as religious affairs together with the smaller number of lay officials (*shodrung*) in the secular section. Since the emphasis in education and government purpose was religious, it was this ecclesiastical bureaucracy that gave the political as well as the religious structure its cohesion and direction. The part played by the grand secretaries in supervising the selection of candidates and their

CHART OF

Dalai Lama
(or Regent)

Lord Chamberlain
(Chikhyab Kenpo)

ECCLESIASTICAL WING
(Sectarian and Monastic
Autonomy)

Monk Officials
(Tsedrung)

Grand Secretariat
(Tseyigtsang)

Peak School
(Tselabdra)

Gelukpa Order
and Monastic
Establishments
in General of
All Sects

General Assembly
(Tshokdhu Gyezom)

Working Committee
of General Assembly
(Tshokdhu Rakdu)

Finance & Mint Dept.
(Drazhi Ngukhang)

Peak Treasury
(Tsechak Lekhung)

Lhasa Supply Dept.
(Lhasa Nyertsang Lekhung)

Dept. of Agriculture
(Sonam Lekhung)

Doipal Craft Center

Commission for Nepalese
Citizens *(Gorzhip Lekhung)*

Treasury of Labrang at Lhasa
(Lachak Lekhung)

Subadministrative Institutions:
Estates   Towns
Elders and Headmen *(genpo, gopa, shepon)*
Meetings *(tsogzom)*

Common people *(Mi-ser: tral-pa,*

TIBETAN POLITY

```
                                    ┐
                 Regent or
                 Prime Minister
                       |
                 SECULAR WING
            Monk and Lay Officials
             (Tsedrung and Shodrung)
                       |
               Central Government
                       |
                    Cabinet
                    (Kashag)
                       |
               Office of Revenue
                  (Tsikhang)
```

Investigating Dept. of Land Taxes *(Babzhip Lekhung)*	Fodder Dept. *(Tsanyer)*
Peak Supply Dept. *(Nyertsang Lekhung)*	Fuel Dept. *(Shingchopa)*
Barley Supply Dept. *(Tsamsherwa)*	Dept. of Pub. Works *(Arpoi Lekhung)*
Dept. of Tea & Salt Taxes *(Jatsa Lekhung)*	West Lhasa Court *(Zho Lekhung)*
City Court of Lhasa *(Nangtse Sha)*	Dept. of Military Supplies *(Zho Phogkhang)*
Dept. of Checking Accounts *(Zhipkhang)*	Dept. of Foreign Affairs (1920)

Local Government

Provinces *(Chikyab)*
Districts *(Dzongs* and *Zhikas)*

du-chung, tsong-pa)

education was therefore of greatest importance.

The task of the grand secretaries extended beyond the training and selection of the monk officials to the management and supervision of the monk bureaucracy as a whole. The vast majority of the monks, however, did not serve in state offices. The monk bureaucracy that gave the Tibetan polity its cohesion and purpose was the instrument through which Buddhism dominated Tibetan life. It was also a broad avenue by which all class distinctions in Tibetan society were overcome; a means of social mobility that was available to all. It is true, as indicated earlier, that the opportunities of trade and business, crafts, and production management had created an urban middle class and a class of well-to-do farmers and herdsmen who, although technically mi-ser, had become for all intents and purposes financially independent. But only monastic service could change one's social status to a highly respected one, that of monkhood.

More than that, monastic service provided Tibetans with a religious ladder of success that could lead to the highest administrative offices and a prestige not only equal but actually superior to that of the aristocracy. This political and social opportunity was clearly a major attraction for the young Tibetans and their families, and it led many of them to enter monastic life.

The highest purpose in entering religious life was, however, a commitment to serve for the liberation (*moksha*) of all sentient beings. For a devout religious person, this service was the noblest end to which one's life could be devoted, and the concept of service was clearly inherent in the monastic system of Tibet. The vast majority of the monks chose the monastic life voluntarily. Actually, since they entered the monasteries as children, usually at the age of five or six, it was the parents who gave their children to the monasteries. The child, however, was at least old enough to agree, and—if one later found himself or herself unsuited for monastic life—a young monk or nun could always become an apostate and either choose a different life, returning to farming or trade, or continue in religious service without the stringent rules imposed by the monastic vows. But the basic motivation was service. It was indeed an honor to give one's life to this highest purpose, and the great esteem in which all monks and nuns were held attested to the general respect for those who gave this service.

This concept of highest service was underlined rather than disparaged by the fact that in addition to the voluntary enrollment that was the rule, monasteries also drafted people to become monks, especially monasteries in outlying areas that did not obtain enough voluntary recruits. In areas where labor was scarce it was a sacrifice to give up the manpower of sons or daughters to the religious institutions, but the draft was accepted everywhere and did not diminish the prestige of the monk or nun. This draft paralleled a similar draft of men from village communities for military service. As with the military draft, the draft of children for monasteries was allotted among the village families by the village elders, and where it was needed, the figure for monastic draftees appears to have been very much higher than that for soldiers.[4] Those families who contributed soldiers were compensated by being given additional, tax-free land. The families who contributed their children for ecclesiastical service received no such compensation—the religious purpose was apparently regarded as a reward in itself. Beyond that reward, however, religious service also provided a special opportunity, for those who were so inclined, to serve in the official or nonofficial management of human affairs. Monastic status opened the way to the highest administrative positions in the central, regional, and local governments.[5]

Only a few hundred of the perhaps half million monks, however, could hold those high positions because they were so limited in number. The large majority of the monks applied their efforts, energy, and interest to managing monastic estates, to work in arts and crafts, or to the respected occupations of teaching, arbitrating conflicts, and conducting religious services. They were the recognized leaders in the society and economy, invested with a singular prestige that all wearers of the monastic robes enjoyed. Had it not been for the Buddhist dictum that humility and modesty must be expressed in bearing and attitude, the monks could have considered themselves as the ruling elite of Tibet.

And indeed the monks had become superior to the aristocrats. In government service, for instance, the superior prestige of the monks may be seen from the fact that some sons of the high aristocracy preferred to become monk officials rather than to assume positions as secular officials, which they were entitled to do. By becoming monk officials, they added the aura of religious commitment to their service in the government. Another example of the special esteem in which monk officials were held is that a special rank was given to sons of Cabinet ministers who entered government service as senior officials, but such a prestige award was not deemed necessary if the same young men entered government service as a monk officials—as such, they gained a higher esteem than any special title could confer.[6] Not only monk officials but all monks shared in this esteem, and many testimonies confirm the fact that for the ordinary Tibetan man, woman, or child, a person in monastic dress was always the object of the greatest respect and reverence, second only to the incarnations.

The special attraction of administrative service, whether for the government or a monastic estate, led many to enter monastic life. In fact, the monks should be classified according to their calling and career. All those who entered the monasteries were called monks (*drapa*). They first took 5 basic vows—binding themselves to celibacy and abjuring killing, indeed all violence, intoxicating drinks, theft, and lying—and in status these monks were novices (rapjung). Between the ages of ten and twenty they took 31 additional vows and became getsul—still a novice category. At the age of twenty-one, with proper preparation and after consultation with their teachers and the abbot of the monastery, all monks could take additional vows to become full-fledged monks (gelong). For the last status, 253 additional vows had to be taken, and they contained many strict disciplinary rules for the daily life of a monk.[7]

Only a minority of the monks, particularly, but not exclusively, those turning to specialized higher religious studies—from logic and philosophy, ethics, and the lengthy study of important sutras to the advanced tantric studies, including meditation and higher yoga practices—would take these last vows and assume the gelong status with its severe disciplinary restraints. A majority of monks, an estimated two-thirds of them, remained novices and prepared themselves for other specialized service.[8] A goodly number in some monastic institutions turned to arts and crafts, became highly specialized in the art of tanka painting, sculptors, carpenters, weavers, goldsmiths and silversmiths, or other craftsmen. These monks provided all the religious art for the monasteries and the lay population, including the architecture, furniture, utensils, ritual instruments, and tools needed by the monasteries and the general public.[9]

The most important group in terms of the religiopolitical system, perhaps a third of the total number of monks, aimed from the outset at administrative careers. From this group the government primarily selected its officials, and the majority of the monk officials were not fully ordained monks. The "novice" monk officials, whether trained at the Peak School or by private tutors, who were the candidates for administrative careers had to come from the monasteries—chiefly, but not exclusively, from the three great monasteries near Lhasa. Since such a career was most prestigious and desirable, it became a special goal for the sons of well-to-do or well-connected subject families. These children entered the most influential monasteries and then extended their studies under private tutors or at the Peak School with this final aim in mind. In a few cases it seems that young men—who were about nineteen, had not entered any monastery in childhood, and had had some private tutoring—nominally entered a monastery, with the approval of the abbot, by enrolling in the monastic membership and taking the novice vows but without participating in monastic life so as to be able to become candidates for government service.[10] This occasional practice demonstrates both the singular attractiveness of an administrative career and the control the monastic institutions had over government service.

That a majority of monk officials or their families regarded this career as the primary reason for entering monastic life may be inferred from the composition of the monk bureaucracy. It has been estimated that about two-thirds of the three hundred to four hundred monk officials were novices and only one-third were fully ordained monks. The difficulty of obeying the 253 strict disciplinary rules as a full-time administrator in government service is a major explanation of the preponderance of novices among the monk officials, but the ratio also indicates the division within the monk community between those who followed a fully religious life and those who aimed at and turned to a life of active participation in mundane affairs. This latter inclination did not, of course, have to affect the second group's religious outlook or the importance of religious beliefs in the handling of their responsibilities. Conversely, that one-third of the monk officials were fully ordained monks provides proof of the religious orientation of the Tibetan government. In fact, the one-third percentage of the fully ordained monks in the bureaucracy held high positions, which reveals the importance that was attached to the dedication and learning of such monks by the Dalai Lama and the leadership of the monasteries.

The same approximate personnel division according to the educational preparation, career development, and eventual activities and assignments of monks existed in most monasteries throughout Tibet. Approximately one-third of the monks were fully ordained and followed a life of academic religious study, teaching, and service; one-third prepared for and practiced arts and crafts and served the daily needs of the monasteries; and one-third became financial administrators, managers of the estates, or managers of other business affairs of the monasteries.[11]

It was the fully ordained monks who provided the greatest service to Tibetan society. They were the teachers, not only of the monk novices in the monasteries but also of the laity in private homes or in communities. They had the prestige to act as arbiters in conflicts if the monastery itself did not become involved, but most of all they rendered most of the religious services to the laity at festivals and in times of sickness, death, and other auspicious or adverse events. Their duties encompassed what the concept of service to humanity, of compassion for all sentient beings, was presumed to be. The managers of the monasteries—who provided charity, arbitrated conflicts, and determined justice in lesser cases—as well as the artists and artisans also contributed, but to a lesser degree, to this concept of service. It was through such service that religious beliefs and the religious organization had their greatest impact on Tibetan society.

As has been true in most premodern societies, the role of government in Tibet was very limited. There were only perhaps five hundred to seven hundred officials for about three million people, a ratio of about four thousand to six thousand people for each official. On the district level, the lowest level of administration and the chief contact between the government and the people, the ratio of about two hundred to two hundred fifty magistrates for the same number of people was even more unequal. This disproportion between the number of officials and the number of people whose affairs they were to manage is itself sufficient proof of the limited scope of government action. It also explains the great extent to which social and economic affairs were carried on outside of the framework of the state and its officials.

Clearly this restraint of government was intended and in line with Buddhist religious philosophy. It meant that only the more difficult issues were brought to the attention of government officials. Most affairs were handled locally—within the communities, the villages, and the camps—chiefly by local headmen with more or less popular participation. In the case of monastic or aristocratic estates, most affairs were handled by the estate managers. It was on the subadministrative local level, the level of the life of the ordinary people, that the monks played their major part. One may describe this nonofficial activity as social leadership, in contrast to the government management of major affairs by the monk officials and their secular counterparts.[12] In this way, the monk bureaucracy dominated not only the state but also the social order, giving Tibetan polity and society their value system, ethics, beliefs, and "other-worldly" aim.

The framework for all this religiously motivated life remained, however, the state government, which dominated the social order as much by suasion and public acceptance of its role based on religious faith as on the exercise of its authority. The very looseness of the political structure was an indication of a system of rule by religious precepts whose tenets were a matter of all-pervasive faith. The important controlling role of the Dalai Lama's government in the ecclesiastical sector consisted of the supervision and support of the monastic estates and the selection, training, appointment, promotion, transfer, recall, and direction not only of the monk-official bureaucracy in general, but also of the abbots of monasteries and the administration of the leading Gelukpa order. This role linked government with the social responsibility of religion. In this area the Grand Secretariat was the primary controlling and coordinating agency of the Dalai Lama's government.

The Secular Section of the Administration

The Dalai Lama's secular administration was headed by a prime minister and a Cabinet. The prime ministers were appointed chiefly during the rule of a Dalai Lama; in the intermittent periods, during the rule of regents, prime ministers were not appointed,[13] and the regents themselves assumed the full management of government. The thirteenth Dalai Lama appointed three prime ministers, two laymen and one monk, who acted jointly in deciding matters of state. The fourteenth Dalai Lama appointed two prime ministers during his rule in Tibet, one monk and one layman, who also acted jointly. The term prime minister (*silon*; literally, "political minister") is somewhat misleading. The position did not include chairing Cabinet sessions, or even participating in Cabinet action, but rather a special responsibility to act as liaison between the Cabinet and the Dalai Lama, as well as to assume some functions that the Dalai Lama wanted to avoid, such as final action in criminal cases. All final authority remained in the hands of the Dalai Lama, and the position of prime minister was therefore not as important as the title implies, although the prime ministers enjoyed considerable personal influence and held second rank.

Most of the executive work in the secular field was handled by the Cabinet (Kashag), which was composed of four ministers (*kalon*). Three of these ministers were secular officials, and one was a monk.[14] They held the third rank and were known as the "four outer pillars." They were appointed by the Dalai Lama or the regent and worked together six days a week, making joint decisions. In cases of disagreement, discussion carried on until any dissenting member would eventually accept a majority decision.

The Cabinet ministers, acting jointly, had the same functions of selecting, appointing, promoting, and recalling secular officials as the grand secretaries had over the ecclesiastical bureaucrats. The prime minister who was a monk participated fully in these decisions, which indicates the religious role and its importance in the secular aspects of government.

The secular officials were derived from the aristocratic families, who held their estates in exchange for the obligation to provide at least one son per estate to serve as an official in the government. The candidates received practical training in the Tsikhang, the Office of Revenue; were tested by the heads of that department jointly, and if found adequately prepared, recommended to the Kashag for appointment to official rank. From this group of officials-in-waiting, the Cabinet selected its appointees to administrative positions in the central government as well as in the provinces and districts.

The major function of the Cabinet was to appoint, promote, transfer, recall, and supervise those officials. It received reports from all central, regional, and local officials, acted on their requests, and issued directives and orders. Each year the Kashag issued a general directive to the governors and local officials, admonishing them to maintain standards of fairness and justice in their treatment of the people and to keep the welfare of the public always in mind. This yearly exhortation, which repeated in substance the chief principles of the central government, was simply a reminder that those principles were not to be taken lightly.

The Cabinet decided on all aspects of taxation—the rates, new taxes, local or specific tax exemptions. It dealt with questions of allocating funds for

Kalon Juchen Thubten, Cabinet minister and former ritual dancer in Rajpur (photo by Franz Michael and Eugene Knez).

secular purposes, considering revenue and expenditure in a budgetlike manner, although not as systematically as under modern budget planning. In the same field of financial management, the Cabinet authorized the printing of paper money and the minting of coins. It also directed the printing of postage stamps.

The Cabinet also dealt with the allotment of income for secular positions. As stated earlier, the sons of well-to-do aristocratic families were expected to render their service in exchange for the estates that provided them with ample income. But some secular officials held positions to which income was attached, regardless of the status of the official—whether monk or secular.

Such offices were the regional and local positions of governor and district magistrate, as well as a few positions in the central government such as handling storage supplies or the treasury.

The records for those income payments were kept by the Cabinet, which also fixed the rates. In a few exceptional cases the Cabinet would decide to add income to the nonincome positions of aristocratic officials, because their estate income was regarded as too meager to provide for their office expenses. One such case was the grant of extra income to one of the three secular aristocratic Cabinet ministers in the 1940s. That case, like others, was decided by the Cabinet with the approval of the regent.

The Cabinet supervised regional and local administration. Minor matters were left to the discretion of the local officials, but all important matters had to be reported regularly for the Cabinet's decision, and if necessary, the Cabinet would initiate its own investigation, sending investigators and requiring further reports, before taking action.

To carry out their functions, the Cabinet ministers had the aid of a rather varied staff. Each minister was served by a personal staff of six—one lay official as aide-de-camp, one chief of protocol, and four attendants. These staff members were all laymen without official rank; they were in the private service of the minister and lived in his residence. In addition the minister had his own domestic servants—a manager, a secretary, steward, maids, kitchen staff, and grooms. The personal staff had to be paid out of the minister's pocket, supposedly provided for by the minister's private income except for the monk (and exceptional cases), for whom a special income was provided.

The Cabinet as a whole had the assistance of three or four secretaries, three or four protocol officers, and three or four officers who prepared and distributed documents and orders. These were unpaid lay officials, who were presumed to have an adequate private income of their own. They also would count on receiving gifts from applicants and complainants, which were not regarded as bribes as long as they were within recognized limits. The lower-level nonofficial staff of the Cabinet—including scribes, messengers, and numerous other attendants—received payment for their work.

In its political role, the Cabinet would call upon and be supported by the General Assembly (Tshokdhu Gyezom) and the Working or Standing Committee of the General Assembly (Tshokdhu Rakdü). Both of these assemblies were called into session by the Cabinet, but the Cabinet ministers did not participate in the assembly sessions. The General Assembly, or Great Assembly, was composed of all officials, both lay and monk officials, including military officers; the abbots and representatives of the three great monasteries; representatives of professional secular groups such as artists, craftsmen, tailors, blacksmiths; and representatives of some special middle-class associations such as traders, nonofficial secretaries, and semireligious lay groups—a total of about seven hundred people.

The assembly was regarded as representing the nation and was therefore called into session during times of crisis or for major national decisions. One of its functions was to nominate the regent during a Dalai Lama's minority by discussing the candidates and selecting three finalists. The final decision among the three candidates recommended for the regency was made by lot. Each name was written on a piece of paper, rolled into flour balls, and placed in a bowl for a churning ritual in a special temple. The ball that dropped out first contained the name of the selected candidate.

The assembly was jointly chaired by the four grand secretaries and the three or four lay chiefs of the revenue department, a half-ecclesiastical and half-secular chairmanship of the most broadly representative secular institution. Every member of the assembly was able to speak and did so, but the main voices were those of the representatives of the three great monasteries.[15]

Since the Great Assembly was called only on special occasions, its Working Committee was the regular representative body. The Working Committee was also called by the Kashag for important decisions. The conflict with the Panchen Lama, border troubles with China, the investigation of a former regent, a 1945 declaration that demanded the return of territory from Nationalist China and a reaffirmation of Tibet's independent relationship were among the issues taken up by this Working Committee, or Small Assembly. The Small Assembly consisted of about fifty representatives of officials of various ranks, both ecclesiastical and secular; military officers; and the three leading Gelukpa monasteries—a predominatly ecclesiastical group. Their decisions carried great weight with the Cabinet and the Dalai Lama or regent. In both the Great Assembly and the Small Assembly, the ecclesiastical leadership provided the decisive influence in the management of worldly affairs.

Government Agencies and Procedures

Management of Economic Affairs

The most important secular agency under the Cabinet was the Office of Revenue (Tsikhang). Its most important function was to maintain up-to-date records of the government's as well as the estates' lands and herds and of the revenue derived from them. It supervised payments and informed the Cabinet about them. The department was headed by four lay officials (*tsipon*) of the fourth rank, who acted jointly. As aristocrats they were believed to have sufficient private income from their estates to make a salary unnecessary. The position of tsipon was regarded as a stepping-stone to becoming a Cabinet minister, and the department served also as a training school for aristocratic lay official candidates. These candidates usually entered the department at the age of fifteen or sixteen after previous private schooling for a period of three to four years.[1] After their schooling, they had to pass one test on the system of accounting and other administrative work and another test on the writing of documents, which were given by the four tsipon. If the candidates passed, they were recommended by the tsipon to the Cabinet for official appointment.[2]

The revenue department often had an important investigating role assigned to it by the Cabinet in civil suits or serious charges of corruption or exploitation filed by subjects against district magistrates or estates. Although other departments were also occasionally assigned such investigating roles, the Tsikhang was the chief instrument for the Cabinet's supervisory control over government agencies and the economy. Together with the four grand secretaries, the four tsipon chaired the General Assembly and its Working Committee, a further indication of their key secular administrative position. The administrative staff of the Tsikhang was headed by four lay accounting officers, who supervised the work of the fifteen or more student trainees acting as scribes and office staff.

Directly under the Cabinet was the Finance and Mint Department (Drazhi Ngükhang), which was established in 1920 and located at Drazhi near Lhasa.[3] It handled the printing of paper money, in denominations of two, five, seven and a half, ten, twenty-five and one hundred sang (one sang being equal to one-fifth of a rupee); the printing of postage stamps; and the coining of money in silver and copper, in denominations of one, one and a half, and three sang; one, five, and seven and a half kar; one, three, and five zho (ten kar equaled one zho; ten zho equaled one sang). The department supplied cash to the various government agencies under the direction of the Cabinet. The department also bought gold for a gold reserve held in the treasury of the Potala. This purchase was in addition to the gold tax imposed on the private gold miners (before 1920).

Like so many of the agencies, the Finance and Mint Department was headed by four chiefs, who were officials of the fourth rank. Two of them were monks, the other two were lay officials. As a rule, one of the monk officials was a grand secretary, which indicates the importance of the department and the power of the ecclesiastical structure in the field of economic affairs. The staff consisted of about half a dozen ranking officials, secular as well as ecclesiastical, and nonofficial lay secretaries. The department had its own military guard.

To assist the government in the management of revenue, an Investigating Department of Land Taxes (Babzhip Lekhung) was created in the 1940s to check the payment of land taxes in kind from estates and government mi-ser under guidelines issued by the Cabinet. This department was also assigned the task of investigating some of the civil suits before the Cabinet. The department was headed by some of the highest monk and lay officials, namely, one of the grand secretaries and one chief of the Office of Revenue, working with a staff of about half a dozen ranking officials, both ecclesiastical and secular.

A similar function was handled by the Department of Checking Accounts (Zhipkhang). Its task was to review the accounts of the government departments for errors or falsification, and it also occasionally dealt with civil suits. It was headed by one chief of revenue and two high-ranking monk officials, working with a staff of two lay officials and one monk official.

Another central government department was the Department of Tea and Salt Taxes (Jatsa Lekhung). It supervised the tea and salt tax collectors and checked their accounts. The collectors were monk or lay officials appointed by the Tsikhang or the Cabinet. They were posted at the salt mines and on the caravan routes to collect a tax in kind, which was generally very modest. They had also a Cabinet license to requisition transportation service. The department—headed by one monk, one lay official, and a combined small staff—simply supervised and checked the accounts.

Loans were made available to officials and common people by a committee of the Namgen Treasury (Namgen Mangül), which met once a year at the Potala Palace, or by other departments such as the Finance and Mint

Department, the Treasury of Labrang, and the Peak Treasury. The interest rate was 10 percent to 12 percent per annum, whereas private loans were usually at a 50 percent higher rate.

The management and distribution of funds and materials were carried out by a number of supply departments, which dealt with the allocation of funds in kind to the chief religious and secular agencies. The Peak Treasury (Tsechak Lekhung) supplied the Dalai Lama's personal, palace, and secretarial material needs, such as rice, tea, butter, fruit for people and offerings, clothing, and furniture. The treasury was headed by two monk officials and one lay official of the fourth rank. The staff consisted of a principal secretary (chakdrung) and about twenty staff members (chaknang), who held quasi-official rank. They were recruited from ordinary middle-class people, government mi-ser, scribes, and court dancers–people who could hold positions only within these supply departments. They were not among the ranking government officials.

The Peak Treasury assigned personnel for low-level work in other agencies, and it was also in charge of and maintained lay groups of dancers, the court dancers (fifty in number), the lay mask dancers, and various folk-opera troupes. The dancers performed inside the palaces, especially at New Year's and on other important occasions.

The Peak Supply Department (Nyertsang Lekhung) provided the chief staple food, ground barley flour, to the palaces and temples. It was headed by three monk officials of the fifth rank and staffed by nonranking laymen and secretaries.

The Treasury of Labrang at Lhasa (Lachak Lekhung), named after its location, provided supplies–barley flour, butter, woolen cloth, stationery, and the like–to the various government offices, such as the Cabinet and other government agencies, and also to monasteries and nunneries around Lhasa for religious offerings, as ordered by the Grand Secretariat. This department was managed by four officials of the fourth rank, two monk and two secular officials. Their staff was the same as that of the Peak Treasury.

Of special importance among the supply departments was the Lhasa Supply Department (Lhasa Nyertsang Lekhung), which had the same supply functions as the Peak Treasury for the agencies in Lhasa. It was administered by four officials of the fifth rank, two monks and two laymen, and a staff like that of the Peak Treasury. The Lhasa Supply Department also had the important duty of supervising the maintenance of the main temple in Lhasa, the Jokhang, built in the seventh century by the Nepalese princess consort of King Songtsen Gampo. The department handled the flood control work of the Lhasa river, the Kyichu, and the upkeep of the underground sewage drainage system, managing the necessary corvée labor, which was made up of government mi-ser from the Lhasa region and mi-ser from monasteries and

Jokhang temple and view of the Potala (photo by David T. Parry).

aristocrats' landholdings. As in the outlying regions, the supervision and management of flood control and irrigation were thus in the hands of government agencies.

Other regional departments located in Lhasa included the Barley Supply Department (Tsamsherwa), which distributed staple food to the monks during the Mönlam festival, when the monks from the big monasteries assembled in Lhasa for three weeks. The department was managed by one monk, one lay official, and a nonranking staff. There were also a Fodder Department (Tsanyer) for the Dalai Lama's stable, which was managed by two lay officials, and a Fuel Department (Shingchopa), which supplied the common kitchen during the Mönlam festival in February and was managed by two monk officials.

For the management of the government's land reclamation policy, there was a Department of Agriculture (Sonam Lekhung). Established under the thirteenth Dalai Lama as part of his reform program,[4] it had the task of administering a project for the cultivation of unused land. To increase production and government income, the Dalai Lama's government had decreed that vacant land could be occupied and cultivated by anyone, and to make this offer more attractive, a new occupant was to be exempt from land tax for three years. The department was directed by four monk and secular officials of the fifth rank, with a ranking staff of four or five and some secretarial assistance.

Interested potential farmers could apply to the department for allocations of land. For the tral-pa and dü-chung this was one way to increase their income. In this way a landless person (dü-chung) could become, in fact, a tax-paying government tral-pa, a status that was more attractive despite the taxes.

Of regional importance was the Department of Public Works (Arpöi Lekhung). Its function was to build and repair government houses, temples, and monasteries in and around Lhasa[5] under the direction of the Tsikhang and the Cabinet. The department was headed by one ranking monk and one ranking lay official and had a small staff. Its functions included supplying material and funds as well as supervising the work and hiring the workers. The architectural and design planning was done by lay builders, who were privately trained and paid for their work.

Of special interest was a government department that handled business relations with the craftsmen and artisans in Lhasa. The Doipal Craft Center, located at the foot of the Potala, assigned commissions to individual craftsmen or guilds for work on the palaces and government buildings in Lhasa. The existence and functions of this government agency substantiate the fact that an independent middle class was very much a part of the social structure in the capital city. In other cities, which were not the seat of the central government or of a government agency, this social middle class dealt directly with its clients. The craftsmen and artisans—silversmiths and goldsmiths, painters and sculptors, carpenters, tailors, blacksmiths, and weavers (not under this department)—were mostly organized into associations or "guilds," were much more numerous than the respective professionals in the monk population, and worked not only for their secular public and private clients but also often for monasteries.

Laws and Legal Procedure

The first Tibetan law codes of the "sixteen pure human rules," expressed within the confines of Buddhist ethics,[6] and the "four fundamental laws" were ascribed to King Songtsen Gampo, together with laws of punishment against the "ten sins." The last attribution may have been made in order to justify, from a historical and an ideological point of view, the codification in 1346 of a similar code of chal by Changchub Gyaltsen, the lama king. The original text of each legal code was expanded several times and combined with additional matter. In the view of a most astute student of the codes, the introduction of a legal system can, in essence, be regarded as a part of Songtsen Gampo's great administrative accomplishment.[7]

The sixteen-article code and the later code of chal remained in use until the end of Tibetan polity, brought about by the Chinese takeover in 1959. The punishments applied for major crimes, such as murder, theft, sexual misconduct, false testimony, or banditry, were harsh. As in other premodern Western and non-Western legal systems, the punishments included several forms of capital punishment, mutilation, incarceration, fines, and flogging.[8]

The application of the law, both civil and criminal, was a function of the Lhasa government, and the cabinet functioned as the highest court of the country in both civil and criminal cases. It dealt with interdepartmental and interpersonal disputes in the administration. In cases of major crimes, capital punishment and mutilation (before they were abolished) were decided on by the Cabinet alone. (As an exception, the governor of Kham had this authority too.) Mutilation was no longer practiced after the 1920s,[9] and even after capital punishment and mutilation were abolished, the Cabinet still acted as the criminal court for cases of treason and sacrilege. In civil cases, the Cabinet functioned as a court of appeal for decisions made by the dzongpon or governors. Usually the parties either came in person to Lhasa or sent representatives to take their case to the Cabinet and/or to the prime minister or regent. In the latter case, the regent or prime minister would approve or alter Cabinet recommendations. In the most serious cases, the Dalai Lama himself, if of age, could be appealed to. His decision was final.

In preparation for its decision or recommendation to the Dalai Lama or regent, the Cabinet assigned an appropriate department or its own staff to investigate a case. Each decision, stamped with a black square seal, was read in the reception corridor of the Cabinet to the parties concerned, who then received copies of it. If the Dalai Lama decided the case, his own seal was affixed to the case, which was then handled by the grand secretaries. In criminal cases involving capital punishment before 1920, the Dalai Lama had avoided any personal role because of his religious position.

The judicial authority over major criminal matters rested in the person of the Dalai Lama and was managed on the central government level by the Cabinet. All major criminal cases were regarded as secular matters. If a major crime was committed by a monk, he was expelled by his monastery and then handed over to the respective secular authorities in the district or province. The final adjudication of a case was in the hands of the Cabinet, the prime minister, or the regent. Before making a decision on the central level, a more complex case was assigned to the Criminal Investigation Department (Sherkhang Lekhung). It was up to that department to investigate the case and to collect testimony and data to be submitted with its recommendations to the Cabinet. For this investigation, the department depended on the cooperation of the respective dzongpon, who had to present the accused, the witnesses, and the necessary data. If the issue involved an accusation against a person or persons by a group of persons, as happened frequently as a result of local quarrels and violence, then the accused party or parties and the complainants would appear before the department to argue their case. The investigating judges (*sherpang*) were two lay officials assisted by a small staff of clerks.

Although for Tibet as a whole, the first instance of judicial authority was the dzongpon, in Lhasa and a neighboring suburb, special local courts were set up. The City Court of Lhasa (Nangtse Sha) dealt with crimes committed in the inner city of Lhasa. This court used a small number of constables, about fifty, to deal with criminals and to maintain security and order. Under the thirteenth Dalai Lama, a modern police force for the city was set up in the 1920s, after the British model.[10] Its full strength was to be five hundred men, but it never enrolled more than some two hundred officers. The judges of the court were three lay officials of the fifth rank, assisted by a staff of three secretaries and about fifty civilian inspectors as well as some prison guards.

A similar criminal court, the West Lhasa Court (Zhö Lekhung), had jurisdiction over the area west of Lhasa, below the Potala Palace. Its three judges consisted of two monks and one lay official of the fifth rank. Their staff was the same as that of the city court, but they commanded a smaller number of constables. In addition, they were in charge of a purely ceremonial force: two regiments of infantry in splendid ancient uniforms that took part in the parade at the official prayer festival (Mönlam festival) in February when the monks of the three great monasteries came to Lhasa to conduct the ceremonies. The regiments also participated on that and other occasions in the ceremonies honoring the two chief guardians of the Buddhist religion, the Red-Black Religious Protectors, at their respective temples.

The criminal court of Lhasa and the suburban court were both under the direction of the Cabinet, to which they had to report and which, in cases of dispute, acted as a higher court of appeal.

The Military

The Cabinet was also in charge of the military forces, which were garrisoned in and around Lhasa and on the borders, particularly in eastern Tibet along the Chinese border. Traditionally the official number was about 15,000 men, but the actual total was only about 12,000 men. The force was composed of regiments, designated by letters of the Tibetan alphabet, and the regiments were of uneven strength. Most of them contained 526 men, but others had far more than that (see adjoining table).[11]

The modern Tibetan military system differed substantially from that of the earlier period of Tibetan history. Under the kings—when Tibetan power extended into northern India, central Asia, and western China—the

Tibetan Military Regiments

Region	Regiment	Number	Recruited from
Lhasa	Ka	500	Ü region
Lhasa	Kha	1,056	Ü and Lho
Shigatse	Ga	1,000	Shigatse, Gyantse, Aungden Palbar
Ngari	Ca	1,000	Ngari Province
Ngari	Cha	526	Jarra, Dakpo, and Kongpo in the Southeast
Ngari	Ja	526	Ü region
Kham	Nja	526	Ü region
Kham	Ta	526	Ü region
Kham	Tha	526	Ü region
Kham	Da	526	Ngari (Lhatse, Ngamring, and Phuntsok Choling)
Lhasa	Na	1,800	Drongdrak[a]
Kham	Pa, Pha, and Ma	1,550 (combined)	Kham
Changtang	Tsa	800	Changtang
Kham	Tsha	1,000	Kham (Sho-tar-Lho sum)

[a] Sons of aristocrats and wealthy families; dissolved in 1935 because of resistance by those families.

Tibetans were an armed people. Their military units, divided into center, forward and backward, and right and left wings, were an administrative as well as a military organization. The civil administrators of the districts were primarily responsible for the supply of the military forces. The center of the district, the dzong, was originally a fortress and military supply base. Because of the character of organization as a "nation in arms," warfare was chiefly seasonal so that it would not interfere with the labor needed for agriculture.[12]

The old system changed after the establishment of ecclesiastical rule by the fifth Dalai Lama and also because of Chinese influence under the Manchu emperor K'ang-hsi in 1721. The so-called patron-priest relationship was introduced as well as the new organization of a Tibetan army. This was the beginning of a professional army, which had the much more limited function of securing internal order and guarding frontiers rather than of building up a Tibetan power in central Asia. It was this organizational change, rather than a change of character of the Tibetans under the influence of Buddhism, that ended the military role of Tibet in central Asia. True, Buddhism was against military action for the sake of military conquest, but the fighting quality of individual Tibetans, including the monks, was not lost.

As a tool of government, however, the professional army was clearly neglected. The military commanders were not professionals but sons of the aristocracy, and they received their service assignments with no training that was even comparable to that which their civilian counterparts were given in the government schools and as apprentices in the government agencies. There were no military schools. Lower officers rose from the ranks, and higher officers were assigned without training. Soldiers were expected to have a knowledge of firearms and were drilled. Their later performance against a superiorly equipped enemy was proof more of their individual spirit and valor than of their training.

The military system was incorporated into the bureaucracy under the Cabinet. Two commanders in chief were appointed, a monk and a lay official, and they held the position of third rank. Together they formed the military headquarters and were in charge of maintaining the army, training, deployment, and the acquisition of weapons. In times of emergency, they were also presumed to be in charge of the militia and the often large number of monk soldiers.

The soldiers received their food supply and uniforms from the government and from the estates and communities from which they had been drafted. (In case of transport difficulty, cash was provided instead of supplies.) The soliders were also paid a small amount (three sang per month) by the Department of Military Supplies (Zhö Phogkhang), which was managed by two paymaster generals, one monk and one lay official. This department received the food grains and woolens from the estates and communities for the soldiers and sent them to different areas to be stored and distributed.

Both the commanders in chief and the paymaster generals had personal and administrative staffs. All told, there were four fourth-ranking monk and lay officials (*khenchung* and *rimzhi*), six monk and lay staff officials, and a substantial clerical and administrative staff. In addition, each commander in chief had his own personal staff; the same was true for the two paymaster generals.[13]

This military bureaucracy was all under the control and direction of the Cabinet. Although the Cabinet's control was consistent with modern Western concepts of civilian authority over the military, there was in Tibet little professional military knowledge or contribution to the religiopolitical direction of the bureaucratic system. To a large degree, the survival of the polity was entrusted to faith rather than to preparedness. During a program of military reorganization that was carried out in the 1920s, under the thirteenth Dalai Lama, the role and the attitude of the military commanders became political issues that led to the removal of the military commanders. The importance of this incident in relation to Tibet's military ability to resist the Chinese invasion later is still a matter of argument.[14]

Foreign Affairs

In the absence of a foreign office, which existed only for short periods at the turn of the twentieth century and again in the early forties, the only agency to deal with foreign affairs—aside from the Cabinet—was a Commission for Nepalese Citizens in Lhasa (Gorzhip Lekhung). The large number of Nepalese traders in Lhasa—who lived in Lhasa city, made a good living, and paid no taxes—were dealt with by this commission, which also handled occasional crimes, disputes involving Nepalese, and problems arising between Nepalese and Tibetans. The commission was headed by a joint team of Tibetan and Nepalese officials, the latter from the Nepalese diplomatic delegation in Lhasa.[15]

Foreign affairs—insofar as they existed, at first mainly with China, India, and the Tibetan border states—were handled by the Cabinet, as were any other political issues. Only at the beginning of the twentieth century and because of the impact of the Western powers, especially British and Russian, did the thirteenth Dalai Lama establish a Department of Foreign Affairs under the control of the Cabinet. That department did not alter Cabinet decision-making procedures or the orientation of the religiosecular bureaucratic structure. Economically a base for the emergence of modern statehood may have been in the process of development, but the political and particularly the military understanding of the new and dangerous elements threatening Tibet's survival came too late.

The Art of Healing and the Role of Oracles

Included in the ecclesiastical sector of the administration was the field of medicine. The historical reason for this combination was partly that the art of healing came chiefly from India at the same time as and combined with the introduction of Buddhism. The Indian medical system, known in India as the Ayurveda, was used by both Hindus and Buddhists and was the chief source for four Tibetan esoteric texts of medicine. This theory of the art of healing was based on anatomical explanation, medicinal herbs, fruits, and the use of assumed medical properties of precious stones, minerals, animal products, and water. Illness, believed to be caused by an imbalance of the "three humors"—bile, phlegm, and air—which was in turn based on psychological imbalance caused by delusion, lust, and hatred, had to be treated by restoring the balance. Also required, however, was the removal of the deeper cause through psychoreligious methods that changed the behavior of the patient.

That Indian medical tradition became combined with the indigenous tradition of the herbal treatment of diseases and was also influenced by Chinese medical methods, especially the diagnostic use of pulse feeling.[16] Minor surgery was performed as well as acupuncture and moxibustion (burning of the skin as a counterirritant), but the major treatment consisted of the prescription and use of pills and powders and dietary control. Pills, containing many ingredients, were used for treatment as well as for general health and longevity. Some were produced by the Dalai Lama's or other incarnations' court physicians and were given out to the faithful as gifts, along with the incarnation's blessing.

The training of physicians in Lhasa was conducted in two institutions. One, on Chakpori (Iron Hill) opposite the Potala, was known by its location. It was entirely ecclesiastical in nature, and its six or seven teachers were monks who were also medical practitioners. The approximately two dozen students were also monks. This institution was under the general supervi-

Jokhang temple with view of ruins on Iron (Medical) Hill (photo by David T. Parry).

sion and direction of the Grand Secretariat. The other medical college, called the College of Medicine and Astrology (Mentsikhang), was located in the center of the city of Lhasa. In recent times, its two leading physician teachers were monk officials; of the fifty or more students, about one-half were monks, and of the lay half, the majority were military men. This institution was established only in the 1920s by the thirteenth Dalai Lama. In addition to institutional training, there was a long-standing tradition that each practicing physician trained his own student apprentices.

Any examination of the religiopolitical structure would be incomplete without a discussion of the role played by the state oracle in deciding important policies that affected both the secular and the religious world. The practice of using oracles can be traced back to ancient societies in most parts of the world. In Tibet it existed in pre-Buddhist times, and the practice was taken over by the Buddhists. It was used throughout the country in the monasteries and by the lay people. The oracles were lay professionals — with the exception of a minority who were monks — and they were consulted on most personal decisions, such as marriages and other family matters or business ventures and journeys.

In the same tradition, state oracles were selected for political advice and appointed as monk officials. There was one chief state oracle and two lower state oracles. The question of which of the three oracles would be consulted depended on the importance of the matter under consideration. For most important matters, the Dalai Lama would invite the chief state oracle to his residence, and the oracle would go into trance and then answer questions addressed to him by the Dalai Lama in person. The most important questions were dealt with in secret by whispering into the ears of the oracle and the Dalai Lama. Other predictions were given at different places, mostly at the Nechung monastery where the chief state oracle resided.

The questions asked dealt with such matters as the selection of a new incarnation of the Dalai Lama, asked by the regent or the grand secretaries and the Cabinet, or what policies to follow in a time of national crisis, such as an imminent Chinese invasion. The same officials also asked routine questions during their yearly visits to the Nechung monastery about the health of the Dalai Lama and the regent and the peace and security of the country. Abbots and leading lamas also consulted the chief state oracle for advice on problems at their institutions.

The influence of the Nechung oracle as a sort of spiritual political adviser must not be underestimated. The oracle was regarded as a medium through whom the spirit spoke. The delicate nature of the task demanded physical well-being and spiritual strength, and the oracle was required to lead a dedicated religious and secluded life. The predecessor of the present state oracle constantly predicted the imminent pending disaster threatening from the East, and the present incumbent accompanied the Dalai Lama on his flight to India. The faithful believed that the chief state oracle was seized in his trances by the very powerful force of the protective deity, Pehar. In a way, the state oracle personified the very concept of religious dominance in the affairs of man.[17]

5
Provincial and Local Government

Limited Government

In theory, the central government of Lhasa had complete authority over the whole of Tibet. The border of Tibet toward the South and West—today's India including Ladakh—though contested in some areas, had remained basically unchanged since the fifth Dalai Lama. But the eastern border of Kham and eastern parts of Amdo and Changtang had suffered over the years from a continuing and growing Chinese encroachment that brought more and more territory under Chinese control and administration. The extension of the territory of the Chinese province of Yunnan and the creation of the provinces of Sikang and Chinghai in the 1920s pushed back the Tibetan frontier by hundreds of kilometers. One reason for the uncertainty about Tibetan population figures is the great difference between the political and ethnic boundaries as the former came to be drawn during the last century. When the Chinese occupied Tibet, the Tibetan Autonomous Region of China was formed, but it comprises only the central and western parts of the former Tibetan state.

Until 1959, Tibet included central Tibet, the western province of Ngari, most of Kham in the east, and the larger part of the steppe pasturelands and deserts of Changtang in the North. In view of the great distances in the eastern, northern, and western parts of Tibet, the difficulty of premodern communication on horseback or by runners, over large stretches of land with no or little population, would have made central control over the whole country on a regular daily basis problematic under any governmental system.

Under the Buddhist religiopolitical system, an intensive form of central control and government was not even sought. The concept of limited government was inherent in this Buddhist system and concerned not only the question of central control but also control by regional and local governments. The small number of officials in proportion to the population, which has already been pointed out, and the almost complete absence of any police force demonstrate that the government was based on a voluntary acceptance of its authority—a basis for authority that is rarely found in political systems of such substantial size. In essence, it was the religious faith of the Tibetans that inspired them to accept and support the authority of a religiopolitical order that, in their belief, was sanctioned by a supreme spiritual power.

It is often written that the powers of the governors of the provinces and the *dzongpon* ("district magistrates") were very great (one author has used the word "enormous")[1]—the more so the farther away the governor or magistrate was from Lhasa. Such language must be tempered, and the image of authority reduced to its proper proportion, by considering how the government actually operated in its Buddhist setting. The authority of the officials depended entirely upon their acceptance by the people within the framework of the Buddhist concept of human relations. Each official sent out by the Dalai Lama's government was given a letter of instructions in the name of the Dalai Lama and with his seal (or else by the regent and with the regent's seal). These instructions spelled out in general terms how to treat the subjects—to be fair and compassionate, to be just in adjudication and the collection of taxes and services—and they especially warned against any harassment of the people. If deemed necessary, special instructions were added.

The substance of these letters was general knowledge, and the subjects and their village headmen or camp leaders, in spite of all deference shown to authority, knew well whenever a magistrate misused his authority. They were quite capable of protesting and resisting, and they had the possibility of recourse to Lhasa and the Dalai Lama—a practice that was not uncommon. A distant official might be quite greedy, oppressive, and brutal for some time, but he would eventually be recalled to Lhasa and taken to task. The opportunity to make a fortune during their tenure in such positions was, of course, tempting to many officials—perhaps more so for monk officials than for the aristocrats, who were as a rule rather wealthy—and there were periods in which corruption was rampant and other periods in which reforms were introduced to prevent abuses. But even in times of declining standards, the Tibetan people did not tolerate for long large excesses of power, which, after all, could not be backed by police or military force. As one study has put it, "With their strong sense of self-reliance and firm conviction of what is traditionally right, the Tibetans are a people whom it is extremely hard to oppress, unless one subjects them with armed force, and this their own rulers and administrators never did."[2]

The reason for this self-reliant attitude was not only the absence of police power, but even more so the social organization of the villages and camps under the dzongpon's administration. In order to function, the magistrate had to work with and through the headmen or elders, who were nominated by their communities, sometimes by rotation. They were consulted on the distribution of taxes or services, which they would assign and supervise, and they would assist in the arbitration of local conflicts, provide a posse for the capture of criminals or bandits, and occasionally select men for service in the regular army. In some frontier areas like Kham, the headmen or elders led the men of families of their community in fighting as a militia force. Without such community support, the magistrate would not have been able to carry out his functions. It is such popular participation that helps to explain the small number of local government officials.

Provinces and Districts

Kham

In the framework of government, the largest regional administrative unit was the province. For reasons of geographical convenience and political tradition and exigency, the country was divided into seven provinces, which were managed by governors (chikyab). In size, population, economy, and political prominence the seven provinces were of uneven importance. Aside from the central part of the country, the most important area—in population, economic development, and strategic importance—was eastern Tibet, the region known as Kham. The area actually contained two provinces: Kham, with its seat of provincial government at Chamdo, and the province of Hor, with its provincial headquarters at Drachen Dzong. As far as population and the economy were concerned, Kham was the main province of eastern Tibet. If the total population of Tibet, including some of the territories lost to China, has been assessed at six million,[3] the population of Kham may well have made up one-third of that figure. The people, the Khampa, were well known for their sense of independence and their fighting qualities. It was a Khampa rebellion against the Chinese that started the uprising of 1959, which was suppressed by Chinese military force. After suffering heavy losses in the early guerrilla warfare in Kham, some of the Khampa units moved into southern Tibet, and it was with their help that the Dalai Lama escaped to India.

Kham was also a major trading area for the caravans that carried Tibetan wool and handicraft products to Lhasa for the India trade and to the border areas of China, and brought Chinese tea, silk, brocades, and other products from China and cotton goods and consumer goods from India. A number of towns in Kham were famous for their handicrafts, especially silver and gold ornaments, jewelry, ritual objects, and swords. The wealth of the province was greatly enhanced by such trade and craftsmanship, as was the sense of independence of its population. In fact, several of the areas of Kham were governed by autonomous rulers (gyalpo; "princes" or "kings"), whose political

Angam, former Khampa leader (photo by Franz Michael and Eugene Knez).

Former Khampa leader (photo by Franz Michael and Eugene Knez).

dependence on the governor and Lhasa was somewhat tenuous.

Unfortunately the very autonomy of those rulers provided an opportunity for Chinese encroachment. Between 1914 and 1950, that is, before the final Chinese onslaught, most of these kingdoms were in whole or in part taken over by Chinese provincial administrations. Nangchen in the North was incorporated into Chinghai Province, much of Derge in the eastern part of Kham was incorporated into Szechuan, and Muli and Trichu in the Gyalrong area of eastern Kham were also incorporated into Szechuan.[4] The territories of Drau Pön in the Ga (Jekundo) area became part of Chinghai; Litang, Batang, and Chatreng (or Changtreng) were incorporated into Sikang Province. Only Lingtsang, with its ruler's seat at Markham on the Sikang border, remained Tibetan and under the governor of Kham. As long as they remained in authority, each gyalpo or king had his own administrative staff, consisting of some "ministers" appointed by the king and headmen called *ponka*. The latter were in fact local hereditary aristocrats, and they were responsible for the collection of taxes, services, and security, which was maintained by their leadership of a militia formed of all able-bodied men. Nominally at least, the kings accepted the authority of the governor and Lhasa, to which they paid taxes in kind and service.

For one such principality in Derge, which was formally annexed by China in 1931 but which informally retained its loyalty to Lhasa and maintained its system of government until the final Chinese onslaught, this system of local government has been described by a local headman or ponka.[5] According to this ponka, his "king" ruled over eighty thousand families and a territory that included five large monasteries and about four hundred smaller ones, chiefly Sakyapa but also some Nyingmapa and Gelukpa. The king had eight ministers (*nangha*), "intelligent people," who were chosen by the king after "referring to the people" and consulting high lamas. The king also consulted the forty-five ponka, who actually administered the king's territory, a local hereditary aristocracy, and had their own estates of nomadic or agricultural people. Under the ponka were 180 "subleaders." The informant's estate contained two hundred families, a number that was above average, indicating that perhaps more than half of the families were direct subjects of the king. The ponka's duty was to collect taxes and provide security by selecting and leading one hundred militia soldiers from among his two hundred families. The informant had led his force in fighting the Chinese Communist forces, had been wounded, and had eventually escaped. The ponka's estate, like the rest of the kingdom, produced beautiful handicrafts—especially those worked in gold, silver, iron, brass, and copper—and the income from crafts was greater than that from land or herds. We may assume that this description, coming from the principality of Derge under the governor of Kham, was rather typical for the state of affairs in eastern Tibet.

The informant provided a lively picture of a rather prosperous society with a high level of education. According to him, the wealth from crafts and trade brought affluence to the population, and in the towns of the craftsmen, literacy was very high. There were private schools at Derge Poma, the king's residence, and in other towns and villages; the schools were coeducational. For the ponka's sons, there was a special school, which was obligatory. Only the nomads who lived in twenty-seven of forty-five pons had no schooling, except for the nomad ponka.

The ponka informant claimed that there was never any question about his king's loyalty to Lhasa or his acceptance of the authority of the governor of Kham, to whom the taxes in grain were regularly transmitted, even after the formal Chinese annexation. Because Derge was located on both sides of the river Drichu, which became the border with China after the eastern part of Derge had officially been claimed by China, its position was precarious, and for that reason alone allegiance to Lhasa would have been crucial. But from all information, it is apparent that the Khampa's strong religious faith and passionate loyalty to the Dalai Lama, as demonstrated by their sacrifice in his behalf during the fighting in 1959, left no question as to their sense of belonging to the Dalai Lama's polity.

Supplementary data provided by other informants confirmed the ponka's story.[6] The population of Derge, given as eighty thousand families in the old chronicles, was believed to have increased to as many as one hundred twenty thousand families before the Chinese conquest. Great emphasis was given to any population increase, and local administrators were rewarded or reprimanded according to the increase or decrease of the population under their control. The increase of wealth from crafts and trade was stressed. The people in the capital of one district, Lhündrubteng, specialized in woodblock printing and received a great deal of revenue from such sales. The district of Peyü specialized in working in silver and other metals, and the district of Khasundo produced pottery. The craftsmen of these districts were not only trained in their respective crafts, but an estimated 99 percent of them were educated and literate. In addition to public schools, over 10 percent of the families engaged a tutor to teach their child or children at home, and usually the servants' children received the same home education. Often a monk taught members of his family. Since at least 40 percent of the male population of Derge were monks and a substantial number of women were nuns, the educational level of the people who were nonnomads (*yülpa*) – over 60 percent of the population – was very high. Indeed the informants believed that Derge had the highest rates of skill and education in all Tibet and could have easily advanced to a modern economy and life-style had its development not been cut short by the Chinese conquest.

The informants claimed that the purpose of this advancement and of the education was essentially religious. The high percentage of young men – and also women – in the area who entered monastic life bears testimony to this religious inclination. The informants also pointed out that the large profits obtained from crafts and trade were used for religious ceremonies and services, for the upkeep and renovation of the monasteries, and most of all for the support of the monks as teachers and their religious studies and pursuits.

Successful managers of the incarnations' labrangs and monasteries (*chiso*) were given great credit in the records, and after retirement, when all the property was turned over to their successors, they received lifelong pensions from their monasteries. To the informants, who were former managers, it was a matter of great personal satisfaction and happiness to have contributed to this effort, a feeling of achievement that most social activities would not engender. The last Derge ruler, a young man of nineteen when the Chinese finally invaded and still guided by his mother, was an "unusual king" as he spent most of his revenue on monasteries and educational purposes. He was quoted as citing an old Tibetan saying that he "cared more for one old lady's welfare than a horn filled with gold." If not always practiced, this attitude may well characterize the dominant religious theme in this enterprising and lively eastern border region of Tibet.[7]

Another special area under the governor of Kham, over which his control was rather tenuous, was Golok. The feeling of independence among the people of that area was reflected in the words of one of the refugees from there. According to Dodrup Chen Rinpoche, there was no political or judicial authority by Lhasa or the governor of Kham over his monastery of three thousand monks or the community linked to it. The Rinpoche himself decided all issues, together with the elders of his community. Once a year, the thirty or forty elders (*ganpochi*) would gather for an annual celebration at which all disputes were resolved. Conflicts could be settled between the leaders of two groups, but if no agreement was reached, it was the lama who had the final say after "considering the feeling of both sides." For this incarnation, his only country was Golok; he was a Golokpa. Tibet was only a cultural concept, sharing a common religious tradition and literature. He denied any social or political relationship with other monasteries, even those of his own Nyingmapa sect. Visitors, though treated hospitably, would be kept outside the organisation of his monastery. The underlying policy could be expressed in one word, *damtsik*, the "sacred bond" of individual human relations, such as parents to children, teacher to student, or ruler to subject.

The incarnation stated that even when the Chinese attacked, no help from Lhasa was asked or given. The Golokpa themselves fought, and so did he. When the Chinese started to execute people and made the monks beat up the incarnations, the Rinpoche left. This assertion of independence does not correspond with other available information. It may simply express the attitude of an exile, no longer bound to any political authority, but it does indicate something of the spirit of defiance and independence that is characteristic of a Golok.[8]

Derge and Golok were but two of the semiautonomous principalities under the governor of Kham. Each principality had a history and a contemporary situation of its own, but all of them, although not completely incorporated into the religiopolitical order, were still clearly organized in a way that fitted into the administrative system of Lhasa. Although they were aristocratic principalities and inherited positions of power, the monasteries defined the attitude toward human relations and the purpose of government. Politically the governor of Kham was the vital link between Lhasa and this early type of Tibetan institution.

Because of its location on the Chinese border and the constant danger of Chinese annexation, the position of the governor of Kham assumed special importance in the eyes of Lhasa. Thus the governor of Kham was the only governor to hold a special rank above the fourth rank, which was held by the other governors. His was the rank of *dzasak*, just below but close to the third rank held by the Cabinet ministers. In time of war or grave danger, the regent or the Dalai Lama sent Cabinet ministers to act simultaneously as governor of Kham and commander in chief of the Tibetan forces in the region and to link that provincial administration directly to the government in Lhasa. In earlier times, the position was sometimes filled by a double appointment of two governors, one monk and one secular official, who acted jointly. The governor or governors were invested with both civil and military authority, as indicated by the official title, chief of civil and military administration (*dhokam zhidrak chikhyab*), as well as with judicial authority, which was more independent than that of the other provinces.

The governor's headquarters was at Chamdo, town of some ten thousand people and an active trading center. The governor was clearly in charge of his administration. His executive staff members—two high officials, one monk (*khenchung*) and one secular official (*rimzhi*), both of the fourth rank—were appointed by the Dalai Lama or the regent on the recommendation of the grand secretaries and the Cabinet, but they were usually selected by the governor himself. The same was true for the dzongpon under his administration and his official staff, which consisted of a fifth-ranking monk official (*tsedön*), a fifth-ranking lay official (*letsenpa*), a lay master of ceremony, and a lay secretary. Because of the importance of his position, the governor of Kham thus had a retinue of officials drawn from the central government roster; none of the other governors were given such an official administrative staff. The governor's personal clerks and servants were, of course, altogether his own appointments and were paid out of his own pocket. The only limitation was that the governor could not dismiss his chiefs of staff or a dzongpon without consulting the grand secretaries or the Cabinet in Lhasa. He met daily with his administrative staff to conduct the administrative and judicial functions of his domain. He could and did assign specific administrative tasks to his subordinates.

The governor's most important administrative tasks were to maintain law and order and to safeguard the frontiers. For the latter purpose, he was commander in chief of the regular government troops stationed in his province. A unit of five hundred soldiers and officers was stationed at Jamdol in the district of Dzakyab; another of the same size was at Markham; a third, again of five hundred men under a colonel, was garrisoned at Riwoche; and a force of one thousand was stationed at Jeda in Derge—all on the Chinese border. A larger force of about three thousand men was at or near the capital of Chamdo.[9] These troops did not prove as effective in resisting the Chinese invasion as were the irregular Khampa militia fighters.

In peacetime, the governor's most important responsibility was to collect revenue from this wealthy and highly populated province. The taxes were paid to the governor by the dzongpon; chiefs (kings), and other heads of principalities; tribal chieftains; and other officials in charge of administrative units within the governor's provincial domain. The taxes were paid in kind—mainly in barley; salt; animal products such as butter, cheese, and yak hide; and some special items such as paper or minerals from districts where they were manufactured or mined. Tax paid in services, such as providing transportation, was already assigned to the districts and other admintrative units, but authorization for all specific cases had to be given by the governor. At the time of his original appointment and in yearly directives, the governor was admonished not to overburden his people with such obligations and to be constantly considerate of the welfare of the people in his province. As in all regional and local administrative positions, the governor's tax income was fixed by the land records, copies of which were held in Lhasa by the Tsikhang and were therefore known to the central government, as was the amount needed by the governor to supply the army units, pay his staff, and cover other government expenses. But there were many other opportunities for special income.

The governor had the judicial authority to adjudicate civil and major criminal cases, including murder, armed robbery, banditry, intertribal conflicts, and family feuds, which were frequent in an area where tribal life and traditions of family loyalties were still strong. The major criminal cases were brought to the governor by a dzongpon or another local administrator for adjudication in the first instance; in other cases, his was a court of appeal. The governor's decision could in turn be appealed to Lhasa, i.e., to the Kashag, and in final instance, to the Dalai Lama or the regent.

In civil litigation or intertribal conflicts, the governor's authority for decision making was very crucial. In these cases, the governor's judgment was as much a political as a legal decision. Family litigation would often result from questions of inheritance of property, complicated distinctions of lineage related to second and third marriages, children and stepchildren, or uncertainties about the status of a proclaimed heir who had been a monk but had renounced monastic membership in order to gain his inheritance. In many such cases, a great deal of Solomonic wisdom, rather than strict legal concepts, was needed. Similar political decisions were needed in the settlement of tribal quarrels. Conflicts over grazing rights, disputes arising from intertribal marriages, any insults or damages done to a member of one tribe by members of another would not remain individual quarrels but involve both communities. Of special importance were quarrels between villages over water rights. These and many similar problems either came directly or from a dzongpon to the governor for his decision. He was the highest arbiter of social affairs and in many instances, the higher court for a dzongpon's deci-sions. The governor also often became involved in disputes over business deals between trading partners and over financial deals between creditors and debtors, in cases of insolvency or usury, and the like.

The judicial function of the governor was also a major source of income for him. Before submitting legal cases to his office, the parties petitioning the governor would give presents in kind or in cash. Such presents, regarded in general as perfectly proper and in line with social custom, could of course become excessive and amount to bribery and corruption. The governor's reputation, time of tenure, and support by the population would, however, be affected by a general knowledge of the size of presents or gifts, the fairness and wisdom of his decisions, and reports about his local reputation reaching his superiors in Lhasa. Even without a press, public opinion could be a restraint on marked dishonesty. It was, however, quite acceptable that the three or four years of tenure would be quite advantageous for any regional or local office holder.

In addition there was no barrier by any government regulation or by any moral or religious objection to an administrator engaging in private business ventures as long as he remained honest and honorable in his trading, finan-cial, or other business ventures. In these dealings, the governor would also receive help and often gifts from private traders and merchants, to whom the connection with the governor or lower administrative officials was of great advantage. A great deal of the profit made by the governor and other officials came from such private enterprise. The result could well be com-pared with the relationship between politics and private business in modern free-enterprise societies, with the distinction that in Tibet there was no con-cept of conflict of interests.

What made the situation in the province of Kham unique and so in-teresting was not only the military and security situation on the Chinese frontier, but also the great variety of social, political, and linguistic groups in the province. The examples of the Derge ruler and the survival of that prin-cipality and of Golok chieftains' and monastic defiance of outside authority have already been mentioned. Much of Kham, however, was locally ad-ministered, like the rest of Tibet, by appointed district officials, the dzongpon. One such district was Riwoche, which may serve as an example.[10]

Riwoche, a district with an estimated population of several tens of thousands (exact data are not available), was perhaps typical in its mixture of population groups. Two towns of well over two thousand people each were made up of middle-class traders and craftsmen, many of whom were still farmers. The majority of the population were farmers, mi-ser of the government or of religious estates. There were seven and one half "tribes,"[11] which were composed of people who were both farmers and nomads. The term *tribe* (*tshopa*) in this case is used to describe a group that did not live in concentrated village communities or camps but were scattered over an area, while maintaining a social cohesion. Their mixed farming and nomadic life explains their dispersed form of settlement. Seven of the tribes were large, one—the "half tribe"—was smaller. Together they contained over twelve thousand people.

The political and economic center of the district was the large Riwoche monastery. With over fifteen academic units and a monk population of over six thousand, this Gelukpa monastery clearly dominated the life of the district. Indeed, the chief administrator of the monastery, a monk official who was sent from Lhasa, was also appointed the dzongpon of the district, a particularly close relationship between church and state. The economic class structure of the population has been estimated by a former magistrate as 8 percent very wealthy; about 60 percent comfortably off; 30 percent living from hand to mouth—presumably landless laborers, porters, and the like; and 2 to 3 percent beggars, meaning professional beggars (whose livelihood was secure in this Buddhist society, in which charity was an important way of gaining merit).[12]

To collect taxes in kind or service, the dzongpon dealt with the village elders of the government mi-ser and with the heads of the tribes. Each tribe had two such heads or representatives, who were appointed by the dzongpon from two candidates recommended to him by each tribe. These were people who were literate and had proved managing ability and the respect of their people. The "half tribe" had only one representative.

The dzongpon also collected taxes from the monastery as well as from the labrang of the incarnation. As chief administrator of the monastery, the dzongpon also had to care for the welfare of the monastic community, manage its economy, and see to the construction and repair of the buildings. As administrator of the monastery, he handled minor conflicts within the monastery; as dzongpon, he had to deal with minor conflicts and disputes among the communities under his care. As was true for the governor, the dzongpon's authority was a source of income for him. Larger issues had to be referred to the governor, and the same was true for all disputes between a dzongpon's district and any neighboring one. The governor was also the court of appeal for a dzongpon's decisions. The administrative system of Riwoche may serve as a model for all the dzongs in Tibet, as they all had, in the opinion of its former dzongpon, the same system of taxes, judicial authority, and management.

What distinguished Riwoche, in the eastern province of Kham, from districts in other areas of Tibet was the problem of military security posed by the closeness of the Chinese frontier. As indicated earlier, Riwoche was a garrison district for five hundred regular army men, who were under the command of the governor of the province. For this reason alone, the dzongpon had to keep in close contact with Chamdo on all problems concerning relations with China and other security matters.

A list of the other local units under the governor of Kham[13] will indicate something of the variety of Tibetan local social life, especially in that eastern frontier region.

1. At Kathok, a territory near Derge and the location of a famous Nyingmapa monastery, the largely nomad poulation was ruled by a chief—similar to the ruler of Derge—who was given the title of dzongpon and as such was responsible to the governor, to whom he had to transmit taxes.

2. The territory of Denma, with a monastery of the same name, was administered by a monk official, who was simultaneously administrator of the monastery and a lama executive (*lanyer*). His relationship to the governor was the same as that of a dzongpon, as was the case with all other heads of such units, whatever title they held.

3. The Gonjo estate consisted only of government land worked by government mi-ser. Units formed by such estates, usually smaller than dzongs, were called *zhika*. They had clearly defined boundaries and a uniform system of taxation in kind and service for all inhabitants. Gonjo was alternately administered by a monk and a lay official (*zhikapon*).

4. The territory of Trayap, a large area on the Chinese border, was dominated by two strong monasteries. One called Chetsang was near the town of Jamdol, and the other, Chungtsang, was not far from Chamdo. The territory was administered by the manager of the Chetsang labrang. A regular military force of five hundred soldiers was stationed at Jamdol.

5. The territory of Markham, also close to the Chinese border and located south of Trayap, was situated around the town of Markham, an important trading center. Because of its strategic location and economic importance, the lay official who administered this territory was not called a dzongpon but held the special title of *theiji*. His rank was slightly higher than that of a fourth-rank official, next to the governor of the province. A security force of five hundred regular army men was stationed in Markham.

6. The estate of Mengung in the area of Tshawa had been granted to the aristocratic family of Zhölkhang by the Lhasa government in recognition of distinguished service rendered by members of that family. The estate was administered by a personal representative of the Zhölkhang family, who paid regular taxes to the government.

7. The Zogang estate in the same area of Tshawa was a government estate administered by a monk official.

8. The government estate of Tshawa Drayül was administered by a monk official.

9. The territory of Tshawa was under a lay official, who not only administered the remainder of Tshawa but also administered the three Tshawa estates just listed as they paid their taxes to him. His title was therefore higher than dzongpon. He was appointed as a *tok makpon* ("chief administrator") and was responsible to the governor.

10. In the south, the district of Sangngak Chödzong on the Burmese border was administered jointly by two dzongpon, a monk and a lay official.

11. The large area of Poho was divided into three units; one, the dzong of Poho Tö was administered by a monk dzongpon.

12. The dzong of Poho Me was administered by a lay dzongpon.

13. The government estate of Poho Chödrung was managed by a lay administrator.

14. The territory of Dzayul along the Dzachu River was given as a grant by the government of Lhasa to the Kundeling incarnation and was administered by a representative of the Kundeling labrang.

15. The district of Lhodzong, southwest of Chamdo, was administered by a lay dzongpon.

Kalon W. G. Kundeling—former administrator of the Kundeling labrang—with family and friend in Rajpur.

16. The territory of Dzi Tho and its monastery were jointly administered by a monk official and a secular official.
17. The dzong of Shopa Dho (or Shobando), west of Chamdo, had been granted by Lhasa to the Kundeling labrang and was administered by a representative of the labrang with the title of dzongpon.
18. Tardzong was administered by a lay dzongpon.
19. Benkar Dzong of Gyalshö was administered by a monk dzongpon.
20. The territory and the monastery of Lharigo were administered by a monk manager.
21. The large area of Khyungpo Tengchen in the northern steppeland was divided into four dzongs, two of which were later attached to the neighboring province of Hor. One, the dzong of Khyungpo Tengchen proper was jointly administered by a monk and a lay dzongpon.
22. Another, the dzong of Gertsa Tashiling was administered by a monk dzongpon.
23. The two districts of Hor Drachen and
24. Hor Yetha, later transferred to Ho Province, were administered by lay dzongpon.
25. The district of Arza Besog was administered by a monk dzongpon.
26. The area of Sog Tsanden Gön, with a monastery of the same name, was located in the Northeast. It was an area of ill repute because bandits lived on the loot from their raids on caravans that had to travel through the region. It had a lay dzongpon.
27. The territory of Sangen in the same area was also administered by a lay dzongpon.
28. Chamdo itself, the seat of the governor, was administered by the incarnation of an important Gelukpa monastery, the Phakpa Lha, with the assistance of a large staff.
29. The territory of Riwoche has already been described as a typical example of a combined monastic and district administration.
30. The special case of Golok area has also already been described.
31. The case of the kingdom of Derge, lost to China but loyal to Kham and Lhasa until the final Communist onslaught, has also been told through the account of one of its ponka leaders and guerrilla fighters. What was left of Derge after the Chinese annexation of the territory to the east of the Drichu River was formed into the dzong of Derge under a lay dzongpon, who resided in the little town of Jeda, where a military unit of one thousand regular soldiers was also garrisoned.

The governor of Kham was thus in charge of thirty-one different administrative units, which typified in their diversity of organiztion the variety of Tibetan institutional life. Under whatever form of local organization, however, the basic aspects of the social order were the same. There were agricultural and nomadic mi-ser communities under local headmen or elders; large and small monasteries with estates on which the agricultural and nomadic mi-ser rendered tax or service comparable to that given directly to the state by the majority of the mi-ser who lived on government land; a few aristocratic estates, similarly managed; a large monastic population; a substantial group of part-time and full-time traders and merchants; and a group of highly skilled craftsmen. The last two groups formed an economic middle class. All these various social units were held together by the extraordinary strength of Tibetan Buddhism and its tremendous faith in rule by incarnation.

Ngari, Lho, Dromo, Hor, Changtang, and Tsang

Ngari. Other provinces were similar as far as the variety of administrative and social units was concerned. In the far-flung region of western Tibet, a region known as Ngari, two regional administrators had their seat at Gartok, which was a small town—in fact more a temporary camping ground with a few houses than an established community. The two administrators, both laymen, did not hold the title of governor (*chikyab*) but simply that of *garpon* ("chief" of Gartok). They had no full authority over the dzongs in Ngari, which dealt directly with Lhasa, only over the many nomadic tribes of Ngari that were not organized into dzongs. This function was yet all the more important, since Ngari was largely a nomadic area. However there were a large number of agricultural dzongs in Ngari, in fact twenty-three of them, a number comparable to that of the much more populated province of Kham.[14] The reason may well be the fact that the agricultural dzongs of Ngari were smaller, irrigated, oasistype units in a large area of barren mountains and steppe country, which provided the basis for the nomads' animal husbandry.

As in the other provinces, the garpon, the dzongpon, and the other officials and estate owners who were managers of their estates acted in concert with the people in their respective domains. The decisions that affected the communities—such as tax and service allotments; the settlement of disputes and, in the case of the officials, minor criminal adjudications; decisions on water rights for the agricultural communities and grazing rights for the nomad camps; and any other official actions—were taken in consultation with the elders (*genpo*) of the villages and the headmen of the nomad camps. Those leaders were mostly elected, but in the case of the nomads, those positions were sometimes inherited and held by members of usually well-to-do and literate families, who were recognized leaders and strong personalities. As in the other regions, governmental authority was not based on military or police force and had to count on the cooperation of the people. Aside from the strong religious factor, participation through representatives assured the people's cooperation.

There were a number of important monasteries in Ngari. One, a Kagyupa monastery, Tashichöling, belonged to a branch of the Karmapa sect. Another, Kyedrong Samtanling, a Gelukpa monastery located in Kyedrong Dzong on the border of Nepal, was a famous trading center that was also visited by many Tibetan pilgrims on their way to and from holy places in Nepal and India. The monastery of Arung Gonpa in Rutok Dzong was an intellectual and educational center for the communities on the border of Ladakh. These and many smaller monasteries influenced the life of the agricultural and especially the nomad population, and all participated very strongly in and profited from the lively trade of the area.

Because of Ngari's favorable western frontier location—on the borders of Ladakh, western India, and Nepal—and because the province was not threatened by any military danger from across its borders—as the province of Kham was—Ngari became a major trading area, and "everybody traded," not only the monasteries and the professional traders and merchants, but also the farmers and especially the nomads. There was trade between farmers and nomads, a bartering of butter, wool, and salt in exchange for grain, and trade in those and other commodities with India and Nepal. There were small and large private traders, and many mi-ser families became very wealthy. There was very little tax on trade, only a small customs fee at the frontier on wool, but the traders—especially the big merchants—gave

Tikse monastery on the road to Hemis monastery in Ladakh (photo by Franz Michael).

substantial gifts to the monasteries and individual monks, according to the fortunes of the year and their belief in the blessing of their faith.

Because of the trade and the passage of pilgrims, the educational level of Ngari appears to have been relatively high, as was the cultural life of the population. Once a year, a famous folk-opera troupe went from Ngari to Lhasa to participate in the festival the monks held to celebrate the end of their summer retreat.

Lho. The province of Lho, to the south of Lhasa, was the oldest cultural area of Tibet. It was in the valley of the Yarlung River, a tributary of the Tsangpo (Brahmaputra) River, that King Songtsen Gampo held his court before he moved on to Lhasa. The Phamo Drukpa lama king and his successors also ruled from Lho, and Tibetans always regarded it as a highly cultured area. It has a high literacy rate among the nonmonastic population and was the seat of many monasteries of all sects.

Samye monastery, where the Great Debate between the Indian monk and the Chinese monk is believed to have been held in 792–794, became a sacred pilgrim center for all Tibetans. In the caves near Samye and southward, near the seventh-century temple of Tsedong, and in the sacred Crystal Mountain in the Yarlung River valley, the Indian saint Padmasambhava had meditated, and he had consecrated those areas for future meditations. At Tsetang itself and at Traduk nearby, other seventh-century temples attracted many pilgrims.

It was a well-populated and very productive area, both in agriculture and in animal husbandry. For both farmers and nomads, the off-seasons were times for handicraft work. There was a lively barter trade between agricultural and nomadic communities, and once a year, people came from the whole province and other provinces to camp and trade at a place called Jampaling in the south.

Lho borders Bhutan and Arunachal Pradesh (North East Frontier Agency) in India, and the trade across the borders with those countries was another valuable economic factor for the province. Aside from grain, salt, butter, and wool, the commodities traded included products of the Tibetan cottage industry, such as woolen blankets, leather saddles and other leather goods, and cane and bamboo products. The products of the handicraft and home industries and the trade carried on by farmers and nomads as well as by important merchant families contributed to the creation of an upper social layer of well-to-do farmers, nomads, and an urban middle class, with many different levels of wealth and income. Trading centers in many of the dzongs held their markets more than once a year, for instance, the district town of Lhakang on the Bhutanese border.

The governor of the province of Lho was traditionally a monk official whose headquarters were at Nedong. The governor had full control over all the dzongs and zhikas of his province; thirty-eight such administrative units have been located.[15] As in all such cases, the dzongpon transmitted tax revenues to the governor, received his instructions, and referred to him criminal cases and litigation that were beyond their authority. Both the position of chikyab and that of the dzongpon were regarded as lucrative posts because of the fees and gifts those officials received. Their tenure was usually three years, but it could be prolonged for another three-year term by "popular request," which appears to have been occasionally solicited by the official.

In spite of its great cultural and religious tradition, reports indicate that Lho was one province where monasteries sometimes did not obtain enough *nachwuchs* ("young recruits") by voluntary enlistment and therefore had to rely on conscription, which was handled by the dzongpon in cooperation with the elders of the respective communities. The reason may well have been that agricultural labor was in short supply, nomadism and many other opportunities were lucrative, or physical well-being had weakened religious ardor, at least in isolated cases.

As the original Tibetan culture area, Lho was also the cradle of the mythological origin of the Tibetan race. In the Yarlung Valley near Zothang, the legendary first ancestors of the Tibetans, a mountain monkey and a female ogre, were supposed to have lived.[16] In the same valley, there is also a sacred mountain, Yarlha Shampo, where—according to legend—the first Tibetan king descended from heaven to be welcomed by twelve elders as their king, a legend that has led to several speculative attempts at historical interpretation.[17] Although the center of Tibetan culture moved to Lhasa, the Tibetans of Lho remained proud of their ancient traditions.

Dromo. The Chumbi Valley (Dromo), which projects like a beak into the Himalaya mountains toward the most important caravan pass leading to Sikkim and India, is small in size, but it was of extreme importance as a Tibetan link with the outside world. The valley and its chief trading center, Yatung, formed the province of Dromo. Its headquarters were at Yatung, the seat of a lay-official governor. In times of peace, this valley was the main route for Indian, Bhutanese, Sikkimese, and other foreign traders going to Lhasa. It was also the route taken by the Younghusband expedition to Lhasa in 1904[18] and many other Western travelers. Yatung, other towns, and the people along the road profited from that trade and the transport service that was related to it. Before the final Chinese conquest the Dalai Lama sent many mule caravans carrying loads of xylographs with the irreplaceable texts of Tibetan religious and philosophical writings over this road to preserve them from the expected Chinese destruction. Those writings have remained the basis for the Tibetan culture among the refugees in the Himalayan borderlands.

In this crucial post, the governor's role was of strategic as well as of economic importance. He had direct control over his limited domain, which was not divided into dzongs or other administrative units. The realization of the importance of this chief route to India came only with the political events of the twentieth century. The position of governor was created in the 1930s and filled by an official who had been an important and successful Khampa businessman. He was neither a monk nor of aristocratic background, another eloquent indication of the open-mindedness and practicality of Lhasa toward trade and business.

Hor. The northeastern part of Tibet was organized as the province of Hor. The governor had his seat at Drachen, a small town known for a famous fortress that is linked to the epic hero Gesar, who fought a battle at Drachen and incorporated it into his domain. The battle and its hero have become the theme of epic songs of Tibetan bards. The legendary Gesar was born in Makhamling to a poor nomad family, and he had to struggle in his youth to survive the fighting of clans and tribes, a story similar to that of the youth of Genghis Khan. According to the popular legend, Gesar lived during the time of the early kings. His exploits ranged from the area of eastern Kham all the way to Ladakh and even to the south. In time Gesar become the hero of the causes of righteousness against the forces of darkness. His story became more and more intermingled with Buddhist themes, and Gesar himself became the incarnation of Avalokitesvara. The ballads about his heroic feats and conquests were sung all over Tibet, but it was the bards from Hor who carried on the epic tradition and the religious beliefs linked to it. In Tibetan eyes, Hor was the domain of Gesar.

Initially the region of Hor was directly administered by a governor without any subdivision into dzongs or other administrative units. A large part of the area was nomadic, although the valleys to the east contained a sizable amount of fertile farming land. The larger part of the Hor region was annexed by China in the nineteenth century and incorporated into the Chinese province of Chinghai.

Once the entire region of Hor comprised thirty-nine divisions of nomadic tribes under hereditary chieftains. What agricultural settlements existed were included in the nomadic tribal organizations. Each tribal division consisted of one thousand to several thousand people, amounting to an estimated population of sixty thousand to one hundred thousand. Some of the tribal divisions carried historical names such as the Yellow Hor, the White Hor, and the Black Hor. The larger ones were subdivided; the Yellow Hor, for instance, had five subdivisions.

The large majority of the nomads and settlers in the tribal units were direct subjects, mi-ser, of the central government and paid taxes in kind, chiefly butter and cheese, to tax collectors from the office of governor. They also rendered transportation service for officials and other authorized travelers. The tax was light, and the region was only lightly governed. Between the governor and some tribal chieftains, three administrative subunits similar to dzongs, with officials called dzongpon were established in the northeast at Adrak Dzamar, Arza Besog, and Khyungpo Tengchen, the location of a famous Bon monastery. Only in the 1940s, when the government in Lhasa attempted to strengthen its administrative structure and control over the outlying regions, were a few additional dzong administrations introduced.

The character of the landscape and the nature of the people of Hor were very similar to those of the neighboring province of Changtang to the west. Both regions were largely high plateaus and steppe country thinly inhabited by a subgroup of Tibetans with a Tibetan dialect of their own, with an intonation and pronunciation of words that made it difficult for people from other regions of Tibet to understand it. For the sophisticated people of Lhasa, these simple nomads with their sheepskin gowns, unkempt hair—braided at the back into a pigtail—and awkward politeness were a kind of country bumpkin, the butt of good-humored jokes. These people had a strong religious faith in Buddhism and—more than in other parts of Tibet—in the original Bon religion. In their constant battle with the hardships and privations of a harsh climate and the danger to themselves and their herds from predators and dacoits that survived in this wild country, they had developed a high esteem for such qualities as valor, fearlessness, shrewdness, and tenacity. In their battle for survival, they developed character traits of calmness, generosity, and kindness to the poor and weak. As nomads they loved animals and cared well for them.

Although largely illiterate, these simple nomads showed a great natural talent for eloquent and figurative speech, which lent itself well to the folktales and stories that were so popular in this area. The women—as elsewhere in Tibet—enjoyed complete equality with the men and shared in the work and in the dangers of the nomad life. Aside from attending the herds and fighting when necessary, the women did most of the milking and preparing the butter and cheese. They also spun the yarn and wove the cloth for the famous black tents, the chief abode of the nomad families. The nomad camp was centered around a large tent in which the chief and his family lived and the community gathered, and the smaller tents of his followers were pitched closely in a circle for community life and protection. The evenings were filled with songs and dances or religious chants.

Changtang. The province of Changtang, to the north of Lhasa, was formally created only in the 1940s, when the head of the administration of the region located in the town of Nagchukha was raised to the rank of governor. Actually the post of governor was filled by two officials, a monk and a secular governor, acting as elsewhere always in tandem.

The plateau of the Changtang region was sparsely populated, mainly by nomadic tribes. As in Hor, the tribes were headed by hereditary chieftains, and the relationship between the chieftains and the herdsmen was a close one, due to the community of work and fighting and of the common periodic peregrinations from campsite to campsite.

Because the position of governor was created only in modern times, there were more administrative subdivisions in Changtang, carried over from preprovincial states, than there were in Hor, where subdivisions were later added to the governor's direct administration. In Changtang these administrative units—Nagchu, Nagsho, Nagtshang, Namru, Yangchen Lathok, Phödho, and Jeri Taktse—were, with the exception of Nagchu, not called dzong. Nor were their officials called dzongpon but *gopa*, which indicates the absence of fortresses (*dzong*) in these nomadic areas, in contrast to the more settled regions of Tibet.

One important area was Dhamzhoong, south of Nagchuk, the territory of eight nomadic tribes administered by a monk official sent from the Jae College of Sera monastery at Lhasa. Dhamzhoong was situated in an important strategic location, and it was a stopover point and trading center on the chief caravan route between Lhasa, Amdo, and Mongolia. It was formerly the summer campsite of the Mongols during several of their invasions of Tibet in support of various religious orders, and it has, since 1959, become the site of an airfield for the Chinese military forces.

Southeast of Dhamzhoong were two other monastic domains, based chiefly on nomadic tribal pastureland. One was the Kagyupa monastery Taglung Gonpa, built in 1179 by the Kagyupa scholar Thangpa Tashi Pal, the founder of this subsect. The monastery became the center of not only religious service but also medical counsel and treatment for the nomadic population of the surrounding area, and its incarnations became famous for this special tradition.[19] The other monastery, to the northeast, was Rading monastery, built in 1058 by Gyalwa Drom Tonpa, known as Dromton, the founder of the Kadam order, which was later incorporated into the Gelukpa order. Gyalwa Drom Tonpa was a follower of the Indian Buddhist master Dipankara Atisha.[20] A dialogue between master and disciple has come down to us, and it is of interest not only for its esoteric religious content, but also for its unabashed praise of the great scenic beauty of the mountain retreat where the monastery was located. Both master and disciple acclaimed the beauty of the mountains, the sparkle of the crystal-clean river, and the fragrance of the juniper and pine trees—a setting of natural beauty that caused the Rading hermitage to be singled out as a pivot for the spiritual activities of bodhisattvas throughout the cosmic realm.

The mystical link of the great beauties of the Tibetan landscape with a faith in the sublime role of the Buddha is clearly an inherent factor in Tibetan Buddhism; its connection with the snow, the ice, and the entire scenery is shown by the location of hermitages, mountain retreats, monasteries, holy mountains, holy lakes, and stupas on the mountain ridges and mountain passes. The carvings of mantras, the Buddhist images, and the ever-present strings of prayer flags express, for the believers, reverence for the Buddhist presence in the natural landscape.

With its reputation, Rading monastery was the center of Buddhist learning and meditation in the North up to the present century, revered by Mongols as well as by Tibetans. Disciples of the founder established many monasteries, nunneries, and hermitages in the surrounding area, all to be absorbed by the Gelukpa order, the successor of the Kadampa sect. Eventually the Dalai Lama gave Trichen Tenpa Rabgye of Ganden monastery, the head of the Gelukpa order, Rading monastery for his permanent residence, establishing a powerful position for what then became a new Rading incarnation.

In these monastic domains as well as in the vast administratively unsubdivided areas of Changtang's nomadic steppe country, the Buddhist religion was strongly supported by the simple nomadic people. The nomads were known to be very generous in their offerings to the monasteries and individual lamas, offering animals, wool, felt, and dairy products; gifts of cash, obtained by trade; and valuable gifts of gold or silver. The traveling monks, who acted as gift collectors, in turn provided the services that the nomads required. Aside from the proper religious ceremonies for important occasions, such as death and sickness, the monks served as physicians (healing diseases) and as weathermen (praying for rain for pastureland or diverting snow or hail). They also procured good fortune with their blessing and protection from epidemics, and they performed special religious services to fulfill the hope of childless couples for the birth of sons. The more successful they were believed to be, the greater was their prestige.

Tsang and Ü. The regions of Tsang and Ü, Shigatse and Lhasa, formed the central part of Tibet and its religious and cultural heart. Tsang, of earlier importance than Ü, was the seat of Tibetan kings of the sixteenth and seventeenth centuries, popularly known as *depa Tsangpa* ("rulers of Tsang"). They resided at the ancient fortress at Shigatse, called at that time Samdrup Tse (Wish Fulfilling Peak). Later the seat of the governors was located at Shigatse.

Next to the governor of Kham, who administered the most populous and prosperous province on the critical frontier with China and was at times a member of the Cabinet in Lhasa, the governors at Shigatse were in an almost equally sensitive post because of the delicate relationship between the Dalai Lama in Lhasa and the second-highest incarnation of the Gelukpa order and of Tibet, the Panchen Lama, who had his seat in Shigatse at the monastery of Tashilhunpo. The Panchen Lama was recognized by the fifth Dalai Lama as a reincarnation of Amitabha in the person of the teacher of the "great fifth" (fifth Dalai Lama), and he was a most venerable personage. He was not, as often assumed in the West, of a higher incarnate rank than the Dalai Lama, and he held no temporal power, but the Panchen Lama's high religious authority could, and did on several occasions, pose a problem within the ecclesiastical order under the Dalai Lama. The political consequences of this internal tension could be and were exploited by outside Chinese influences.

Because of his exalted position, the Panchen Lama's wealthy and extensive Tashilhunpo labrang had a large ecclesiastical and secular staff, similar to that of the Dalai Lama, though smaller. The Panchen Lama's estates were under the authority of the governors at Shigatse and under Lhasa, but they were largely tax exempt. Therefore when Lhasa extended its tax control over the Panchen Lama's estates in the 1920s, in connection with the Dalai Lama's reforms, the resulting opposition of the Panchen Lama's establishment led to the Panchen's flight to China and the Chinese attempt to exploit the split between Lhasa and Tashilhunpo to China's advantage.

Actually the governors at Shigatse (there were always two of them, one monk and one secular official, appointed by the Dalai Lama) were not only responsible for the administration of the province of Tsang, but they had superior authority over Tashilhunpo as well in matters of maintaining the law, adjudicating criminal cases, arbitrating civil conflicts brought to them, and collecting land taxes, including taxes from the subjects of the Tashilhunpo estates wherever the tax exemption was lifted. Their authority, however, had to be used with discretion while maintaining the authority of Lhasa and the Dalai Lama. It was this relationship that had to be considered in the nominating of the monk and secular official for the governorships at Shigatse. Shigatse was also (next to Lhasa) one of the few internal posts where a regiment of regular soldiers was stationed under a Lhasa general.

In contrast to Hor and Changtang, Tsang's economy was largely agricultural, based on the cultivation of wheat, barley, millet, peas, and buckwheat, but that was complemented by animal husbandry and cottage industry. The administrative structure was therefore much more developed than in the nomadic steppe areas of the North. Under the overall jurisdiction of the governors were a number of dzongs, many administered by two

dzongpon, a monk and a secular official, appointed by the central government at Lhasa.

In the towns, especially in Shigatse, a substantial number of middle-class
subjects resided, living on trade, business, finance, handicrafts, and the arts.
As an old cultural area, Tsang was the home of many religious orders and
their monasteries. Aside from Tashilhunpo, the Sakya sect's chief monastery
was located only fifty miles to the west of Shigatse, and Zhalu, Palkhor
Chöde, and Gawadong were among the most celebrated religious centers.
The Kadampa monastery at Narthang, Jangchub Ling, was known for its
woodblock printing, and it housed the printing blocks as well as the important texts of Buddhist literature.[21] The earlier Bon religion was represented
in Tsang by the monastery of Menri Gön, located at Thopgyal in the Rong
area.[22]

Literacy in Tsang, as in the Lhasa area and parts of Kham, was very high,
and so was the intellectual tradition among the secular population. The
small town of Dhojung produced a famous mathematician, whose books
and charts were studied until recent times by schoolchildren and monks
throughout Tibet, and the Karleb family of Shigatse produced a famous
grammarian, Karleb Drngyik, a layman who lived in the middle of the nineteenth century. He was known for his essays on language structure and
grammatical points, in which he challenged the writing of an equally famous
eighteenth-century lama scholar, Situ Panchen Chökyinangwa, in a written
argument that stimulated an interest in and the development of knowledge
about the structure of the Tibetan language. These writers and others
characterized the intellectual level of Tsang, which equaled the sophistication of scholars in Lhasa and other towns in Ü.

The arts and crafts were equally highly developed. Tsang was well known
for its rug weaving, leather goods, silversmiths and goldsmiths, jewelers, and
painters. The so-called Mendri school of tanka painting originated in Tsang,
and its founder, a lama named Menla Donyö, studied with a layman painter
named Dhopa Tashi Gyalpo. The art of this school is still to be seen in
museums and private collections the world over. A copper mine, Rangjung
Zang, produced the high-quality copper used by the skilled craftsmen for
making decorative and utilitarian articles. The concentration of monasteries
in Tsang also resulted in architectural schools that were comparable to those
of Lhasa and Derge.

The wealth of Tsang was in part the result of a booming trade based on
agriculture, animal husbandry, and the crafts—a trade that linked Tsang
with other parts of Tibet and especially with the Himalayan border states
and India. The main trade route led via the trading center of Gyantse in the
wide valley of the Rongchu River down to Yatung in Dromo Province and

Monks pray to the newly unveiled tanka of Kyopa Jigten Gonpo, the founder of Drig
monastery, at the eight-hundred-year celebration of its founding (photo by Eugene K

Temple dances in Phiang monastery at the eight-hundred-year celebration of the founding of Drigung monastery (photo by Franz Michael and Eugene Knez).

then to Sikkim and India. Gyantse, a key commercial and political center, was also at a fork in the road that led to Lhasa and Shigatse. It was the most important and most populous of the dzongs under the jurisdiction of the Shigatse governors. The most famous of the monasteries of Gyantse was Palkhor Chöde, which combined a number of orders in sixteen colleges.[23] The importance of this monastic complex in Gyantse can be inferred from the fact that its monastic manager, sent from Lhasa, was eventually appointed to the position of magistrate of the dzong while retaining his office as monastic manager.

Other well-known dzongs included Rinpung Dzong to the north of Gyantse, the location of the palace of earlier kings (the dynasty of Depa Rinpungpa that ruled Tibet from 1407 until its last ruler was overthrown in 1565 by the counselor Zhingshak Tsheten Dorje, who installed himself at Shigatse and became known as the first king of Tsang). Gampa Dzong to the southwest of Gyantse was a fortress town where the Tibetan troops tried to resist the advancing British military force of the Younghusband expedition in 1904, suffering tremendous losses. Phari Dzong was still further south on the trade route between Gyantse and Sikkim, a marketplace for barter trade between Bhutanese and Tibetans. Nearby, on the Phari plateau rose the high snowpeak of Mt. Lhari. Other well-known districts of Tsang Province were Panam Dzong, Nyanam Dzong, Lhatse Dzong, Namling Dzong, Khunam Dzong, Oyuk Dzong, Rintse Dzong, Pedhi Dzong, and Nangkar Tse Dzong as well as the estates of Dujung Zhika, Lhomo Zhika, and Aungden Zhika.

Tsang and Ü were known in the Tibetan popular manner of reference as the "regions of religion," but Tsang was also the "region of trade and sophisticated culture."

Lhasa

Lhasa has been the capital of Tibet since the seventh century, when King Songtsen Gampo moved his government from the Yarlung River area to Lhasa. On the rocky hill where the Potala stands today, King Songtsen Gampo built a castle, the walls of which still stand below the Potala. When the king moved to Lhasa, the ladies of his court—the Nepalese and Chinese princesses and the Tibetan queens—built their Buddhist temples in and near Lhasa. Soon the city became a center of Buddhist temples, monasteries, and pagodas.

A rivalry developed early between Lhasa and the other great Buddhist center, Shigatse, which also had been the capital of Tibet at times. Lhasa's main importance became intimately connected with the establishment and growth of the Gelukpa sect. It was Tsongkapa himself who selected Lhasa as the focus for the practice of his faith. On the large grounds of the Jokhang temple, built by the Nepalese queen of Songtsen Gampo, Tsongkapa instituted a yearly three-week prayer festival held in February, and all Gelukpa monks, other monks, and many Tibetan men, women, and children streamed into Lhasa for the great festivities. At and near Lhasa, the three most important Gelukpa monasteries, the serdegasum, and the "five ling" monasteries were founded by Tsongkapa himself and his disciples. Their combined monk population was over thirty thousand.

During the sixteenth century, Shigatse was the capital of the Tsang kings. Their downfall and the establishment of rule by the Dalai Lama under the fifth Dalai Lama finally made Lhasa the capital, and it remained the seat of all the religious and secular offices of the central government and their staffs after that time. Lhasa became a city of fifty thousand to sixty thousand people, not counting the monk population. It contained many monasteries other than the great Gelukpa institutions. Its scenery was dominated by the Potala Palace, built by the fifth Dalai Lama, which was visible from afar with its white walls and shining golden roofs. It had lovely parks along the river, which were used for picnicking by the people of Lhasa and the nearby areas. The Dalai Lama's summer palace, Norbu Linka, with its beautiful park, was about three miles from Lhasa, westward and down the river.

View of the Potala (photo by David T. Parry).

The city of Lhasa itself was under the control of the Nangtse Sha, under two secular magistrates. What was remarkable was that until the 1920s, a city the size of Lhasa could be administered without the help or need of a police force. It is plausible to assume that the discipline and teachings of the monasteries were the factors that made it possible to govern without the use of force. A nominal constabulary of five hundred men, always about half under strength, was introduced in the 1920s under Western influence, but it was more decorative than a true law enforcement agency. The city had no real estate or income taxes, which was one of the reasons that Lhasa, like other Tibetan cities, became so attractive for craftsmen and traders of the growing middle class. Houses were privately owned by members of the middle class, some of the aristocrats, and the monasteries, the last for the purpose of housing the multitude of monks that streamed into the city for the great festivals. At other times, some of the houses were for rent at very reasonable rates. There were some regulations as to the location and height of buildings to keep structures from obstructing the view of the chief temples. A main sewage system with an underground canal served the city. In the twenties, an electric-lighting system was introduced, which was based on a local power station, but it does not appear to have ever been very efficient.

For the area below the Potala, outside the actual city of Lhasa, a second administrative office was established, and it was also managed by two officials, one monk and one layman. Their functions were similar to those of the Lhasa officials, but since they had a much smaller constituency, their responsibilities were much lighter. Both the city and suburban magistrates functioned as local judges for the handling of crimes. They were authorized to impose fines, some jail sentences, and flogging, but crimes demanding

Street scene at entrance to Jokhang temple in Lhasa (photo by Betty Goff C. Cart-wright).

heavier punishment were transferred to the central authority of the Kashag, which also served as a court of appeal.

Among the population of Lhasa were many foreigners, chiefly Nepalese and Bhutanese traders who enjoyed the equal protection of the law. There were also a small number of Chinese businessmen. Some members of this foreign community were Muslims or Hindus, and there were also Tibetan Muslims. Many of the Muslims were professional butchers, a profession that an orthodox Buddhist would avoid. In all cases there was complete religious tolerance.

The writ of Lhasa went beyond the city and its suburb. Some of the districts and the estates of the surrounding area were not under any provin-cial administration but were directly governed by the central authorities in Lhasa.

East and southeast of Lhasa was Taktse Dzong, which was dominated by a fortress that played a part in the political intrigues and struggles after the death of the fifth Dalai Lama. It was the power base of a regent, Lhagyal Rapten, who was installed by the Dzungar (a warlike Mongol tribe) when the Chinese captured the sixth Dalai Lama (who died as a captive on the way to China). When the Manchu came back to Lhasa with the incarnation of the seventh Dalai Lama, they removed the regent, and thus ended the

Old-style Tibetan house in Lhasa, view into courtyard (photo by Betty Goff C. Cartwright).

short period of glamor of Taktse Dzong, an agricultural district with a number of smaller monasteries.

South of Taktse and across the river was Meldro Gongkar Dzong, an area of mixed agricultural and nomadic life. At Lake Zichen Tsho, renowned for its beauty, an ancient cult of the serpent god was practiced by some people of the area, who regarded the lake as the abode of that powerful deity. Not much further west, the estate of Lamo was under direct central government administration, and it was managed by a *zhidö* (head of a smaller district), who collected the land taxes for the government. Neighboring that estate were the Lamotsherseb monastery and the temple of the Lamo oracle. That oracle, occasionally consulted by the Lhasa government, mainly served the Panchen Lama, but the land tax of the monastic estate went to the Lhasa government through the management of the neighboring Lamo estate of Zhidö. East of Meldro Gongkar Dzong was Gyama Dzong, and further to the southeast were six dzongs—Gyadha, Tsebla, Gyatse, Zhoga, Jomo, Gyatsha—and one zhika, Gyal. Toward the north were Lingbudzong and Langthang Zhika; toward the west, Gyatsho Zhika and Kyarpo Zhika. South of Lhasa was Neu Dzong. All of these dzongs and zhikas were under Lhasa administrators and contributed their taxes directly to the coffers of the Lhasa government. Aside from being the capital, Lhasa therefore had some territory under its direct control.

With this structure of provinces and districts, the government of the Dalai Lama had established a centralized system throughout the country. If this system was loosely administered and was based on religiously expressed exhortations rather than on force, it functioned as intended, and there was unquestioned acceptance by all of the authority of Lhasa. The monk bureaucracy, both in government and in the monastic system, was the mainstay and the ideological force of the polity. The secular popuation participated, however, in the political and social order, full of confidence in the justice and all-encompassing religious purpose of the system. In the final analysis, this faith in the system rested on trust in the Dalai Lama as the incarnation of Avalokitesvara. One could always appeal to him or his government in Lhasa, and, in the words of one informant, "this happened many times."[24]

6
The Social Order

Religious Autonomy: Sects, Estates, and Tax Exemption

Whether there was any autonomy within the central system of the Lhasa government is uncertain and at best a matter of argument, but in the religious arena the sects, monasteries, and leading incarnations clearly had a historically established and fully agreed upon autonomy. Through its religious government departments, Lhasa financially supported all religious institutions of any sect and backed their disciplinary authority. It also sent out monk officials to construct and repair temples and monastic buildings and to enforce discipline.[1] Even more important, in most cases the Dalai Lama made the final decision on the recognition of the correct candidate for the succession of an important incarnation. However the internal affairs of a sect or any monastery—their rules of discipline, government, educational curriculum, specific interpretation of doctrine, preservation of sectarian traditions such as the manifestations of deities—were matters in which the Dalai Lama and his ecclesiastical departments in Lhasa would not have dreamed of interfering.

In a sense, the administration of a monastery could be compared with that of a constitutional monarchy. The head was usually an incarnation or else an abbot, and in most cases he was appointed by the Dalai Lama from a number of candidates selected by a committee of monks, which was usually elected by the fully ordained monks for that very purpose. But the management of the affairs of the monastery was in the hands of an assembly of fully ordained monks, whose authority extended over all matters of liturgy, curriculum, and disciplinary rules and most of the day-to-day affairs. It was this autonomy that provided the vitality to monastic life.

Twice a month all of the fully ordained monks assembled, the abbot[2] presiding, to recite the *pratimoksha* sutra, which contained the monastic vows. While reciting the sutra, each monk analyzed his own shortcomings for self-purification. While reciting each passage, each monk was therefore made aware of his personal shortcomings in relation to the precepts contained in the text.

Monastic affairs were handled by different internal organizations.[3] Important matters were decided in a formal assembly, which was usually held once a month and chaired by a senior monk, or in special sessions called by the abbot. In small monasteries, all the fully ordained monks participated; in large monasteries, such as the serdegasum, each unit sent a representative. In addition, each college or institute had two types of special officials: religious and economic. Religious affairs were handled by a prior or prefect (gekö), who was in charge of discipline; a chanting master (umdze), in charge of liturgy; and a master of ceremony (chöpon), in charge of rituals. Economic affairs were handled by three or four treasurers, who were in charge of finance; one or two stewards, in charge of supply; and a kitchen supervisor. Both types of officials were under the direction of the abbot and supervised by the assembly. In handling their religious community life under such a constitutional system, the monasteries of all sects were autonomous in the ecclesiastical sphere.

Beyond the general autonomy that was valid for all monasteries, the sects and the establishments of leading incarnations had a special autonomy. The best known but often misunderstood case was that of the Panchen Lama and of the authority of his Tashilhunpo labrang at Shigatse. The province of Tsang was governed by two governors, who were appointed by the Lhasa government and under Lhasa's authority. Their headquarters were at Shigatse, the location of the Tashilhunpo monastery and the Panchen Lama's labrang. In theory and in practice, the Panchen Lama's labrang and monastery were under the authority of the governors, but the Tashilhunpo labrang had a more developed personnel system and a more extensive control of its estates than was the case with most other ecclesiastical or secular administrations.

The organization of the Tashilhunpo labrang was indeed very similar to that of the Lhasa government. The labrang was staffed by both monk and lay officials—the latter Shigatse aristocrats—and their number and titles gave the labrang at least the appearance of being a smaller duplicate of the Dalai Lama's establishment at Lhasa. What was more, the Lhasa government had granted Tashilhunpo not only specific estates but whole dzongs and zhikas to serve as sources of income for the expenses of the labrang and its religious activities. When the Panchen Lama traveled—and he traveled frequently and widely—he was accorded honors similar to those accorded to the Dalai Lama himself. And when the Tashilhunpo ecclesiastical and secular officials traveled to Lhasa, they were received and accorded honors in ceremony and seating arrangements that were equal to those reserved for the ministers of the Kashag and the Dalai Lama's ecclesiastical agencies.

Still, all this extraordinary deference did not indicate any bestowal of political authority. The estates granted were, in essence, no different from

Tashilhunpo monastery at Shigatse, entrance way (photo by Betty Goff C. Cartwright).

the grants bestowed on other monastic establishments and aristocratic families, and the higher rank of the Panchen Lama's secular officials, in comparison to most of the managers of other estates, was a matter of prestige rather than of function. As far as the bestowal of dzongs was concerned, the dzongpon transmitted the income to Tashilhunpo, but they were still responsible to the governors and to Lhasa in jurisdictional matters. And although the Tashilhunpo authorities handled minor misdemeanors, offenses, and criminal acts and arbitrated local disputes, as did other estate administrations, major criminal acts fell under the jurisdiction of the governors and of the Lhasa government.

The most important aspect of local privilege was not political in the legal sense but economic, the privilege of tax exemption. A number of estates, especially those granted to high religious dignitaries or families of aristocrats who were believed to have rendered special service, were granted tax exemptions. Such exemptions did not include the obligations to provide transport service for government officials, messengers, and guests, which still had to be rendered, but they did cover the tax in kind on agricultural or nomadic products. Tashilhunpo enjoyed this special status until it was partly removed by the thirteenth Dalai Lama in the 1920s, when a reform program, which aimed at gaining more central control and central income in connection with the formation of a stronger military force, led to the reorganization of the whole tax collection system. It was this action by the thirteenth Dalai Lama that led to the flight of the Panchen Lama to China, which created almost a panic in Lhasa and resulted in giving the Chinese a pretext for their interference in Tibetan political affairs. Thus the political conflict originated not because of a conflict over territorial jurisdiction or power and authority, but because of a conflict over the privilege of tax exemption and the question of revenue.

Next in importance to the Panchen Lama and Tashilhunpo was the Sakyapa sect and its estates. It has already been indicated that the appointment of the head of the Sakya ruling family from candidates of the two branches was confirmed by the Dalai Lama.[4] The latest such decision was made in 1952 but was appealed by the contending branch, a procedure aborted by the Chinese invasion. Although the Sakya administrative organization had a smaller staff and did not rank as high as that of Tashilhunpo, its religious prestige was great. The ruling Sakya hierarch was recognized as an extremely powerful tantric master, and he was often called upon to perform special Sakya rites in Lhasa for the benefit of the Tibetan state. Indeed, many of the sect's rituals and teachings—including the golden doctrine (serchö)—were incorporated into the Gelukpa sect's body of texts and widely respected.

The Sakya's two ruling families each had their "court," a palace (phodrang), and some of their estates were managed by dzongpon appointed by the Sakya court. However in jurisdictional matters, the two families were responsible to their respective governors the same way the dzongpon under Tashilhunpo authority were to theirs.[5] Some of the estates (those belonging to the chief monastery) of the Sakya ruling families were also exempt from the land tax, but their subjects, too, were responsible for the transportation tax to the Lhasa government agencies.

Other leading monasteries and labrangs also enjoyed substantial tax exemptions. Among the other sects, three great monastic establishments of the Kagyupa sects were given this special recognition: Tsurphu, the principal monastery of the Karmapa tradition, which was situated to the west of Lhasa; Drigung, of the Kagyupa sect, to the north; and Sangngak Chöling, the leading monastery of the Drukpa sect, to the south on the Indian border. Drigung had a large staff with special titles and ecclesiastical ranks to serve the sect; it also had two incarnations and separate labrangs. Sangngak Chöling received special treatment from the Lhasa government as the result of the political role played by one of its incarnations during the Tibetan-Ladakhi war of 1679–1684. The Karmapa sect's political role in backing the kings of Tsang preceded the founding of the Gelukpa order. The Karmapa was therefore regarded as the most prominent of the Kagyupa monastic hierarchies, and because of its special position, the central government of the Dalai Lama never imposed the full range of taxation upon it. In addition, of course, all Kagyupa monasteries enjoyed full autonomy for their religious doctrinal and ritual observances.

A similar deference was accorded the famous Nyingmapa monastery of Mindoling in southern Tibet. Mindoling monastery was founded at the time of the fifth Dalai Lama by the highly respected discoverer (*terton*) of concealed esoteric texts Terdak Lingpa, who shared them with the Dalai Lama. After the middle of the eighteenth century, Mindoling was given special treatment by the Lhasa government, in addition to the general freedom of the Nyingmapa sect to practice its own rituals, liturgy, and teaching.

Similar privileges were also accorded to the leading monasteries of the Gelukpa sect, and the three large monasteries (the serdegasum), the "five ling," and other large Gelukpa establishments, at one time or other received the favor of greatly reduced tax obligations. In addition all of the monasteries, although paying taxes, were accorded the privilege of retaining substantial amounts of the taxes for their own religious use.

Another category of tax-exempt estates were those belonging to aristocratic families. As a rule, each family's main estate was tax exempt because of the family's obligation to provide the service of one son to the state. Additional estates, acquired or granted, were taxable to different degrees.

Lastly, similar to the aristocratic estates were those given to the families of Dalai Lamas. These families had been simple farmers, but with the discovery that one of their children was the incarnation of the Dalai Lama, they were moved to Lhasa and given sizable estates, which remained thereafter in the family. They became aristocratic families whose sons were to serve the government in exchange for ownership of and a tax-exempt status for their estates. These families, known in Tibetan as *yabzhi*, became a major part of the Lhasa establishment.[6]

Except for the tax privileges of their estates, the autonomy of the sects, monasteries, and labrangs was indeed religious, not political, and the secular estates had, of course, no autonomy in either sphere.

Local Community Leadership and Participation in Government

The basic economic division in Tibet was between agriculture and animal husbandry—between farming and nomadism. In the quantity of production and in the numbers of people involved, agriculture was clearly predominant, but agriculture and animal husbandry were interdependent. Mixed economies of herding and agriculture existed in estates and in other communities; only the pure nomads of the northern steppe areas of Hor and Changtang depended on regular barter to obtain the grain for their staple diet. Both nomads and farmers combined their primary economic activity with handicraft and trade. For the nomads, leather work, felt making, tent-making, and tanning were the major crafts that provided a supplementary income; for the farmers, they were spinning, weaving, and carpentry, and making agricultural implements, bamboo work, pottery, metalware, and jewelry. Both groups received considerable income from trade and other business ventures. Both were obligated to pay tax in kind and service to the state or their estate owners, but they were economically self-sufficient enough to enjoy a large measure of social and political autonomy.

Agricultural Tibet consisted of an estimated twenty thousand villages and hamlets, varying in size from a few dozen to over a thousand families. These villages formed the basic administrative units for tax collection and economic management. For such purposes, the villagers formed a team. They had to deal with the government for equitable treatment in the payment of taxes and corvée labor and the allocation of the required number of children for the draft of recruits for the monasteries or of men for military service. They had to manage the planning and building of irrigation works, the grazing of village and individual herds on the village's grazing lands, and usually the operation of a water mill. The villagers acted in unison in cases of complaints to the government against oppressive burdens imposed by the estates or, if they were directly under the government, against government taxes in kind or in service. In these cases, they fought legal suits that sometimes became prolonged. They also acted together in defense against bandits and formed—when needed—posses to apprehend criminals. Finally, the villagers joined together in religious rites and for certain religious festivities and services, though their personal religious needs were mostly dealt with in each household.

It was, however, the household that formed the basic unit in the villages, as in the towns. Although estate ownership among the aristocratic families and the tenant farmers' ownership of their own land were contingent on service (as government official or as estate cultivator) being carried on generation after generation, there was no corresponding ideological reason for stressing family continuity. Buddhism precluded any ancestor worship, since rebirth could occur anywhere and in any form. Each household was therefore a temporary unit, and in spite of its status distinctions and traditions of exogamy, the ideological stress on individual existence was strengthened by the considerable social mobility of individuals (perhaps with the exception of a small outcast group of yawa).[7] This mobility was, of course, chiefly facilitated by the opportunity, open to all, to enter monastic life, the most revered status for men and women. But aside from this open ladder for both spiritual and mundane advancement, the status structure was even less constraining than is sometimes believed.

The *mi-ser* class, here translated as "subject," included the vast majority of the nonreligious part of the population—perhaps 90 percent of the farmers, nomads, artisans, and traders. Among them, however, there were distinctions so that the application of the term *mi-ser* to all people in these various sectors of economic and social life conceals more than it explains. For instance, the situation in the villages differed greatly from that in the towns, and there was also a substantial difference between agriculturalists and nomads and between both of those groups and the townspeople.

As stated earlier, the mi-ser in the villages were fundamentally divided into two quite divergent groups: the tral-pa and the dü-chung. The former made up the upper group in the villages and were a slight majority—according to one study, 54 percent.[8] The most wealthy families among them were sometimes regarded as a type of rural aristocracy. These were the taxpaying tenant farmers. The dü-chung, a somewhat smaller group—43 percent according to the same study—were landless laborers who were free to sell their labor.

The tral-pa farmers were obligated to cultivate the land (or tend the herds) of the estates to which the village (or the nomadic settlement) was assigned—which could be government, monastic, or aristocratic estates. Actually the majority of the tral-pa were on government estates and under the direct management of government officials of Lhasa, the provinces, or the districts. Of the remainder, a large number were allotted by the government to monasteries (or labrangs), and the rest were allotted to aristocratic estates. Aside from their obligation to cultivate an estate's land, the tral-pa owed—together with the other village families—a transportation tax to the government, i.e., they had to provide animals and manpower for the transportation of goods or persons whenever required. In exchange for the obligation to cultivate estate land, a tral-pa was granted a plot of land for his private use, and it was his by written contract. The obligation to provide service to the owner of an estate was linked to inheritable ownership of his own plot of land in a somewhat similar fashion as an aristocratic family's obligation to provide a son for government service was linked to the ownership of the aristocratic estate. Among nomads, the mi-ser's personal ownership of a herd was linked in similar fashion to his obligation to herd an estate's animals.

Tral-pa could not leave the community without written permission of the estate owner, be it the government or the ecclesiastical or aristocratic landlord. Therefore the tral-pa were "bound to the soil." In principle there was no difference between the tral-pa of government estates and those of private monastic or aristocratic estates. When estates were given by the central government to monasteries or aristocratic families, the position of the tral-pa on those estates was not basically affected. Instead of paying their taxes of agricultural and animal products to the state, they paid them to the estate, if it was substantial, and the estate in turn paid a percentage to the central government. The same was true for long-established private estates. Whether tral-pa of government or of private estates, the tral-pa held their land or herds on the basis of a written contract and bequeathed it or them to their children. In addition all tral-pa were free to buy and sell their own goods and to carry on trade, a very important economic opportunity. They could also acquire additional land or herds.

The limitation of the tral-pa's status was that they were not permitted to leave their estates. The reason for wanting to leave might often be because of a desire to enter monastic life or to marry into the village of another government or private estate,[9] but there were often other reasons[10] — especially the attraction of a life in town, with its opportunities for income from trade or craft. In general an estate manager was reluctant to let a tral-pa or the members of his family go, because of the chronic shortage of rural labor. If a tral-pa intended to enter monastic life — as was often the case — it was difficult for the estate to refuse permission, since that would have meant interference with a meritorious action. The same was true in cases of women intending to marry into families outside the estate or of bridegrooms intending to marry into families without male descendants. In those cases, permission to leave was easily granted in exchange for the payment of a *mi-bog* ("retainer fee"), in practice a very small amount.[11] The same retainer fee was then also applied to others who wished to leave the estate in order to become traders, craftsmen, or even laborers in the towns, provided they received permission, which depended on the estate manager's assessment of each person in question and the manager's ability or inability to hold the tral-pa back. In many such cases, the agreed-upon retainer fee, nominal in comparison to the former tral-pa's other income, might still be paid by him regularly as a gesture of respect for the estate owner rather than as any real obligation.[12]

If tral-pa left without such permission, as apparently happened frequently, theoretically they could be brought back and sometimes punished. However, this right of the estate owners was difficult to enforce since there was no police force, and it was even more difficult to apply when the defector entered a monastery. The tral-pa would, however, lose the right to his or her land, which would be given to another family willing to assume the obligation. It was the comfortable economic position rather than the fear of punishment that kept the large majority of the tral-pa from abandoning the life in their communities, except for religious reasons or marriage.[13] But for those who did leave, there remained a legal uncertainty, which was apparently the reason why the thirteenth Dalai Lama decreed that any claim to the return of such a defector became invalid after a period of five years.

On government estates, there appears to have been very little effort to keep a tral-pa from leaving. His property was simply assigned to another tax-paying family, and that was very likely the main reason why most of the tral-pa did not exchange their comfortable position for greater freedom, unless they had found better income and life-styles as traders and entrepreneurs in the towns. Most of the tral-pa in the rural communities were not solely or even chiefly dependent on their land. They were rural entrepreneurs in trade and business, activities that were free and practically untaxed. They were free to sell their products of agriculture, animal husbandry, or their specialized craft or merchandise obtained through trade at home and abroad, and many of them became financially independent and wealthy.[14] When they became well to do, they could hire dü-chung as an agricultural labor force or engage them as sharecroppers; the tral-pa's own time could then be used for trade and business and related travel. Some of their profits could be invested in additional land, and in this way members of this status group became the elite of the villages. Their tax burden, cultivating the estate land and providing corvée transport, could be transferred to hired labor, so most of the tral-pa had little reason to leave unless, as indicated, they turned to religious life or were attracted by the higher business profits that were available in the towns.

The dü-chung had no such tax obligation, and some are said to have actually preferred their freer status to the restrictive responsibilities of the tral-pa. The dü-chung were also free to move, and a substantial number of them went into the labor market of the towns. In the villages, they were almost as numerous as the tral-pa. Aside from rural work as laborers or sharecroppers, some worked also as paid porters in trade or engaged in business activities. Enterprising and able dü-chung might move up to tral-pa status, or they might become traders or make their fortune in the crafts. Many moved up through marriage, appointment, or enterprise. Their lesser status was, however, indicated by the fact that as long as they were dü-chung, they had no house names. And when the tral-pa wanted to shift the burden of the draft of young monks or recruits for the military, such service could be allotted to dü-chung families, though it must be kept in mind that most families gave their children voluntarily to religious life as a matter of faith and of merit and that the tral-pa families were regarded as the most religious element among the population. For the monk or nun, social origin was, of course, no longer relevant.[15]

In the towns, a third important group was the tsong-pa, the traders and private entrepreneurs, who could become very wealthy. Although most of them remained nominally mi-ser, their mi-bog—if any—was negligible in comparison to their practically untaxed income from trade and business. Many tsong-pa came from rural origins but did well with their enterprises, so their income matched or surpassed that of the wealthy aristocratic families.

It has been estimated that the tsong-pa and dü-chung of the towns each composed 40 percent of the town population.[16] As traders and businessmen and as craftsmen and artists, the tsong-pa—and even some of the dü-chung—formed the urban middle class of Tibetan society, which had its counterpart in the well-to-do upper group in the villages.

Trade and business were vital and growing parts of the economy.[17] In the villages and between the villages and towns, there was local trade in agricultural and nomadic products and the products of the crafts, a lucrative source of income for all participants. The towns were the centers for the countrywide trade and for the organization of caravans that went to the Himalayan border countries, India, and China. The towns were therefore the center of residence not only for the tsong-pa but also for a substantial number of dü-chung who were needed for transport and labor.[18]

These three groups—the tral-pa, the dü-chung, and the tsong-pa—were the mi-ser, and they differed in status, wealth, and social importance. They formed a rather stratified society, but there was a built-in social mobility, which appears to have increased in contemporary times as a shift occurred from the original predominance of agriculture and animal husbandry to a greater role for trade, business, and the crafts. For this reason, it appears that the term *mi-ser*—whether tral-pa, dü-chung, or tsong-pa—designated a social, legal, and economic position that was entirely different from that of the serf in the medieval European or pre-Meiji Japanese traditions. Mi-ser is best rendered by the English term *subject*, a status comparable to that of subjects of any other premodern bureaucratic state.[19]

The agricultural communities, whether directly under the government or under a private estate, were headed by elders who represented the villagers in dealing with officials and estate managers. The villages were very uneven in size, and the large villages were usually scattered over a considerable area, with government and private estates sometimes interspersed. The larger villages and communities were usually represented by a number of elders—a good example is Chushul Dzong in Ü, southwest of Lhasa, in which there were communities with varying sizes of population headed by their respective elders.[20]

The elders (genpo) were tral-pa, and they were sometimes elected within their villages or communities, but very often they were selected by a system of rotation among the heads of the families. In some outlying areas, as in Kham, these positions were sometimes hereditary among the leading families of a village.

The nomads of the steppe country moved from one campsite to another according to the season, and nomad families usually grouped their tents together in camps. Sometimes a large central tent housed the tribal chief, his family, and a number of followers. As a rule, the nomads of the steppe were still organized in tribes, and the tribal chieftain, a hereditary position, was the link between the government officials and the members of the tribe. Below the chieftain, units of the tribe were under the leadership of local headmen (*gopa*), who allotted and organized government transportation services and other tasks of the unit under the direction of the chieftain. These gopa were in some cases elected by their units, in others appointed by the chieftain. Among the nomads, the gopa fulfilled the role the genpo fulfilled in the agricultural communities.

The herdsmen, who lived in units interspersed with the agricultural communities, usually no longer had a tribal organization. They formed smaller groups of a few families each, which were usually headed by a headman called a *shepon*, who was often appointed by an estate manager or official. The shepon played the same intermediary role the genpo and gopa played.

The functions of these various local leaders were in essence the same. It was their responsibility to manage the transportation service, the cultivation of government or estate land, the caring for government or estate herds, and the allotment of labor for those services among the members of the group. When necessary, they also managed the local irrigation works. In the steppe, it was the chief and for the herdsmen, it was the shepon who determined the dates of the seasonal movements and organized and led them. The elders, the chiefs, and the headmen arbitrated disputes and conflicts among members of their groups and negotiated with other groups for resolution of intergroup conflicts to avoid having to submit them to a higher authority. They also dealt with misdemeanors or minor crimes and organized the apprehension of culprits. In case of general invasion, they were responsible for forming local units of the militia.

Aside from their individual role of leadership in their respective communities, these headmen—genpo, gopa, and shepon—acted together in representing the communities of their estates, their districts, or their areas. To discuss common problems, they came to meetings called *tsogzom*.[21] In principle, there were two kinds of these meetings, those called by the elders themselves and those called by the district officials or estate managers. The former dealt with lesser local problems that could be handled without involving a superior authority, such as minor intervillage disputes; the latter were part of the regular responsibility of the district magistrates or of the managers of estates, who had to handle their affairs in cooperation with the representatives of the local communities. The larger meetings called by a dzongpon included not only the genpo of the villages and hamlets and the gopa of the camps, but also the managers of the estates within the district and one or two representatives of the so-called village aristocracy, the *tsoda*. This village aristocracy consisted of well-to-do families—who might be farmers or herdsmen or traders—who had not only practically but also legally risen from the status of mi-ser to one of social prestige, which they transferred to their children. The very existence of their status is an indication of the social mobility in the agricultural and nomadic communities.

The district meetings were held regularly,[22] and they allowed the people to participate in the management of their community affairs. Matters often taken up in the meetings were the allotment of labor for the cultivation of government or estate land; the herding of government or estate herds; and the distribution of the services required for the transportation of government officials, products, messengers, and other privileged travelers. The authorities would also use the meetings for consultation in cases of arbitration of conflicts, especially when the conflicts involved neighboring villages or estates; in cases of criminal action, especially when such cases involved the apprehension of accused offenders; and when a threat to security demanded the raising of a local armed force. In agricultural regions that were dependent on irrigation, the dzongpon had the authority to decide on matters of building and upkeep of the irrigation system, but he would consult the elders and managers about the planning of and the allotment of labor for construction and repair work and the manner of supervision. If soldiers had to be recruited, men were selected from the communities with the help of the elders, who in turn relied on the cooperation of their respective units. In the rare cases when children had to be recruited for a local monastery because its membership had seriously declined, the recruiting assignments among families would be handled by the elders with the community's cooperation.[23]

This cooperation among the government officials, the private managers of the estates, and the elders and headmen of the agricultural and nomadic populations gave the people a form of participation in the management of their affairs and their government. It is noteworthy that in Tibet's premodern, basically agricultural society, there were in all its history no "peasant rebellions" or similar uprisings as an expression of discontent, if not with the system at least with the ruling group. Many refugees from all status groups who escaped the Chinese invasion of 1959 by fleeing across the Himalayas to India—and some eventually to other countries—asserted that there was no conflict or acerbity between the Tibetan people and their governors and managers. That there was a relationship of trust and human directness in Tibet[24] may largely be ascribed to the fact that there does not seem to have been the same gap between the rulers and the ruled that in other premodern (and modern) societies has created unrest, discontent, and finally rebellion.

What was true for the agricultural and nomadic countryside was even more applicable in the towns, where nonecclesiastical social mobility was even more in evidence. The few major towns in Tibet at the beginning of the twentieth century had nonmonastic populations of an estimated sixty thousand (Lhasa), twenty thousand to thirty thousand (Shigatse, Gyantse, Chamdo), and two thousand to three thousand in the smaller towns[25] – an estimated two hundred thousand people. Together with the well-to-do families in the large villages, this overall group, totaling perhaps a quarter million people, could be described as the middle class of Tibetan society. Still government or estate mi-ser for the most part – some of them still paying modest sums for services due or out of loyalty – they were economically independent. Their income – from trade, business, arts and crafts, or the professions – was practically free of taxation.

Many people from this middle class made major contributions to religion, and they were voluntary. From all accounts, the percentage of people's income given to monasteries or incarnations or for religious services and purposes varied greatly from small amounts to very large contributions of one-half or more of one's yearly income, according to the strength of faith and the belief in the importance of an invocation for success or for compassion.[26]

Although independent rather than led by elders, the urban population had its own community organizations. There were associations for arts and artists (*kyduk*), craft centers such as the Doipal Craft Center, craft associations, professional groups, financial groups, cooperative banking groups, women's groups, many socioreligious groups, and simple friendship groups – some of which had as their main purpose the arrangement of joint picnics. All these groups functioned in the urban community life with a natural acceptance of the religious setting. There was, of course, human nature, there was exploitation, there was brigandage, there was corruption. But there also was in Tibet an open course of appeal against exploitation and injustice, leading to the Dalai Lama, and there was the religious way of life itself, the life of the monk and the nun, which was regarded and revered by all as the most honorable service for all sentient beings.

For the common people, the rituals of daily life were the most important part of their religious support, and they invited the services of religious practitioners to carry out the rituals. Indeed, in some parts of southern Tibet such religious practitioners formed a special profession, the *ser-kyim*. The ser-kyim were ecclesiastics who had been trained in the rituals but had not accepted the monastic vows. They were married and lived in communities of their own, making their living from land that they owned and cultivated and regularly providing the ritual services to their lay clientele.[27] The rituals were recommended and carried out under the direction of the lama teachers.

Religious life was thus carried on on all intellectual, spiritual, and practical levels, and it was an all-pervasive and integrating factor of life in the villages, the camps, the towns, and the monastic communities themselves. The strong common commitment to the Buddhist religious purpose unquestionably cemented society and state; indeed, it may have been the pervasive

Buddhist faith not only of the ecclesiastical but of the secular section of society that brought about the cooperation between people and government. Whichever came first, religious faith and social cooperation complemented each other.

What held this complex social system together was the common faith in the tenets of Tibetan Buddhist religion, which reached the families and the individuals in many forms. In the house or the tent, there was a shrine or shrines, which were the places of daily worship. (Wealthy families frequently engaged a resident monk, who was responsible for taking care of the shrine.) Then there were the many rituals, designed to avert illness and damage to the crops or the herds, bring health and good fortune, and help the dying on the way to a future existence.

To carry on these rituals, the commoners depended not only on the chief monasteries of the Gelukpa and other sects, but also on the many smaller and larger religious centers that had been established all over the countryside. Even during the last and present centuries, religiously trained and committed ecclesiastics continued to establish their own centers and attract disciples and lay followers, which attests to the continuing vitality of religion. To many villagers and herdsmen as well as to the urban people, the lama teachers provided a focus of belief and religious succor.

H.H. Drigung Chetsang Rinpoche leading a prayer session for purification at the eight-hundred-year celebration of the founding of Drigung monastery (photo by Franz Michael).

Marriage and Family

The Buddhist attitude toward the family differs fundamentally from that of Western religions or indeed most other Asian religions or philosophical systems. The difference is inherent in the Buddhist belief in rebirth. In Tibetan Buddhism, where this belief found its strongest expression in the personification of living incarnations of saintly beings (*bodhisattvas*), the individualism of liberation acted against the concept of family continuity. Reincarnation could occur anywhere and in any family; indeed, the highest incarnation, the Dalai Lama, could be and was found in families in any part of the country. Although the parents of an incarnation were honored and the family given privileges and status, this distinction did not provide any continuity in a spiritual context. Liberation was a matter for each individual—progressing through many rebirths on the path toward final freedom from existence and suffering to the undefinable bliss of Nirvana—but the family was not based on any spiritual bond. The concept of rebirth was in direct logical contrast, for instance, to any ideas of ancestor worship, one of the strongest spiritual foundations of family continuity in many other early societies. In a spiritual sense, Tibetan Buddhism was therefore not concerned with the family as a permanent social unit. The family was simply a biological unit, recognized as a reality of human life but not as a sacred institution.

For the compassionate human being, concerned with the liberation not only of self but of all sentient beings, on which indeed one's own liberation depended, service to all these beings, not any special service to the family, was the highest moral and religious goal. To retire out of compassion from an ordinary life within a family to the life of a monk or a nun was the highest service that any being could give to all others. The large number of monks, one-third or more of the male population, and the substantial number of nuns demonstrates the importance that was attached to this dedication by a very large part of Tibetan society.

Other religions have developed similar institutions of monastic life and regarded them as a superior sacrifice for the individual, but in those religions, marriage was also a sacrament and the family was a blessed institution. In Tibetan Buddhism, there was no religious ceremony connected with marriage or, for that matter, with birth. At the most, when the wedding festivities were going on in a house, a couple of monks would be invited onto the roof to provide offerings to the gods (guardians) for prosperity and good luck (*lhasang*), and the name of a newly born child might be selected by a lama. But the family itself had no place in religion. The Three Jewels of the Buddhist faith in Tibet were the Buddha, the wheel of law set in motion by Gautama Buddha, and the community of the faithful, the monks. There

Mrs. Thachoe Nayang, Tibetan housewife and businesswoman in Mussoorie (photo by Franz Michael and Eugene Knez).

was no religious prescription for the organization of family life.

In addition Tibetan Buddhism believed in the equality of all human beings in their temporary individuality and did not, in principle or practice, recognize any sexual discrimination. The equality of women in Tibetan society—already inherent in earlier tradition—was strengthened by this religious concept and resulted in the acceptance of a freedom for women rarely known in any other premodern society. As one of our informants, Mrs. Thachoe Nayang, a successful businesswoman, phrased it, "We had no 'equal rights' for women, but it was up to the woman to prove herself, and she would be treated even more gently by her family because of her contribution." Mrs. Dolma Chozom Shatsang stated that most of the trade and the stores were managed by housewives. Women also went along on caravans and pilgrimages. As elsewhere, there was sometimes an issue over the relationship between a new wife and her mother-in-law, but after the first child was born, the new wife took over, and the mother-in-law retired. Mrs. Dennyertsang also stressed the role of women in business, for which they often were specially trained.

This equality was also seen in the attitude toward sex. In Buddhist theory, sex is regarded simply as a biological fact, and there is no concept of original sin. Sex is a natural part of human behavior, and as in other aspects of

Kungo Dennyertsang and Mrs. Dennyertsang (photo by Franz Michael and Eugene Knez).

human relations, proper forms of behavior between men and women have to be maintained. In the criminal code of the Tibetan government, there was a stipulation against what has sometimes been translated as "adultery" but is better rendered as "sexual misconduct." This stipulation was derived from the moral rules of the *Vinaya Pitaka*, the first of the *Tripitaka* [Three baskets], the basic texts of Buddhist doctrine of morality,[28] which proclaim the negative principles and the "virtues" of moral conduct. There is no command in these prescriptions—no "Thou shalt" or "Thou shalt not"—but simply the moral precepts to be followed by any religious person. These rules condemn sexual misconduct (adultery) and advocate the observation of proper behavior in the relations between men and women. This proper behavior depends on the respective social situation. In essence all people have the obligation to live up to any given commitment. For the monks and nuns, "proper behavior" requires the observance of the vow of celibacy. For the lay people, the observance depends on the particular marital arrangement.

Although monogamy was the rule in all Tibet,[29] polygyny and polyandry were both historically established. The major reason for those arrangements was primarily economic or political. In earlier Tibetan history, Tibetan kings and aristocratic families often engaged in polygyny to build up political power or alliances. The case of King Songtsen Gampo has been referred to, and his reported Chinese, Nepalese, and three Tibetan marriages were obviously of great political importance. There are numerous examples of such cases of polygyny among the kings and principalities in earlier history. These marriage arrangements often led to intrigues and power struggles at court, conflicts over succession, and rivalries between wives and sons, which sometimes led to murder.[30] In such cases, the role of the women in question was as important as that of the men. Although such intrigues were well known in the harems of Oriental rulers, the role of the Tibetan queens appears to have been quite different from that of the Oriental harem women. Officially the Tibetan queens were "sisters," and if there was family infighting, it involved sons and brothers and other relatives. There were also no eunuchs at the court of Tibetan kings or princelings.

Polygyny was more widely practiced because of the need for offspring to maintain the landed property in a family, as without an heir, the property would return to the state or estate. This need for continuity of blood relationship in order to keep property in a family was seen as a biological matter and not as a matter of spiritual continuity and therefore of ancestor worship, as in the Chinese tradition. If there was no male heir, a son-in-law could be brought in as the blood relationship could be carried on through daughters as well as through sons. In such a case, the son-in-law would become a member of his wife's family. An interesting case is that of one of the leading aristocratic families of Lhasa. When the head of that family, a leading political figure of the time, was murdered, together with his son, a protégé of the Dalai Lama married the widow to carry on the family name. But since that marriage did not in fact continue the blood relationship of the family, the new head, at the insistence of other aristocratic families, had to also marry the daughter of the former husband. The offspring of that union then continued the bloodline of the family.[31]

In such cases, polygyny was practiced by aristocratic families to assure that there would be a family representative to serve the state. The same requirement was true for mi-ser families, whose inheritable right to their personal land depended on offspring to carry on the obligation of service to the government or estates.

The importance of keeping property together was also a major reason for polyandry. There was in Tibet no system of primogeniture, which was practiced in medieval Europe, not only among aristocratic families but also sometimes among the families of ordinary property owners, to prevent the dispersion of family property.[32]

In Tibet, dispersal of property was frequently prevented by one or two sons of a farmer family entering monastic life. How much this practice was related to the issue of family property can be gathered from the fact that in some cases, a farmer without offspring or lay brothers would die young and a monk brother would be permitted to leave monastic life, marry the widow of his brother, and take over the landed property.

Although meritorious for the individual and the family, the loss of one member to religious life was a considerable sacrifice for the remainder of the family because of the serious labor shortage that prevailed in most of the rural areas of Tibet. For the less well-to-do families, hired labor, if available, was an undesirable expense. Thus the other solution for families with more than one son was for several brothers to marry one wife and continue to live as one household. In such cases of polyandry, the children were regarded as the offspring of the oldest brother, maintaining, however, equally close relations with their "uncles."[33] The parallel to that type of polyandry was the marriage of several sisters to one man, a type of sororate. In such settings, sexual misconduct referred to any breach of personal commitment between individuals or groups of individuals.

Such marital arrangements would, of course, not always work well. A polyandrous wife might prefer an older or a younger brother, and the union might break up with one brother taking another wife and moving out. Polygamic marriages could not be maintained by force, and the relatively free popular attitude toward breaking marital relationships and engaging in other ones indicates a general social tolerance toward marital arrangements and sexual relations for both men and women.

That tolerance extended to the attitude toward sexual behavior between unmarried men and women. It is true that aristocratic families in particular would discourage younger daughters from engaging in sexual relations with young men, but there was no disgrace or social censure attached to extramarital sexual relations by either sex.

On the other hand, the parents played a decisive role in the choice of marriage partners for their sons or daughters. Usually the parents would select three or four suitable candidates and then consult an oracle or an astrologer or both about the compatibility of the respective young people. The family lama could also be brought in to make the final choice. The marriage itself was closed on the basis of a contract signed by the two fathers and witnesses at a meeting at which the boy and girl also met and had to give their approval. This important agreement was only one part, if an important one, of the parents' responsibility for their children, which was regarded as a natural rather than a religious obligation.

A special attitude toward sexual matters was apparently more common among the nomadic people of the steppe. The long absences of men from their own camps and the migratory form of life encouraged and permitted a greater leeway in sexual relations for both men and women. Among the Khampa, it was reportedly an honor for a male visitor to be offered the host's wife's favors.

There was, however, one area in which sex was related to religious practices: the use of sex in tantric meditational techniques in a so-called inner yoga. Tantrism dealt in general with the use of human emotions to gain a higher consciousness by training in meditational practices. In essence, in tantric practices the world of unreal phenomena was to be overcome through heightened sensory experiences rather than through their denial. Both men and women were initiated into such meditational practices. Inner yoga, with its control of breath, was to bring energy into the nervous centers, a nervous stimulation that would accentuate any emotional experience to its greatest intensity. In this tantric tradition, lay lama teachers who were tantric masters initiated students into practices that used sex, combined with such meditational techniques, to reach a mental ecstasy level in order to gain a deeper insight into the ultimate nature of reality.

It can easily be understood that such sexual rituals led to a violation of vows and to excesses, which in turn brought about reform movements. The beginnings of the Kadampa order, the predecessor of the Gelukpa order, were connected with such reforms. But most of all, the founder of the Gelukpa order, Tsongkapa, was very clear about the obligatory restrictions on tantric practices in Gelukpa monasteries. Tantrism in its emotional form was necessary as an inner transformation for higher advancement, but tantric sex was not to be applied, and monks were not to indulge in any such practices. It was the strictness of the Gelukpa discipline that gave it its lasting, widespread appeal. During a time of a general deterioration of monastic standards, this new discipline affected the monasteries of the other orders as well. The tradition of such sexual tantric practices was, however, continued by some lay lamas, especially Nyingmapa followers. They formed esoteric religious communities of lay men and women, practicing not group sex but individual unions combining meditation with sexual action.

Whether as practiced earlier or in its later very limited form, this form of tantric religion had nothing to do with the institution of marriage and family structure. As indicated, the family existed as a natural institution, and its loyalties were based on blood relationship rather than on religious teachings. In the sixteen human laws proclaimed by King Songtsen Gampo, the respect to be paid to one's elders was a major stipulation, and in practice family loyalty extended beyond the nuclear family to the grandparents, married children, uncles, aunts, and cousins of the extended family. These loyalties in no way competed but rather were intermingled with an overall loyalty to religious faith.

Marriage and other family festivities were, however, often occasions for other popular forms of religious ceremonies that may be traced back to pre-Buddhist times. Such ceremonies were performed by *ngakpa* ("professional magicians"), who were believed to use psychic power to deal with phenomena that affected human life. At weddings and other social events, such as celebrations of promotions, or to gain good fortune and safety on long trading journeys or business ventures, a ngakpa would be invited to call on and glorify the five spirits that in this pre-Buddhist belief, were dwelling in each human being. These forces or gods (*ghowai lhanga*)[34] could assure both spiritual well-being and material prosperity (*yangguk*). The ngakpa also performed a rainmaking ceremony (*charbeb*).

In a wedding, the bride (or occasionally the bridegroom) left her (or his) family to join that of the groom (or bride), so the spirits of both families had to be placated. In the family of the departing bride, a lay woman in ceremonial costume traditionally carried an arrow with a five-colored silk tassel through the house just before the bride's departure to gather good fortune and calm the spirits so they would remain in the house. On arrival in the new household, the bride was welcomed by a woman with a jar of milk that was sprinkled throughout the house to secure blessing for long life and good fortune.

The ngakpa ceremonies were, however, not uniformly practiced. For the faithful Buddhist, a wedding, like other family affairs, was an occasion to make offerings at the family shrine. Each family had such shrines, usually one in every room of the house, including the bedroom. To the faithful, any room without a shrine seemed to indicate disrespect for religion.[35] The shrines, made of wood or metal, usually consisted of five chambers, each containing one major image of a Buddha figure, the founder of the respective sect, or other bodhisattva figures surrounded by smaller figures and scrolls. The family members prayed daily before the shrines, mostly in the morning and evening, and each carried a prayer book from which to read parts or all of the prayers. The nomads had portable shrines on belts, which could be slung around the shoulders together with the rifle. In this way, Buddhism was a part of each family's daily life.

The Monks and Society

Before discussing monks and society, it may be useful to deal with terminology. Monk and nun (*gedun*) are the generic terms for all people who have entered Buddhist monastic life. The term *gedun*, meaning "in search of virtue," describes those who devote themselves to the service of the noble ideals taught by Gautama Buddha. This involves service for mankind, and the monks' and nuns' activities therefore aim at and deal with the problems of their fellow human beings. All monks and nuns acting in this service are respected and revered for it. However, there is a hierarchy in the religious community and in the regard in which they are held by the lay population and in the monastic community itself.

Overlapping with the term of monk is that of lama,[36] which is usually understood to mean religious teacher. In this meaning, the term *lama* is narrower than that of monk or nun. Lama implies a teacher of religion, and not all monks or nuns, not even all fully ordained monks or nuns, are lamas. All monks and nuns who deal primarily with the management of affairs, the crafts, or the professions provide a service different from that of teaching the doctrine and would not be called lama. On the other hand, learned religious teachers who are not monks will still be addressed as lamas. These are lay and married lamas, and they may be members of sects that permit non-monastic membership, like the white-robed Nyingmapa or the white-robed yogis of the Kagyupa sect, or simply distinguished and learned laymen of any sect.

However, the large majority of the lamas in Tibet were distinguished church figures, very often incarnates, and indeed all incarnates were trained as teachers. It is obvious that these lamas, as teachers of religion and performers of religious ceremonies, had a great impact on Tibetan society. Aside from the incarnates, these lamas may have been geshes of their orders (holders of the highest academic and theological degree), abbots, lay yogi, or lay teachers. Aside from their general activities, many of them functioned as family lamas. Mostly upper- and middle-class families invited a specific lama to their home for ceremonies of any kind, teaching, or guidance in family affairs. But members of all families, rich or poor, could have had their own lamas, on whom they relied for teachings and personal guidance.

The tradition of the guru-disciple relationship, stressed by the Vajrayana school, found its common expression in the widely spread practice of attaching oneself to one's own *tsawai lama*, usually rendered as "root lama," whose advice and teaching were sought for all aspects of spiritual and material problems. This guru-disciple relationship applied also to the bond between monks and their lama teachers. Even the incarnations retained their respect and reverence for the teachers who had introduced them to the texts and the metaphysical concepts and practices of the faith.

This student-teacher relationship was a personal one, based on the student's choice of the teacher, which was not affected by any consideration of sect on either side, and the teaching itself was nonsectarian, providing a personal blend of concepts according to the teacher's style and choice. The student thus did not receive any rigid doctrine but an introduction to the concepts that made it possible for him to come to his own grasp and knowledge of the common faith.

By the very nature of their calling, all lamas were constantly active in society. All incarnations, for instance, traveled widely, and wherever they went, they were active in giving blessings, teaching, and performing ceremonies. Other lamas who were not incarnations performed the same functions in their home areas and whenever they traveled. Not only these highly revered teachers but all monks performed similar duties. A considerable number of monks, varying from perhaps 10 percent to over 50 percent, were nonresidents of their base monastery, which they would visit only for major festivities or for periods of renewed study. For the rest of the year, they lived in the communities and carried out their religious, educational, or social role. Some of the monks would stay with wealthy families in the towns or on country estates and take charge of the family temple or family shrine. These monks were called *konnyer*, meaning "steward of the Three Jewels." Aside from caring for the temple or shrine, they were expected to perform all necessary religious ceremonies, and they would also give advice and help in domestic matters, including the practical management of provisions. Less wealthy families, who could not afford a permanent resident monk, were regularly visited by a specific monk to look after their rituals. Such monks, called *chöney*, usually visited several families in turn,[37] and providing such services was the chief role of the ser-kyim practitioners in southern Tibet.

Not only for rituals at the family shrines but for prayers on all occasions, the reading of scriptures by such resident or visiting monks—or, in many cases, by monks residing with their own families—was a regular part of a family's life, without which the members of the family would feel deprived of spiritual sustenance. For Tibetans, this particular service performed by the monks was an essential part of their life. Layman and monk had a patron

and priest relationship in which they were inseparably linked, and this relationship could cover many aspects of intellectual life. The monk who stayed
with his own family would teach the younger family members the rudiments
of reading and writing and the basic tenets of the faith, together with the
stories of Buddha's life and those of other religious figures.

For higher guidance, however, the people would turn again to the tsawai
lama for counsel. The questions people asked these lamas embraced every
aspect of their lives. They would ask about the health of a pregnant mother,
how well she would pass through her pregnancy, and whether the delivery
would be successful for mother and child. The lama was expected to provide
spiritual support for a happy outcome. Some parents asked for spiritual
blessing to have the child be a son. Others who had no child asked a lama
who had the reputation of extraordinary attainment to invoke spiritual
power to grant them their wish to have a child. Other entreaties concerned
children's health, advancement in education, a good marriage, matters of
business and trade, a good harvest, protection of the herds from disease, or
indeed any aspect of life. It was also a common practice to periodically send
a questionnaire to a chosen lama to determine the fortunes of the coming
year: whether the family as a whole would have peace and prosperity,
whether there was a danger of disease or mishap, and what should be done
to prevent misfortune. Monks, too, asked their lamas for personal advice
about their studies and their vocation.

The role of the monk in general and of the lama in particular was thus
that of spiritual guide, psychological counselor, and teacher in every way,
from instruction in simple literacy and an understanding of the religion to
the highest intellectual and emotional insight into their own lives and the
lives of others. Of special importance was the service performed for the sick
and the dying. For the faithful Buddhist, the prayers said at the bedside by
the monk were more urgent than the visit by the doctor and his prescriptions. When death was approaching, it was the lama who was to give his
blessing and guide the dying person through the presumed transformation.
Soon after death, the lama conducted a special ceremony, called a *phowa*,
which marked the transference of the stream of consciousness of the dead to
a higher or an enlightened realm. Soon after a death, the family organized
the *getsa drubpa* (the "virtuous service"), which was held in the home and at
various temples and monasteries to give spiritual support to the dead. As a
matter of charity, food and money would be distributed to the poor, and the
deceased's clothes, jewelry, and cash were given to lamas, including the
Dalai Lama, and monasteries for special prayers for the dead. The value of
the gifts obviously depended on the financial means of the family, but it also
depended on their piety.

Lamas also gave their blessing for a child's physical development and good

Drukchen Thuksay, monk from Hemis monastery in Ladakh (photo by Franz Michael).

health, for the growth of its intelligence, and for its spiritual growth. They selected and blessed sacred paintings and sculptures and ordinary household articles or the commodities of trade. There were special rites for the consecration of houses. In those ceremonies, processions carried the 104 volumes of the *Kanjur* around a newly built house to secure spiritual blessing. But the main function of the lamas was to teach the laity and monks an understanding of self and the world of phenomena for the sake of advancement toward liberation. The lama in turn was convinced of his responsibility. As the Gyalwa Karmapa stated: "Buddhism depends on the purity of the teacher. If you profess to be a lama, you have to be one."

The advice and guidance provided by the lamas and/or monks were not based merely on an intellectual process or educational understanding but, in the minds of the devout, on spiritual guidance gained through meditation and divination. For important decisions, both monk and lay oracles would be consulted. The practices of the oracles, both monk and nonmonastic, were carried out in the Buddhist conceptual framework.

Aside from the religious role of the teacher, the monks played an important part in the management of practical affairs. They not only managed the estates of the monasteries and labrangs but served as estate managers for aristocrats and well-to-do middle-class people. As business managers and traders for their monasteries and labrangs, they traveled widely within and outside Tibet and thus played a major part in the economy of the country. The monks were also the custodians of the medical tradition of Tibet. Although there were lay doctors, the colleges of medicine, both old and new, were headed by monks, and medicine remained a very important subject in Buddhist studies.

According to a Tibetan saying, the task of the monk was threefold. The first task was to set the wheel of knowledge in motion; the second, to set in motion the wheel of meditation; and the third, to set in motion the wheel of humane action.

Literacy

For a premodern society, Tibet appears to have had an extraordinarily high literacy rate. Although it is difficult, in the absence of any reliable statistics, to arrive at anything better than a most general estimate, any study of Tibetan society and its social and professional strata indicates that a large percentage of the population had acquired at least the basic ability to read and write and a substantial number of people had, through years of study and application, achieved a highly sophisticated humanist education in the Tibetan framework.

There is no agreement about the size of the total population of Tibet among the Tibetan, Indian, Western, and Chinese authors who have ventured to express an opinion.[1] Taking all the estimates into consideration and our own attempts to add up the data available to us from different regions of the country, we suggest a total population of about six million people. This estimate is based on the territory of the Tibetan cultural area, including the central regions of Ü and Tsang (the area that is now known as Tibet Region of China in the Chinese political scheme); Tö or western Tibet; Kham or eastern Tibet; Amdo or northeastern Tibet; and Changtang or northern Tibet. The major population concentrations are in central and eastern Tibet, and some of the differences in the population estimates can be explained by the respective authors' use of varying political delineations. What is important from the point of view of traditional culture is the fact that the religious and social stratification extended over all these regions in similar proportions, except perhaps for the central city of Lhasa and its environs.

The assumption of a high rate of literacy throughout this whole cultural area is based primarily on the fact that a very large percentage of the male population became monks and received at least a basic schooling, which was a prerequisite for them in order to be able to conduct their religious and secular services. The figure mentioned for the percentage of the male population that entered the monasteries is sometimes given as high as 40 percent.[2]

In our own estimation, that figure appears to be somewhat exaggerated. It may perhaps be explained by the fact that most of the observers were more familiar with Lhasa than with the more distant regions of the country, and the area of Lhasa, where the largest leading monasteries were concentrated, may indeed have had such a high monk population, somewhat in excess of that of other parts of the country. In our own very tentative estimation, not only of Lhasa but also of other areas on which we have some information, the percentage of monks may have been closer to perhaps 33 percent of the male population. Whatever the estimate, however, a very substantial seg-ment of all the people dedicated their life to religion and in order to prepare themselves for their calling, acquired at least a basic education.

In addition to the monks, a segment of the female population became nuns and entered nunneries. Although the number of nuns was perhaps only in the thousands, it indicates not only the concept of the equality of women in the religious scheme, but also the absence of any discrimination in the field of education—as manifested also in other parts of the educational system.

Religious education thus was the major factor in the extension of literacy throughout Tibet. Since the monastic orders and nunneries were open to all Tibetans, regardless of their social background, this large sector of Tibetan life provided total mobility to all strata of the population, and education was thus available to people from all classes.

However, religious education served secular as well as religious ends, and it included subjects such as arithmetic, geometry, management, and finance to prepare the religious elite for the worldly part of their service. That same purpose was also served by the education of a substantial number of Tibetans, both men and women, who were not part of the religious establishment.

The first and most important secular group was the higher aristocracy, the one hundred fifty or so families in Lhasa who, because of their inherited position and ownership of landed estates, were obligated to have some of their members provide government service and who, through their prestige and influence, formed a substantial element of the leadership elite. Their children—both sons and daughters—can be assumed to have all had a basic and in most cases, a higher education.[3] Also, the families of what we have described as the urban middle class in the larger cities, though of common background as subjects of the state or of monastic or aristocratic estates, gave their children—both male and female—the education they needed to follow in the footsteps of their elders. This group, which may have made up 5 to 10 percent of the population, therefore were, to various degrees, part of the educated elite. More important still, a substantial upper group in the villages and camps—the rural aristocracy, the elders, the headmen, and also many of the well-to-do farmers (tral-pa)—was, we believe, for the most part literate. Our information also indicates that a high percentage of the artisans and craftsmen in many villages, particularly in Kham, were also well educated. We have therefore come to the conclusion that an estimated 50 percent or more of the Tibetans were literate.[4]

This broad general literacy among the common people—not only those who lived in the urban centers, but also those who were members of the upper status groups in the villages and nomad settlements—was facilitated by the fact that most monastic teachers remained outside their monasteries and nunneries, had residences in towns or villages, or stayed for considerable periods of time with their families, returning from time to time to their monastic establishments. This looser monastic system, in comparison to Western religious tradition, resulted from the guru-disciple tradition inherent in Tibetan Buddhism. The lamas gathered disciples and taught in their communities and in the families with whom they resided, and so did the ordinary monks. It is therefore extremely difficult to draw an educational borderline for any section of the population. Indeed, many interviews indicated that most education began in early childhood, not in the schools but at home or in the communities through such private teaching by monk or nun relatives or other religious teachers. When and if children were sent to school, then, many of them had already had some education. It is on this basis that it may be assumed that perhaps as many as half the people of premodern Tibet had at least a rudimentary knowledge of how to read and write, enough to read religious texts and popular stories, and thus could participate to a degree in the literary tradition of their country.

Private Schools

Aside from or continuing this early private education, the children of the aristocracy, the urban middle class, and the upper social levels of the rural communities went to private schools in the urban centers and rural towns. These schools were established by secular persons—such as physicians, businessmen, and secretaries in government offices—as a part of their contribution to society. Teaching added to their social standing and from their point of view, gave them added merit, but it did not affect their income in any substantial way as that continued to come from their professional work. As teachers, they received gifts on special occasions from the families of their students, but the gifts do not seem to have been large enough to cover more than the costs of their teaching. These teachers taught reading, writing, arithmetic, the chanting of religious texts, vocabulary and grammar, and general religious and moral precepts.[5]

Children were sent to private school at the age of five or six. According to

Mr. Rabden Chazotsang, principal of the Central Tibetan School, and Mrs. Khando Chazotsang, secretary of the Tibetan Homes Foundation and niece of H.H. the Dalai Lama, Happy Valley, Mussoorie, who generously gave their time in arranging for and assisting the authors in their interviews (photo by Franz Michael and Eugene Knez).

our informants, discipline was stricter in the private schools than in the monastic establishments, and, as in the one-room schools in the United States, all children studied together, each according to his or her respective level. The schools were coeducational, and no distinction was made in what subjects were taught either sex. The enrollment seems to have varied from thirty or forty to about a hundred students per school.[6] Aside from practicing writing in three types of script—Uchen, Tshukchen, and Khyukyik— much of the learning consisted of memorizing texts or tables under the supervision of advanced students, who served as prefects or subprefects and had the authority to assign and test the work and to mete out minor punishments for poor performance. Although the curriculum contained some secular subject matter—such as writing, arithmetic, accounting, composition, poetry, and the reading of epics and folk stories—it was heavily religious in content. The day began at dawn, and most of the morning was taken up with the chanting of religious texts. These texts contained prayers, invocations, and eulogies of the most venerated Buddhist deities, in prose or verse, and they were chanted in unison under the direction of a student chanting master.[7]

The private schools were attended not only by the children of aristocratic and what we have called middle-class families, but also by children of common farmers and herdsmen. In many cases, children of servant families of the aristocracy or the urban middle class went to school with the children of their masters. Thus, those children grew up, played, and went to school together, and remained companions in a quasi-family relationship through life. Several informants reported that as a practical matter, the heads of their families had seen to it that their servants' children received not only a basic but also a higher secular education, which made it possible for them to serve later as stewards or managers of their patrons' estates. Loyalty to the family was thus enhanced, and the policy contributed a great deal to the absence of educational class distinctions in the nonreligious sector of society.

Religious Texts

Among the most popular liturgical texts chanted in verse by students in school, and thus forever ingrained in their minds, was *Dolmai topa*, a eulogy in praise of the Green Tara, which was recited daily in many schools. The Green Tara was believed to be an emanation of Avalokitesvara, the most venerated bodhisattva, who symbolized Buddha's compassion for all sentient beings. The eulogy praising the Green Tara was supposed to demonstrate the powers of the enlightened mind on several levels of symbolism, but it was also believed to protect devotees from evil and from every sort of danger.[8] Legend has it that the prayer's text was composed by the Buddha before he appeared as the Gautama incarnation.[9]

Another liturgical text of equal or perhaps even greater importance was *Gaden lhagyama*, which was chanted in veneration of Tsongkapa, the founder of the Gelukpa sect. It included an invocation and glorification of Tsongkapa and a synopsis of his teachings. It described the religious law, the value of human life, its transitory nature, the conditions of life, its misery, its agonies, and death; it expounded the understanding of one's own nature, personal liberation through observance of moral principles, and development of wisdom through meditation; and finally it enounced the Mahayana principles that require the devotee to develop "spiritual enlightenment" (*bodhicitta*), compassion for the good of all others, which became the essence of Mahayana Buddhist teachings in Tibet.

There were other such religious chants in verse: the *Gangloma*,[10] a eulogy commending Manjusri, the bodhisattva of wisdom; *Sampa lhündrupma*, a text of the Nyingmapa sect containing an invocation to Padmasambhava, the eighth-century teacher from India, for fulfillment of religious aspirations; and *Thabkhey thukjema* and *Kabsumpa*, both texts containing eulogies in praise of the Gautama Buddha. The substance of all these chants, which were recited daily during the impressionable years of childhood and adolescence, was clearly instrumental in shaping the strong faith and religious attitude of each educated secular generation.

Secular Material and Popular Literature

However memorization was by no means limited to religious texts, nor was reading limited to religious literature. A versified lexicon was to be memorized and tested and so were charts of multiplication, measurements, money, grain, calculation, etc.–all in all about nine to ten charts had to be committed to memory along with the religious literature. Once a week, the head of a school appeared to test the students and distribute rewards and punishments, the former consisting of small gifts of ceremonial scarfs; the latter, a beating with small bamboo canes for both boys and girls, with the one distinction that the girls were slapped more gently than the boys.

Reading also included popular literature: stories used in folk operas, heroic epics, stories of kings and their consorts, and love stories, which often ended in tragedy. A few such stories became well known. *Drowa sangmo* was the story of a king's favorite who incurred the jealousy of the chief queen. The queen imprisoned the king, but the lady escaped in a miraculous manner and ascended to heaven. Her children by the king avenged their father by killing the bad queen. In another tale, Lady Ache Nangsa, the daughter of a middle-class family, was seen at a public festival by the king of Tsang when he was looking for a bride. Taken by her beauty, he had his men enter the crowd and, according to custom, place an arrow into the back of her shawl. Although she was very religious, she was forced to marry the king, but the king's sister was jealous and spread slander about the lady, convincing the king that she was guilty of some alleged crime. Eventually the lady escaped to a remote area and became a nun and a religious teacher. Hearing of this and realizing his error, the king went to her, confessed, and became her disciple. *Pema hobar* [Radiating lotus] is the story of a boy, an incarnation of Padmasambhava, who went out to conquer an evil king and eventually succeeded. Chogyal Norzang was a ruler who loved a pretty woman and married her. When he went on a military campaign, his other concubines made life miserable for the lady, and under the threat of death she escaped to her parents, who were lower celestial beings. When the prince returned, he was disconsolate and went in search of her, expressing his sorrow in love songs that became very popular, but he finally found her so the story had a happy ending. Another such story concerned Milarepa, the famous eleventh-century poet-saint. Once when he was living in a cave, a deer took refuge from a hunter, and the saint protected it by quieting the dog and assuaging the hunter. The hunter then recognized the saint.

In these and other stories, such as the heroic stories of Gesar, the epics of the past became intertwined with religious legends and concepts to form a popular literature. Avidly read by the young, the stories, together with the folk operas, formed a counterpart to the massive amount of religious literature in the monastic and private libraries. In fact, the epics and tales of animals and similar stories became popular enough that some religious teachers admonished their young students not to read the stories too much, because they might distract the students from their religious concentration.

Monastic Schooling

Monastic education, which produced the large majority of the more educated elite, was of much higher importance, both in numbers and in its impact on society. As indicated earlier, even the monks and nuns in the small monasteries and nunneries in distant rural or nomadic areas were literate, at least to the degree of being able to read and write and to apply the religious texts needed for the services and liturgy. There was no limitation on entering monastic life; not even the great monasteries in and near Lhasa or the other major centers at Shigatse and Chamdo had quotas or other restrictions on the enrollment of novices. The only requirements for acceptance were that the candidate must be of the proper sex and have normal physical and mental abilities.

Before the parents requested that a monastery admit their child, they arranged for a suitable monastic guardian (*shaktshang gegen*) to care for the candidate's well-being by providing board, lodging, and guidance. In turn, the guardian received an endowment (*chögyak*) from the family of the candidate. In the case of aristocratic, rich, or well-to-do families, the endowment could consist of a considerable amount of money as well as artifacts, religious objects (sometimes made of gold or silver), or furniture. Ordinary farmers and herdsmen provided food according to their ability and on a continuing basis. A close relationship was formed between the families and the monastic guardians, who became the "foster parents" of their "adopted children," the novices in the monasteries or nunneries.

Children generally entered the monastery at the age of seven or eight, usually with some prior knowledge of reading and writing acquired from private teaching by family monks or in school.[11] An erroneous view holds that if there were several sons in the family, the eldest had to be sent to a monastery to become a monk. The reason why a child, often more than one and not necessarily the oldest, entered monastic life was essentially the result of a voluntary decision by parents and relatives with the agreement of the child. It was a way of earning merit for the child, the family, and all sentient beings. In practice it was also a great opportunity for a full life of intellectual and spiritual fulfillment in an open-ended career of worldly advancement and, in the strong belief of the faithful, for moving toward enlightenment, Buddhahood, and liberation for oneself and all other beings. Only children chosen as incarnations *had* to enter religious life, regardless of the wish of their parents, but to be so chosen was regarded as an especially great honor, which could not be refused.

Although most of the novices entered the monasteries voluntarily, smaller monasteries, especially those in the outlying areas, sometimes relied on a form of draft to recruit needed new members. Through the district official, the local headmen would be instructed to select from the families under their authority three or four children of proper age to enter the monastery.[12] Because of the strong belief in the importance of religious merit and opportunity, it does not appear that these requests were difficult to fulfill, although some informants spoke of attempts to hide children in order to avoid such drafts. It appears that service, whether military or religious, can be looked at from a personal as well as from a community point of view, in Tibet as elsewhere.

Once in the monastery or nunnery, each child was assigned a teacher to direct the education of the novice. The religious part of the monastic education covered essentially the same material as that taught in the private schools. Reading and writing the three scripts had to be mastered, and much time was spent memorizing religious texts and chanting them. These texts varied in accordance with the sect of the monastery. Arithmetic tables were also committed to memory, as were vocabulary and grammar, liturgy, and, of course, the rules of monastic discipline. Instead of reading folk literature, a young monk advanced faster to memorizing and interpreting the sutras, the sacred texts that were to occupy the major part of his intellectual life.

Higher Monastic Education

After three or four years of basic training, the monastic student, now an adolescent, moved on to higher training and studies. He became first a getsul and then a gelong, and having achieved the latter stage, he was free to choose his own course of study and his teachers. There were several paths of study open to him. One was to engage in academic studies.

Each of the large monasteries consisted of several colleges, each college usually had several institutes, and each student would belong to one of the institutes. These institutes provided courses in the five academic subjects: logic, canon law, monastic discipline, *Madhyamika* and *Prajnaparamita* (the two major treatises of Mahayana philosophy), and Abhidharma (the doctrine of psychology, which dealt with the mind and the mental faculties). The study of each subject began with memorizing the texts, which were then to be interpreted word by word as well as through textual meaning. The study covered the general teachings of Mahayana and Theravada Buddhism in addition to the special teachings of the student's own sect. Monks and lamas who had an eclectic inclination studied the teachings of other sects as well. The syllabus of study contained numerous sutras, eulogies of Buddhist deities, invocations, worship of incarnations, texts of monastic ordinations, other doctrinal texts, and the textual study of *Lamrim*, the stages to enlightenment. The last was based on integrated teachings from both Theravada and Mahayana traditions, and it combined textual study with practice and advancement in meditation.

To study, the student chose as tutors a teacher for each respective field. In the Gelukpa order, these personal teachers had passed the final academic examination and had obtained the geshe degree. Each geshe had a number of students, and those studying the same subject studied together under the geshe's direction, first memorizing the texts and commentaries and then analyzing them critically. The most important method of analytical study in the Gelukpa order was the group debate, in which each student in turn became a defendant to be questioned by challengers from among his fellow students. In this form of disputation, the defendant sat and the challenger stood in front of him, and the questions and statements were accompanied by well-established gestures. These debates, carried on in the courtyard of the monastery in front of the assembled monks, were also used for the geshe examination itself. Each debate served not only as a test of the knowledge of texts and concepts, but also as training in logical thought and argument. (Other sects also used this practice in some of their monasteries.)

The avowed goal of the academic education was to lift the spiritual level of the trainee, who was to learn to subordinate material ambitions to spiritual aspirations. Material wealth was to be looked upon as a means for sustaining the precious human body and facilitating humane actions: The "middle path" was to avoid extreme poverty and riches, self-mortification as well as indulgence. The final aim was to gain transcending wisdom and compassion. The method called *thösamgomsum* ("listening, examining, meditating") was to achieve the immediate purpose of *khetsungzangsum* ("erudition, self-control, and kindness") and ultimately full enlightenment in order to be competent to serve humanity.

For those scholars of the Gelukpa order who passed the geshe examination and obtained the degree, there was the possibility of advanced esoteric studies in two tantric colleges at Lhasa. The emphasis of this advanced training was on meditation and yoga. There were also other tantric monasteries and nunneries with comprehensive or selective programs based on memorizing numerous tantric texts and on applying meditation and yoga practices. In the most advanced stage of esoteric study, a monk or nun could retire for

Geshe Gomo Rinpoche, monastic teacher (photo by Franz Michael and Eugene Knez).

Courtyard in Jokhang temple (photo by David T. Parry).

short or long periods of time to isolated temples or caves. They would live a hermit existence of meditation and occasionally preach to or counsel a growing number of faithful followers, based on the enlightenment gained through their spiritual exercises.

An advanced education was also open to nuns, although their study did not include philosophical debate but stressed tantric education. There was no geshe degree for nuns, though they had less comprehensive examinations of their own. A case in point is that of the well-known incarnated nun Dorji Phagmo of the Samdhing nunnery. The equality of nuns was indicated by the fact that women teachers could teach monks as well as nuns.

The academic training was chosen by perhaps one-third of the students who entered monasteries or nunneries.[13] Those students entered a "life of study," the practical application of which was to teach others, both monks and laymen, and to offer themselves as living examples of the concepts of the religion in which they believed.

The majority of the monks and nuns chose less stringent forms of education and life. Some of them received a more simple schooling, being privately tutored by lamas, which provided them with a condensed explanation of the doctrinal and meditational teachings of the Hinayana and Mahayana schools. Such students usually studied *Lamrim* texts of meditation and some selected books on psychology and other fields of philosophy but did not follow a strict academic course. As monks or nuns, they were, however, also bound by the monastic discipline, unless they left the monastic establishment and continued their studies under their tutor elsewhere. The purpose of such training was to share in the personal benefits of religious education without assuming the full intellectual burden of a monastic life of study.

More important was the education of those monks, perhaps the majority, who accepted the monastic discipline and religious education and prepared themselves for a more practical role in the polity, the economy, and the culture of their society.[14] These monks provided the majority of the administrators for central and local governments and most of the monastic estates. Others served, in many instances, as arbiters of civil disputes or as religious oracles to be consulted on any important decision by the authorities as well as by the secular population. These professionally trained monks truly formed the ruling stratum of society. To prepare themselves for this role, they had to receive not only a thorough religious education, but also training in the composition and writing of official documents, in the keeping of records, and in the management of financial affairs. As described elsewhere, the monastic establishments and religious education, based on Buddhist concepts of the "middle way," were in no way hostile to trade and banking or the profitable management of economic affairs, and a whole administrative structure derived from monastic education had to be prepared to oversee those enterprises.

Aside from the preparation for administrative work provided by the monasteries, there were, in Lhasa, two schools that were set up by the seventh Dalai Lama to prepare students especially for official service in monastic and secular careers. For the monastic side of government service, there was the Tselabdra or Peak School mentioned earlier. Located in the Potala, it educated a group of about thirty boys, ages fourteen to twenty, as monk officials for the highest government positions. The students were selected from the leading monasteries or were sons of nobles, and they had to be recommended by the four grand secretaries. Their three to four years of training included religious education by individual monk teachers and courses in accounting, style of correspondence, calligraphy, and drafting of documents. The secular school, located in Lhasa itself, had about twenty-five students, also fourteen to twenty years old, for three to four years of training in a similar program. Examinations were given twice a year in both schools, and successful candidates were then transferred to government service. From this small number of specially trained religious and secular students came many of the leading administrators of the Lhasa government.

Aside from this educated elite of monk and secular political and social leaders, there was a special group among the leading educated upper stratum, the incarnations. In essence their selection paralleled that of the monks and nuns. Their families were from all strata of society—aristocracy, middle class, and commoners—so in the reincarnations there was the same social mobility as was found in the rest of the religious sector of society. But in the incarnations' religious and political roles, and therefore in their social standing, they were singled out from the rest of monastic and secular society.

The incarnations were believed to be predestined for a sacred mission as "protectors of mankind" to help all beings in their advancement toward salvation. After their predecessors had departed from this life, the incarnations were found among the young children who were born at the proper time and in areas and under conditions indicated by the previous incarnation or oracles. The incarnations were confirmed by a special group of monks from a group of potential candidates by tests of recognition of possessions or other means. At the age of about five, they were taken in special procession to their particular monastery to grow up there and be educated for their calling of religious and social leadership.

To enable the incarnations to carry on their role as religious teachers on the highest level, they were provided with special privileges and a comfortable income, which set them aside from the ordinary monks and often made them very wealthy indeed. As incarnations, they had final authority over their religious establishment, the labrang, which—as indicated earlier—often included large estates given by the government that were exempt from the land tax. The incarnations also received an extra percentage of the gifts presented to the monastery by its patrons. The incarnations' needs were thus amply provided for and taken care of by the managers and stewards of their labrang, who were selected by the monastery from among the nonacademic monks.

The education of an incarnation was, from the outset, directed by a personal tutor (in the case of a Gelukpa incarnation, a geshe), who established a lasting and close relationship with his pupil—a pupil-teacher relationship that was indeed one of the main ways in which higher religious wisdom was orally transmitted. The education of an incarnation began with the same syllabus as that studied by all monk or private students: the learning of the alphabet, writing and reading, and the memorizing and chanting of religious texts—texts of devotion and invocation, eulogies, prayers, and the histories of famous saints and incarnations. These chants included those generally used by all sects, those of the particular monastic order, and those belonging to the monastery and the labrang of the respective incarnation. After this basic training, the incarnation would move on, perhaps faster than ordinary monks, to more advanced religious courses: memorizing texts of sutras and tantras, analyzing them in discourses with the personal tutor and others, and practicing debating and disputing on the basis of the knowledge thus acquired.

An incarnation took the monastic vows—i.e., not to take life, not to lie, not to take without being given, to remain celibate, and not to drink—and there were daily tests by the tutor, who had the right to inflict moderate punishment for a misdemeanor or lack of effort. The monastic experience also included presence at and later participation in the public debates and discourses that played such an important part in the intellectual process. Finally, when prepared, an incarnation (of the Gelukpa order) was tested in the highest academic examination. This geshe exam was presided over by the abbot and held in the presence of the entire assembly of the monastery and dignitaries of the order and the area in general.

Being human in nature, the incarnations represented, as a matter of course, many levels of intelligence and character. But because they were carefully chosen and highly educated, a great number of them appear to have been outstanding personalities, a fact that the faithful naturally attributed to their being incarnations of bodhisattvas. As the guiding figures of the religious elite, they provided strength and durability for the whole religiopolitical system. That role was especially fulfilled by the incarnations of the Dalai Lama, among whom there have been a number of outstanding religious and political leaders—notably the "great fifth," the thirteenth, and the present fourteenth Dalai Lama, whose extraordinary religious, intellectual, and humane development has enabled him to retain his religious, cultural, and political leadership role during the greatest crisis his people and his country have endured.

The educated elite of Tibet created, developed, and managed the political, cultural, social, and economic systems of the country, and that group's guiding role was universally accepted for centuries until outside conquest imposed a new structure. The education of the leaders, based on religion, and their idea of service, as implied in the monastic tradition and the lives of the incarnations, were clearly the basis for the leaders' complete acceptance by a devout population.

Nonliterate Education

The acceptance of leadership by an educated elite did not, however, preclude participation by all Tibetans, whether educated and literate or not, in the religious and cultural life of the country. As in Elizabethan England, the rich language of the illiterates, farmers, and herdsmen used in ordinary conversation, interlaced with proverbs and lucid expressions, has been commented upon by educated observers. When these simple people came to

Lhasa for the great festivals, they often impressed their more sophisticated countrymen with their lucid speech, which was spiced with expressive phrases taken from the great literature.

When Max Weber applied the distinction between elite and masses to the religious sphere as well as to the political and social world, he attempted to analyze the relationship between the two groups. In his interpretation, the elite minority originated the ideas and concepts of the system and represented it, and the majority of the people followed the ordinary interests of practical life but sought reassurance in ritual and belief. In Tibet, the elite made up a large percentage of the total population, and the involvement of religious leaders in mundane affairs as well as that of the general population in religious life clearly helped to soften any sharp distinction between the cultural elite and the common people. Tibetans did not have to be literate in order to share in the country's cultural tradition.

For those who remained illiterate, there were many ways in which they could learn about the religious beliefs and the culture of their country and come to participate actively in their expression and practice. At home, a child would soon learn the mantras, sacred formulas that were perpetually on the lips of all Tibetans. *Om mani padme hum*, the invocation of the bodhisattva Avalokitesvara, so widely and constantly used, became a symbolic expression of religious devotion in all Tibet. Travelers have testified that they continuously heard such religious expressions being spoken by people from all walks of life. This may well be the way a Tibetan child first received its deep impression of the importance of religion in life.

Then there were the prayer flags that fluttered from the rooftops of houses and from mountaintops. These prayer flags (*lungtai darchok*, or "wind-horse flags") were a Buddhist adaptation of an older Bon custom practiced as a means to ward off evil forces and attract benevolent forces in nature. Under Buddhism, the flags continued to be a means of communication with all that is sacred, and they also became silent prayers to the Buddha. Five colors, indicating the five elements, were associated, by rotation, with the calendar years, so each person was assigned the color of the year he or she was born.

Literate or illiterate, everyone could say innumerable prayers by the use of an ingenious device, the prayer wheel. Some of the wheels, in barrel shape, were placed near the entrance of temples where the faithful could rotate them in turn. More common still were the hand prayer wheels, small metal cylinders that contained written prayers, were held by a handle, and rotated clockwise with the aid of an attached metal weight. Other forms of prayer wheels included those turned by the water of a mountain stream; those on rooftops, which were turned by the wind; and those in houses, which were fixed on top of a butter lamp and turned by the heat. It may be significant that in Tibet, where no carriages were used for transportation (perhaps because of the difficulties of the terrain for animal-drawn vehicles), the wheel was known but used almost exclusively for this religious purpose, i.e., to facilitate communion with the Buddha.

For the ordinary Tibetan, education was not altogether dependent on literacy. More perhaps than in other premodern societies, Tibetans learned about their culture and history through spectacles and performances as well as through constant contact with monks and nuns and the religious leadership. During the many religious festivals, the ordinary people were not mere spectators but participated in the activities. At the April processions in Lhasa, in which all monasteries and all sects took part, groups of lay dancers marched along and performed before the Potala. These dances differed in form and substance from the sacred dances of the monks. There were dances with various secular themes, rhythmic drum dances, and numerous forms of folk dances, but all were treated as expressions of devotion. The sacred dances were considered a special form of meditation, and the use of masks was an aid to visualization of the emanations. Such dances were performed as rituals, not entertainment, and they were understood and received as such by the faithful laymen as well as by the monks.[15] Thus the religious processions and dances were an education in the tenets and mythology of the Buddhist faith for both dancers and participants. So, of course, were the festivals themselves. The burning of incense along the routes of the processions and the filling of thousands of butter lamps before the deities were not only signs of devotion but also forms of participation in religious activities.

One of the more important forms of popular education was provided by the many storytellers who wandered around the country, the majority of whom were monks or nuns. They usually carried three or four tanka paintings, which they unrolled when they set up their stand and used as illustrations while narrating the life stories of great Buddhist saints. These *lama maniwa* roamed the countryside during most times of the year and usually went to Lhasa in the fourth lunar month, the sacred month of Saga Dawa (usually in June). They set up their tents and folding tables for offerings and pointing to the tankas with a long stick, indicated the various figures and symbols and chanted their stories in traditional, often beautiful songs. Occasionally interspersed with mantras, their narration took the form of a dialogue. Their audience, which gathered and listened, made small offerings to be taken back by the monks or nuns to their monasteries or nunneries, where such offerings were considered part of the regular income. Other lama maniwa wandered the streets carrying small wooden shrines that contained clay images of deities. With the aid of these images, they told and explained popular religious tales and received offerings. Still other lama maniwa sang religious songs accompanied by a drum. The stories and songs varied accord-

antric ritual mask dances at the eight-hundred-year celebration of the founding of Drigung
ıonastery (photo by Franz Michael and Eugene Knez).

Musicians at the eight-hundred-year celebration of the founding of Drigung monastery (photo by Franz Michael).

ing to sect and monastery, but some were of general appeal, for instance, the legendary accounts of the saint Milarepa.

Equally popular, though not quite as numerous, were the secular storytellers, the bards, who traveled through the countryside. Following a profession they frequently learned from their fathers, they related epic stories of great heroes or romantic tales of fair ladies, usually interspersed with Buddhist legendary occurrences and miraculous events. The bards sang, danced, and acted out the battles and conquests of past great leaders—men like the legendary king Gesar, a noble and courageous fighter who fought in many parts of Tibet and conquered many lands. All these secular epics became part of the oral tradition that, together with the more formal education, provided Tibetans with a knowledge of their culture.

Religion and its language and myths were an inseparable part of life for Tibetans and closely linked to all mundane matters. Not only were religious oracles consulted for state and religious affairs, but the use of oracles was also a regular part of the daily life of the ordinary population. Oracles were consulted for business affairs, for journeys, for choices of bride or groom, and for children—indeed, for any major and many minor decisions. These oracles, who predicted and advised while in a trance, were professionals, and they made a living from their work.

To Tibetans, the ideal was the educated man (the *tam yig tsi sum*)—the learned man who combined the oral tradition with a knowledge of literature (with its massive number of religious texts) and mathematics. In education, as in religious life, there were no status barriers and no sex discrimination. Tibetans recognized a religious and a social elite, but social mobility bridged the gap, and at the top of the educational system was the tam yig tsi sum.

8
Survival of a Culture?

Traditional Society

Was the Tibetan cultural tradition, as Max Weber would have it, "ossified," unable to adjust to the modern world? Did change have to come from the outside—in this case, unfortunately, from a totally different system, "Marxism-Leninism–Mao Tse-tung thought"—or was there another alternative? Were there elements inherent in the politico-religious order of Tibet that would have permitted an internal modernization of the system? The last question may not be entirely abstract and historical, as it may be relevant for Tibetans today—both outside and inside their homeland—and even for other traditional societies faced with the necessity of adjusting to the modern world. The answer to the question of a possibility of modernization within the Tibetan order must be speculative, but an analysis of the Tibetan society as it was before 1959, as well as the story of the Tibetans' adjustment to life in exile without abandoning their strong committment to their religion, leadership, and culture, can provide ample clues for an assessment of past potential and future possibilities.

Although there were clear status distinctions in the traditional society, it was open enough, and the fact that it provided considerabe social mobility to people on the lower levels of the social order prevented stagnancy as well as explosive pressures. There was a good reason why there was never a "peasant rebellion" in Tibet. The obvious road to higher status was to enter monastic life, which provided the opportunity for an education according to ability and inclination and access to a distinguished academic, artistic, or political-managerial career for any male, and in a more limited way, for women. It was for these very reasons that many people entered monastic life, and the monastic elite was clearly the dominating factor in the Tibetan polity.

There was, however, another, often overlooked, way to higher income, living style, and social recognition: trade and business enterprise. Aside from the religious institutions and aristocratic families, ordinary Tibetan people were also free to engage in and prosper from forms of economic activities such as trade, handicrafts, or the professions. These ordinary people were the subject people, the mi-ser. Even in the rural communities, the positions of the mi-ser—the farmers and the herdsmen—varied greatly, as we have seen. The higher level of mi-ser, the tral-pa, was made up of those families who combined their obligation to work on government or estate land or to tend government herds with hereditary ownership of land or herds of their own. The rest of the mi-ser, the dü-chung, were rural laborers who owned no property but were free to sell their labor. But all of the mi-ser could earn other income from trade or crafts and become prosperous. Although there was tax on land and herds, there was practically no tax on trade, crafts, and business. It was from this group that a middle class derived.

The wealthier families may have continued to live in the rural communities, and some of them may even have become recognized as a so-called village aristocracy, but many times, the untaxed profits from trade, business, or a craft surpassed a family's income from agriculture or animal husbandry, so many of these people moved to the main towns. There, together with private artisans and artists, physicians, and craftsmen, they formed the growing urban middle class. Their status as mi-ser of the government or an estate had become nominal (so it was therefore easily discarded by those who later escaped to India). The wealthy property owners and traders who remained in the villages maintained their service obligations, but those obligations were economic and not physical or political. Therefore these people, too, were middle class in terms of living standards and social prestige, and they participated in the political affairs of their communities. These affluent tral-pa and tsong-pa families were regarded as the most loyal supporters of the Buddhist establishment, and they were indeed the strongest link between religion and society in Tibet. Many of Lhasa's central, provincial, and local monk officials came from these well-to-do village mi-ser families, who were able to support their children's education in order to launch them on their careers. Others sought their children's advancement in estate management.

The large majority of the managers of monastic estates, aristocratic estates, and labrangs were mi-ser, and the income and fortune of their religious institutions or patrons' families depended largely on their efficiency and success in administration and profit making. The managers of some of the most famous labrangs in Lhasa, such as the Kundeling or Rading establishments, earned a substantial income and established a professional career for themselves. Those and other labrangs came to be capital-forming enterprises, and they functioned like banks, providing credit for other merchants and entrepreneurs at a—for Tibet very favorable—rate of 10 percent to 12 percent per annum. The main activity of those labrangs was, however, in international as well as local trade, and they especially prospered in the period just before the Chinese takeover.

The religious establishment thus became the backbone of a flourishing commercial world. Rather than being against commerce, profit making, and interest taking, the Buddhists in Tibet not only encouraged the commercial activities of the faithful, but their own institutions engaged in the activities of finance, business, and trade. As has been pointed out, "the Buddhist genesis story not only postulated private property as a 'natural' fact of human life, but also advanced it as the proximal and anterior fact, leading to the formation of regulated society."[1] Trade and business, as much as agriculture and nomadism, thus fell within the scope of Max Weber's famous concept of "elective affinity" between ideology and society—in Tibet, the relationship between the Buddhist religion and Tibetan society and economy.

All classes of Tibetan society participated in the commercial and financial activities. Among the largest trading houses were, aside from Rading and Kundeling, the aristocratic establishments of Yuthok, Surkhang, Tsarong, and others, which also received their chief income from this commerce. For all of them, the income from trade and commercial business was incomparably larger than the income from their estates, which had, however, been the basis for their capital formation.[2] The labrangs were leaders in the trade with India. The important petrol trade, for instance, was almost exclusively carried on by the Rading labrang. To assure an outlet in India, all these Tibetan firms formed alliances and partnerships with Newar families (groups of Nepalese traders and artisans) from Katmandu and other Indian merchants who lived in Lhasa.

Some of the leading Khampa families, such as the Pangdatsang, Sadutsang, and Chamatsang families, belonged to the business community in Lhasa. Those merchant families from Kham had intermarried with the aristocracy and, in practice, controlled much of the large China trade. Rich commoner merchant families also took part in the internal and external trade, and in addition to the merchant houses, the muleteers of the large caravans often came to own their own mules and participated in trading as well as earning their transport fees.

The economic developments could theoretically have led to a change in the legal aspects of the mi-ser versus government and mi-ser versus estate relationships. Nothing in the basic concepts of the Tibetan Mahayana faith would have stood in the way of abolishing the mi-ser contracts altogether, as has since been amply demonstrated in the Tibetan exile communities in India. Indeed, as a result of the fear of the Chinese Communist threat and the knowledge about the events of the "agrarian revolution" in the People's Republic of China, some Tibetan estate owners introduced a policy of distributing estate land to the farmers in the fifties. But like other changes, that measure was not pursued with any sense of urgency, partly because there was no pressure within Tibet from the agricultural population for such reforms. Apparently the established paternalistic relationship, with its economic security, good levels of income, and opportunities for economic and social mobility, was comfortable enough.

Reforms

A realization of the vast political changes outside Tibet and the perceived danger to Tibet from China did, however, lead to some reform ideas and some reform attempts. Most of the attempts led to political ramifications, became mired in factional and power struggles among the leading figures of the religiopolitical elite, and subsequently failed. Perhaps the most important of the late attempts at reform was in the area of military preparedness. As has been described previously, and in contrast to practically all other premodern governments, the authority of the Lhasa government was based on religious faith and commitment, not on any police or military force. The few military units that did exist were mainly located in critical border areas as defense against the outside threat from China. Those small units and their antiquated weapons were hopelessly outmanned and out-equipped by the modern Chinese military force.

The realization of the urgent need for strengthening the Tibetan military defense and for creating a modernized military force preceded the Communist takeover in China. The thirteenth Dalai Lama had broadened his understanding of world affairs during his travels in China, Mongolia, and India, and he recognized the danger to the Tibetan polity from outside and initiated a program of military modernization. In the twenties, Dasang Damdul Tsarong held the favor of the thirteenth Dalai Lama and was, for a time, one of the most influential figures in the Lhasa government next to the Dalai Lama. A short account of his life story is relevant to characterize the potential social mobility for Tibetan commoners, the working of Tibetan affairs in Lhasa, and the interrelationship between internal and external politics.[3]

Tsarong was born as Dasang Damdul to a peasant family in Phenpo, north of Lhasa. His father died when he was young, and Dasang, one of many brothers and sisters, was taken by an aunt to Lhasa at the age of six or seven and placed in a local school for three or four years. At the age of ten, his aunt introduced her nephew to a high lama who was a keeper of the Dalai Lama's summer palace, Norbu Linka, and the lama accepted Dasang Damdul as a student-apprentice. The intelligent youngster came to the attention of the Dalai Lama, joined the Dalai Lama's court as an attendant, and gained the Dalai Lama's confidence.

In 1904, at the time of the British Younghusband campaign to Lhasa, Dasang Damdul accompanied the Dalai Lama when he fled to Mongolia and China. As his personal attendant, Dasang Damdul gained experience and knowledge of foreign countries and their leaders, and he was rewarded for his services with a fifth-rank official title. In 1909, when the Chinese attacked Lhasa and the Dalai Lama fled to India, Dasang Damdul commanded a rear-guard unit of sixty-seven men, whom he had trained over the previous year. Holding back a Chinese cavalry unit of three hundred men at a river crossing (Chaksam Ferry), his unit inflicted heavy losses on the Chinese and secured the Dalai Lama's escape.[4] He then fled in disguise and joined the Dalai Lama in India. A year later, he was sent back as commander of Tibetan military forces (*chinda*) to join two other officials (Tsepon Norbu Wangyal Trimon and General Chamba Tendar) who had organized a secret war department. They formed a volunteer army of several thousand men, including monks and Khampa,[5] and engaged the Chinese in battles for Lhasa that led to house-to-house fighting and lasted for several months. The Chinese revolution in 1911 led to the collapse of the Chinese forces in Tibet, some of whom surrendered through Nepalese mediation and were sent back to China via India.

At this time, before the Dalai Lama returned to Tibet, one of the Tibetan leaders, the head of the aristocratic house of Tsarong, was accused by the Tibetan General Assembly of having collaborated with the Chinese. He and his son were killed, which eliminated the male membership of that prestigious family. After his return, the Dalai Lama was pressured by some of the aristocratic and religious leaders to reestablish the family, and he commanded Dasang Damdul to assume the headship of the Tsarong family, by marrying the widow of the executed man's son as well as his daughter in order to carry on the bloodline, and to assume the Tsarong name and position.[6]

This was the height of Dasang Damdul Tsarong's career. At the age of twenty-five he became a minister of the Cabinet and also minister of finance. Most of all, he was entrusted with the organization of a modern army for the defense of the country. He became commander in chief (*makchi*) and was to recruit an initial force of five hundred men, which was to be rapidly expanded.

The immediate purpose of the organization of a modern army was to force the Chinese out of the eastern areas of Kham, which they had invaded. Equipment was imported, recruitment was speeded up, and modern army drill, heretofore unknown in Tibet, was adopted. Four regiments were formed and trained according to several foreign models. One regiment was formed in Gyantse and drilled in the British military system; another unit was trained in the combined Chinese and Mongol army system; a third regiment under the command of a Mongol officer, who had been trained in Russia, adopted the Russian form of training; and a fourth regiment was placed under a Japanese officer who instructed it in Japanese methods of warfare. In 1913, these four regiments were brought to Lhasa for joint maneuvers and competitive exercises, and they were reviewed by the Dalai Lama, government officials, and the public. The outcome was a decision to use the British system uniformly for all army training. Some officers and soldiers were then sent to Quetta and Shillong to be trained as artillery and machine-gun units, and others went to Darjeeling to be trained as a military band.[7]

The new army was successful in resisting Chinese encroachments in eastern Tibet, but its recruiting and equipment expenses were beyond the ordinary resources of the government. To finance the new army, the thirteenth Dalai Lama introduced a tax reform in the early 1920s that abolished some of the tax exemptions of the privileged monastic estates, including those of Tashilhunpo, which resulted in the flight of the Panchen Lama to China. Apparently some of the other estates were also dissatisfied with the new tax measures.

There were other reforms as well. A school of Western learning was opened in Gyantse under a British headmaster, and another one was established later in Lhasa. A small police force of five hundred men was formed for the city of Lhasa under a Sikkimese commander, who had been superintendent of the British police in Darjeeling. A few Tibetans were sent abroad for technical studies. But this whole reform effort soon faltered because of the opposition of conservative monastic leaders, who were afraid that Western ways would undermine the Buddhist faith of the students.[8] The Western-type schools were closed when the students' attitude was felt to be disrespectful to the clergy and older Tibetan dignitaries.[9]

The major crisis occurred, however, in 1924 in the military reform program. The issue was partly a personal power struggle, but it touched also on the basic question of the role of the new Western-minded military officers in the Tibetan polity. There are different versions of the actual events. What seems definite is that under the leadership of Kalon Tsarong, their commander in chief, the young officers wanted more military representation in the assembly, which was then debating the new taxation of the estates.[10] When the military commanders interrupted a session of the assembly with such a demand, "their ambitious assertiveness created an atmosphere of suspicion and misgiving" not only on the part of the assembly but also on the part of the Dalai Lama and the Cabinet, especially since there were rumors of a secret plan by the military leaders to broaden their role over the civil authorities.[11] According to one historian, the shocked apprehension of the assembly was stirred on by Tsepon Lungshar, "one of the heads of the assembly who was jealous of Tsarong's growing power and encouraged the monks to make a big issue of it."[12]

However, there may have been other reasons for the hostility of the monastic leadership to Tsarong as well. A year earlier Tsarong had, at the Dalai Lama's request, mobilized the army to dispel a demonstration at the Dalai Lama's summer palace of four thousand monks from Drepung monastery who were protesting against taxes being imposed on the monastery.[13] The monastic leadership may therefore have had reason to believe that Tsarong's growing power and such use of the military threatened their own influence over the Dalai Lama.[14]

The outcome of the incident of 1924 was that the Dalai Lama dismissed two of the new army's commanding officers, and Tsarong took a leave of absence and went to India, officially on a pilgrimage. On his return journey, he received a letter from the Dalai Lama that informed him he was no longer commander in chief.[15] Another opponent of Tsarong, Dzasa Dumpa,[16] a nephew of the thirteenth Dalai Lama and commander of his bodyguard regiment, was appointed commander in chief of the new army. After Tsarong was degraded, "the drill and general condition of the Tibetan army was allowed to deteriorate. The police force fell into decay."[17] This change was all the more unfortunate since Tsarong appeared to have gained the confidence of the British, who were apparently willing to support a buildup of military strength in Tibet under his leadership. During his journey to India, Tsarong had negotiated—privately and indeed without Cabinet authorization[18]—an agreement for the training of five hundred Tibetan officers under British direction in Gyantse and in India. Since Tsarong was highly honored by the British in India, who had invited him to visit military installations and review naval maneuvers from a destroyer, he was accused of being too friendly to the British, and the connection with England was ended for the time being.[19] In view of the Tibetan dependence on outside assistance for military training and equipment, that alienation appears in retrospect to have been a tragic turning point in the attempted buildup of Tibet's military strength.

If there have been Tibetan complaints about the limitations of later British military aid—outdated equipment, grudgingly provided; no training; the British yielding to Chinese pressure[20]—one may assume that after the removal of Tsarong, British confidence in his successors was not the same. Although military reform in Tibet was not officially abandoned, there was clearly a lack of leadership and drive, which were needed to get the program that had, after all, only been started, into full gear. As a result, the officers in command of troops were not prepared for modern warfare. The whole effort finally flagged after the death of the thirteenth Dalai Lama, the most powerful source of inspiration behind the whole program. Under the regencies that followed, there was a period of stagnation and corruption, which led to disillusionment and disgust with a regime that was regarded as selfish and corrupt. Only at the last moment, too late for preventive action, was a new outstanding figure, the fourteenth Dalai Lama, placed in authority.

The issue of military reform was affected by personal intrigue and a power struggle in the circle around the Dalai Lama, but that conflict of power raised a deeper issue than that of personalities or even of policy decisions. What was at least felt to be at stake was the role of the monastic establishment in the Tibetan polity.

Any assessment of the ability of the Tibetan system to adjust to the modern world will have to consider not only the general questions of economic and social transformation but also Tibet's ability to defend itself against outside aggression and, for that crucial matter, to implant a modern military force into its religiopolitical order. In weighing the chances for the establishment of a viable military defense that could have avoided the disaster of 1950–1959, it is fundamental to note that all parties concerned agreed on the basic necessity of providing military training, organization, and weaponry—in effect, of building a modern army.

The monks and their leaders were by no means pacifists. Historically monks had fought in internal conflicts and especially in resisting Chinese encroachment, and monks were to continue to fight with valor in the coming battles with China. When there was need, the monks themselves could therefore provide a fighting force, albeit an untrained one. There was also "definitely no opposition, overtly or covertly against military strengthening."[21]

What many of the monks may not have realized was the urgency of the danger and the implications of the need for military professionalism. As a result, their major apprehension was fear of a growing predominance of the military over the religiopolitical system. They naturally were afraid that their eminence would be undermined if modern military leaders were to have the ear of the Dalai Lama and become a factor in his decision making. Indeed the monks believed that any interference in the religious order of things was the primary concern and took precedence over any other policy matter.[22] To many monastic leaders in the assembly and to many monks, it must have appeared that "possession of a well-trained army would enable the Dalai Lama to dominate the monasteries, as he had shown in the military suppression of the Drepung demonstration a year before."[23] It was the establishment of a political role for the professional army that was a threat to the monks' power.[24] There was no objection to strengthening the military if it was under traditional authority, but the creation of a modern military organization that would be in competition with the traditional power structure was clearly unacceptable.

Tsarong, on the other hand, was obviously the most outstanding reformer of the time and a strong and very able person.[25] Through his unusual opportunities for travel with and for the thirteenth Dalai Lama, he had gained a worldwide outlook and a grasp of the realities for Tibet far beyond those of the Lhasa ecclesiastical or aristocratic leaders. That experience and the trust extended to him by the Dalai Lama appear to have caused him to overplay his hand and thus endanger the whole program he had begun so well. Although clearly loyal to the Dalai Lama and the Buddhist religious system to which he faithfully adhered, he appears to have misjudged the balance of forces in the Tibetan order and thus forced his patron, the Dalai Lama, to abandon him and the realistic potential of the program. Tsarong remained to the last a patriot. Out of office at the time of crisis in 1959 and on a pilgrimage in India, he returned to Lhasa to help the Dalai Lama, as he had done before. He was last seen digging trenches at the Potala. He died in Chinese hands, as did so many.[26]

The primary credit for the whole effort of modernization and especially its military program belongs, however, to the thirteenth Dalai Lama. He had the vision and the charisma to inspire and guide a program of modernization that incorporated such diverse aspects as a national literacy campaign and the improvement of monastic discipline, the standards of scholarship of the monastic colleges, and the quality of the appointed abbots. Most of all, he fully realized the great danger to the survival of Tibet's polity and cultural tradition and planned and promoted the military program with a clear grasp of the needs for training, equipment, and a financial basis. Citing the Mongol example, he warned that the "red ideology" would destroy the Tibetan cultural heritage, and he continued to ask for the establishment of a well-trained and well-equipped army until his death.[27] Yet his vision and drive were not matched by those of his ecclesiastical or secular officials, and he clearly could not evade or divest himself of the monastic framework of the Tibetan polity of which he was the head. As Richardson very perceptively has stated, "Yet, the Dalai Lama, although the summit and master of the system, was also its creature," and he could not "ignore determined pressure from the general body of the monks."[28]

How concerned the Dalai Lama remained about the danger he had not been able to prepare for and the petty intrigues of the monastic and aristocratic leaders around him, which had frustrated his hopes and plans, can be seen from his writing at the end of his life. In his political testament, which he prepared in the year he passed away, the thirteenth Dalai Lama expressed a somber warning: "Unless we learn how to protect our land, the

Dalai Lama and the Panchen Lama, the Father and the Son, the upholders of the Buddhist faith, the glorious incarnations, all will go under and leave no trace behind. The political system inherited from the Three Great Kings will become a matter of mere history. All beings will suffer great hardship and pass their days and nights slowly in a reign of terror." Ram Rahul, who quotes this prophetic warning,[29] added his own words: "We know from hindsight how wise and prophetic his words were. It is a pity that the Tibetans, not taking the warning in time, allowed themselves to be over-taken by events."

The Dalai Lama revealed his irritation with his officials in the same document. "It is evident that if you do not devote yourselves to the service of the state but continuously indulge in self-seeking, prejudice, or nepotism, the long-term common objective will not be realized. And then nothing will help, and regrets will be useless."[30] In a letter written shortly before his death, he expressed again his worry and concern about the monk and lay officials: "If they carry on their indulgence in dishonesty and pleasure seeking, a violent cyclone of change will unequivocally arrive, and then it will be too late."[31]

The intention of the Dalai Lama was thus clear and so was the early potential of the military program under Tsarong. But the problem remained of fitting such a program into a system that, because of its isolation, fell behind in its understanding of the needs of the time and opposed any diminution of the religious preeminence. There was obviously no communication and no link between the reformers and the monk bureaucracy. Was there no possibility of reconciling their opposed positions? Assuming a common agreement on the importance of strengthening the military defenses, there need not have been any obstacle to a solution based on the equivalent of what in Western parlance would have been civilian control over the military: monastic authority over and even monastic participation in the military reorganization.[32] The *lapsus* was the lack of communication.

Even at the final moment of truth in 1959, when Chinese forces attacked the Potala and the Dalai Lama escaped to India, there was no coordination among the regular military, the Khampa volunteers, and whatever monks fought against the invaders.[33] The valor of the fighters was to no avail without proper leadership, training, organization, and weapons.

To bridge the gap between the two groups—without surrendering the fundamental concept of the Tibetan Buddhist system of rule by a religious leader to a system that included military participation in government—would have required communication between reformers and monks on the structure of the reform and also a better understanding of the modern world on the part of the monastic and aristocratic leadership. In looking back on his life of important service in government and in the religious establishment, Mr. Kundeling felt "happy for having governed with the background of religion and culture, but unhappy about the lack of communication and the lag in the grasp of world affairs."

The lack of communication, isolation, and lack of time spelled disaster for the continued political independence of the unique Tibetan order, not any basic incompatibility between Tibetan Buddhism and a modernized society. In principal, it seems, Tibetan Buddhism could have adjusted well to the modern world.

The Tibetan Polity in Exile

That assumption is strengthened by the experiences of the Tibetan diaspora. If the growing commercial segment in both the secular and the ecclesiastical sectors of the Tibetan society bode well for the potential of modern transformation, the true test of the adaptability of the religiopolitical order to modern life came when the Dalai Lama, his court, and some one hundred thousand Tibetans from all walks of life fled across the Himalayas into India. In exile, the test was not only continued Tibetan success in commercial trade and financial matters, in the continuation and development of Tibetan crafts, or even in industrial labor and management, but in agriculture, which to some observers had remained the most tradition-bound part of the economy, at least in its social structure. The present situation of the Tibetan refugee communities in India and of their religiopolitical leadership shows an extraordinarily successful ability not only to survive but to flourish.

In his extremely good essay on the Tibetan settlements at Munda Ruppe in India and their relationship to the Dalai Lama's quasi-government at Dharamsala, Melvyn C. Goldstein comes to the same conclusion.[34] After listing all the disadvantages the Tibetan refugees had to deal with in their new surroundings—as an uprooted population thrown into an alien culture in a hostile climate without the technical knowledge or a knowledge of the language to facilitate their adaptation—Goldstein comes to the conclusion that their adaptation has been very successful. Not only did the stereotyped refugee syndrome not develop, but the most successful programs of rehabilitation occurred in the very area that might have been suspected of causing the greatest difficulties, the area of permanent agricultural settlement. Disregarding the long-range questions about the future, Goldstein contends that "in particular, the traditional Tibetan political structure possesses a high 'adaptive capacity' and is the single most important variable underlying the successful initial adaptation of the Tibetan," a conclusion fully shared by the author of this book.[35]

Before dealing with the various elements of the transfer of this traditional society, it should be pointed out that the adaptation of the Tibetans to their new condition as refugees was greatly improved by the generosity and consideration of the Indian government. Not intimidated by Peking's pressure and accustomed to tolerance because of the great variety of ethnic and religious components within the Indian polity, the Indian government not only offered tolerance and financial support, but also permitted the Tibetans to form their own communities. It also offered encouragement to the Dalai Lama and his court and recognized his role as the religious and secular head of the exile communities (and other Tibetan population groups in Ladakh and other parts of India). In spite of that help, it is extraordinary that the Tibetan emigrants have established themselves successfully within the Indian polity. The dramatic adaptation may be described as a situation in which some of the unessential aspects of the Tibetan order – the surface trimmings of inherited tradition – fell off and the essence remained.

What has remained is, first of all, the religiopolitical structure, the *Personal-Union* of the Dalai Lama's religious and temporal authority. When the Dalai Lama arrived in India, the Indian government recognized and accepted that authority. Although not approving of any government in exile, it permitted the establishment at Dharamsala of the Dalai Lama's hierocracy for the Tibetans in India. This government consists of the Dalai Lama's Cabinet with portfolios on resettlement, finance, education, and security; a Tibetan assembly with elected representatives from the different settlements and groups; and a considerable staff to deal with all the problems of the new development. The authority in the settlements themselves is divided in a fashion very similar to that which had existed in Tibet. The heads of the settlements and their staffs, corresponding to the dzongpon in the Tibetan homeland, are appointed and their salaries paid by the Dharamsala administration. Under them, there are elected representatives of family groups (ten families), called *bcudpon*, and – on a higher level – representatives of differing language groups, called *gardu*, from central and eastern Tibet (Ü/Tsang, Kham, and Amdo). The elected representatives are paid by Dharamsala but represent the people of the communities in the same way the headmen and elders did in Tibet. Again it is on the community level that the central government and the people's representatives cooperate in the management of local affairs.

As in Tibet, the Dalai Lama's authority is strengthened by his ability to provide financial support for local religious and community purposes and to attract people from all levels for a government career. And again the real source of authority is religious. It is the acceptance of the Buddhist faith and of the role of the Dalai Lama as the incarnation of an emanation of Avalokitesvara that is the basis of all authority among the Tibetans in exile. This, indeed, is the same system that existed in Tibet until 1959.

If some wonder[36] how it is possible to maintain authority without an army or police force, it must be pointed out that the same extraordinary form of government existed in Tibet, where the Dalai Lama ruled without an army or a police force. And if some wonder[37] how easy it was to end the mi-ser status and disregard the aristocracy, it must be pointed out that without the mistaken notions of "feudalism" and "serfdom," those institutions clearly could not be regarded as a crucial part of the traditional order. In fact, since the aristocracy no longer has any obligation to serve, the vast majority of the Dharamsala officials and, of course, the local representatives are of common and secular background. If there are some questions about the autonomy of the non-Gelukpa sects, that situation, too, appears to have changed little from the former situation in Tibet. But on the whole, a common fate and danger appear to have formed a stronger bond among the sects than existed in the past.[38]

In addition, there may be a new force to cement Tibetan unity in exile that is stronger than any such force prevailing in Tibet: modern nationalism. There has been an ethnic nationalism in Tibet ever since the aristocrats invoked it in the eighth century in their attacks against the Indian Buddhist missionaries the kings had imported. Today this nationalism among the exiles is linked to their hope of returning to their homeland

Dr. Franz Michael and Dr. Eugene Knez in discussion with H.H. the Dalai Lama (photo by the secretary of H.H. the Dalai Lama).

under their own rule, and it transcends the particularist inclinations of the past. The settlements contain population groups from all regions of Tibet, and the Lhasa language has become more of a lingua franca than ever. The nationalism is inextricably linked to Tibetan Buddhism, and the Dalai Lama is its focus and chief symbol.

Questions about the future remain, of course. There is the question of future financial resources for the Dharamsala administration and the monastic life. There are no more estates, and state support, voluntary contributions, and new taxes may pose problems. There is also the question of future incarnations—will they be found in India or will some of the present incarnations not be reincarnated after they have passed away?

Most of all, there is a grave question about the survival of the faith and the culture in the Tibetan homeland, which has been subjected to physical, political, and ideological blows. The signs are that in spite of the vast destruction of temples and monasteries by the Chinese before and during the "cultural revolution" and the harsh suppression of all religious life, the Tibetan people who remained in their homeland have clung to their faith and their belief in the Dalai Lama. This continued tie was demonstrated by their spontaneous, enthusiastic reception of the Dalai Lama's visiting delegations in 1980 and by many other testimonies.

Much, however, will depend on the survival of a religious base outside the Chinese orbit, and so far there are no signs of disintegration. On the contrary, the story of the success in India and the survival of a culture in exile after an unparalleled disaster at home indicate that human faith and willpower are still the chief weapons for national survival, and Tibetan Buddhism has proved its strength in adversity. We may learn even in our time that the cultures that survive are those that can maintain their beliefs and values above the vicissitudes of any outrageous fortune.

Appendix 1

The Last Testament of the Thirteenth Dalai Lama (1876–1933)

Translated by Lobsang Lhalungpa

I was first recognized as the reincarnation of the supreme spiritual guide of the world [the twelfth Dalai Lama] in accordance with the prophetic directions of the great lamas and the state guardians, making it unnecessary to follow the practice of selection through drawing lots from a golden vase. Since that time, following the examples of my predecessors, I studied under holy tutors such as the regent Tatsak Hothoktu, Phurchok Rinpoche, and others. Having memorized daily the religious texts, including the liturgical chants, I received the primary and secondary monastic ordinations and practiced the regular debate on the five major treatises of Buddhist doctrine. Besides, I was given daily—without interruption—profound sutric expositions, the great and the lesser esoteric initiations, the key instructions [including the secret oral teachings], and explanations in accordance with my intellectual capacity.

Despite of the lack of experience, I was called upon at the age of eighteen [1894] to assume the responsibility of the temporal and spiritual power by unanimous appeal of the ecclesiastic and secular communities of Tibet and by the counsel of the great [Manchu] emperor. I have been striving to advance the cause of Buddha's teachings, to strengthen our political system, and to promote the welfare and happiness of my subjects to the best of my ability with honesty and justice, despite the fact that my personal leisure and freedom were thwarted by my constant concern about the heavy responsibility for the well-being of our religiopolitical system.

In the wood-dragon year [1904], the British army invaded our country. I considered that any diplomatic appeasement [of the invader] merely for one's personal safety and welfare would certainly undermine the future of

Text is from the collected works of the thirteenth Dalai Lama. Translated by Lobsang Lhalungpa.

our sovereignty. Ever since a mutually respectful relationship, based on the traditional bond between preceptor and benefactor, was established [in 1653] by the Dalai Lama, the "great vth," [with the Manchu emperor], I found it worthwhile to invoke [the stipulations of] mutual support. So I left for Peking via Tibet's northern plateau and Mongolia. The emperor and the queen mother received me graciously, showing me great honor and hospitality while I apprised them of our situation. Not long after that, the emperor and the queen mother passed away one after the other. Hsüan Tung was installed as new emperor. After having talks with him and his father, I returned to Tibet. [By that time the British troops had withdrawn from Lhasa.]

Sometime after that [in 1909], invading Chinese military forces led by General Chao Erh-feng penetrated Lhasa with the intent to seize power. This invasion was due to the crafty and slanderous report to the emperor by the resident amban.[1] I, the sovereign, and my ministers, who held the power, departed for India. Enduring all the hardships of the journey, we arrived there safely.

Persistently we protested [against the Chinese invasion of Tibet] to the Chinese imperial court through the British government. Meanwhile the civil war in China altered the situation, depriving its forces and their commanders [in Tibet] of further supplies, like a reservoir cut off from its source. They were gradually expelled from the country. This came about owing to the unfailing power of the profound truth of causality connected with our performance of religious services for the preservation of Tibet's temporal and spiritual system.

I returned to the religious land of Tibet that remained under my guidance. A new glorious peace and happiness prevailed from the water-ox to the water-monkey year [1914–1932]. People, high and low, enjoyed tranquility and liberty in a relaxed manner. This was indicated widely since much was known to the people of the various classes in the religious and secular communities. The details are recorded in the documents. If ever there was any beneficial result from my personal and political service it would be a matter of personal satisfaction. I will neither boast about it nor do I have the slightest wish—not even the size of a sesame seed—for any reward and recognition.

Considering my age at the present moment, I feel a strong urge to abdicate from my position as spiritual and temporal ruler in order to devote myself, during the last phase of my life, to virtuous [religious] practice and to secure spiritual support for the long course of my next life. Yet I dare not forsake the complete trust placed in me by the religious guardians—who have associated themselves with me like the shadow of my body—and by my revered lamas as well as my subjects, high and low, who have had both a spiritual and practical relationship with me. I therefore continue striving to discharge my responsibility to the best of my knowledge and ability.

I am now in the fifty-eighth year of my life. Everyone must know that I may not be around for more than a few years to discharge the temporal and spiritual responsibility.

You must develop a good diplomatic relationship with our two powerful neighbors: India and China. Efficient and well-equipped troops must be stationed even on the minor frontiers bordering hostile forces. Such an army must be well trained in warfare as a sure deterrent against any adversaries.

Furthermore, this present era is rampant with the five forms of degeneration, in particular the red ideology. In Outer Mongolia, the search for a reincarnation of Jetsun Dampa [the Grand Lama of Urga] was banned; the monastic properties and endowments were confiscated; the lamas and the monks were forced into the army; and the Buddhist religion destroyed, leaving no trace of identity. Such a system, according to the reports still being received, has been established in Ulan Bator.

In future, this system will certainly be forced either from within or without on this land that cherishes the joint spiritual and temporal system. If, in such an event, we fail to defend our land, the holy lamas, including "the triumphant father and son" [the Dalai Lama and the Panchen Lama] will be eliminated without a trace of their names remaining; the properties of the incarnate lamas and of the monasteries along with the endowments for religious services will all be seized. Moreover, our political system, originated by the three ancient kings, will be reduced to an empty name; my officials, deprived of their patrimony and property, will be subjugated like slaves by the enemy; and my people, subjected to fear and miseries, will be unable to endure day or night. Such an era will certainly come!

At the present time, when we enjoy peace and happiness as well as the admiration of others, the inerrable common cause of religion and polity still remains in our hands. The political stability depends on the devotion of the ecclesiastical and secular officials and upon their ability to employ skillfully every diplomatic and military means without any possibility of regret or failure in the future. It is the bounden duty and responsibility of all my subjects, the religious and lay members of the various orders, to think and work unerringly in unity and cooperation for the promotion of the common welfare and of peace. To do so without deviating will be in accord with the chief state guardian [oracle] when he stated, "There is no need for fear and anxiety [on the part of all concerned] for everything will be all right as long as everyone strives toward fulfilling the express wishes of the master Thongwa Donden, the Fulfiller of Aspirations upon Sight [the Dalai Lama]."

I, on my part, will protect and hold dear to my heart those who devote themselves to serve honestly in keeping with my wish for the common cause of religion and polity. They will be blessed with successful achievement while the unscrupulous will meet with failure and retributions. It is evident that if you [officials] do not devote yourselves to the service of the state but continuously indulge in self-seeking, prejudice, or nepotism, the long-term common objective will not be realized. And then nothing will help, and regrets will be useless.

I perceive that Tibet's happiness will continue as long as I live. In the long run, each of you will suffer the consequences of your actions in the manner I stated. There is no clearer advice which emanates from my innermost perception, experience, and reasoning. If all of you deeply concern yourselves with your duty—as the inner remedy—with sincere repentance for your past omissions and a resolve to do your utmost, we shall not only carry on the religious services as external support, but I shall also try, as long as I live, to bring about an extensive long-term progress in the religious and political system. I shall also support and guide the officials consistent with their positions and performances while striving to maintain peace and happiness as before for all my subjects lasting through this century.

I have recorded this counsel at the request of the entire nation. Of paramount importance for you is to examine seriously and apply unerringly through your four daily activities[2] this my counsel in regard to the importance of the inner remedy for our common cause!

1. Amban, a Manchu or Mongol word, was the title of the resident imperial minister in Lhasa.

2. Movement (*drowa*); sitting (*dukpa*); recreation (*chakpa*); resting (*nyalwa*).

Appendix 2

Gangloma: In Praise of Manjusri

Composed by an Assembly of Teachers

1. Your wisdom—like the sun—is perfect and clear, unclouded by the two defilements [delusion and passion].
2. You perceive the real truth in infinite knowledge, as symbolized by the sacred text you hold close to your heart.
3. To all sentient beings deluded by ignorance and tormented by miseries in the prison of cyclic existence
4. You extend your compassion like a mother to her only son.
5. Your voice, reverberating like thunder with sixty attributes and ranges, arouses [us] from our slumber of confusion and breaks loose the karmic fetters.[1]
6. You hold the double-bladed sword which cuts the weeds of ignorance and misery.
7. From primordial time you were perfect beyond the tenth stage with consummate qualities.
8. Oh! Heroic son of the victorious Buddhas; your manifestation is endowed with a hundred and twelve attributes.[2] I pay my homage to you, the remover of dark ignorance of my mind!

1. The sixty attributes and the tonal ranges refer to the aesthetic qualities, the tonal levels, and the power of the Buddhas' speech. These are divided into ten categories and their specific details are available in the Mahayana treatises such as *Khejug* [The entrance to scholarship] and the commentaries of Uttaratantra.

2. Refers to the aesthetic attributes of the Buddhas. The Buddha figures in Tibetan paintings or sculpture are depicted according to these attributes. Divided into two, the first category consists of thirty-two major marks of perfection. They include naturally curled hair with braids forming a tuft (*tsugtor*) at the center, shining white hair curled up in a right spiral between the eyebrows, and other marks such as the swastika on the chest. The second category consists of eighty minor marks, such as complexion, color of eyes, hair, etc., and the symmetry of the Buddha figure.

From a Tibetan manuscript in the possession of Lobsang Lhalungpa and translated by him.

Appendix 3

The Sixteen Human Principles
(Michö Tsangma Chudruk)

Composed and proclaimed by King Songtsen Gampo in the seventh century. [From the Record of the Seals of Tibetan Rules (Thamdeb)]

1. To worship the Three Jewels and look upon them as the Supreme Guide
2. To believe in the law of causality [karma] and to abstain from harmful deeds
3. To respect one's parents and repay their kindness
4. To reciprocate the kindness of others and not to hurt them
5. To emulate the behavior of refined people while disassociating from impudence
6. To be restrained through one's conscience and honesty
7. To master every branch of knowledge
8. Not to fall under the domination of one's wife
9. Not to cheat through false weights and measures
10. To pay taxes and repay loans on time
11. Not to harm but help others
12. To respect and obey teachers and parents
13. Not to interfere in the affairs of others
14. To fulfill one's pledges and promises
15. To be loyal to one's masters
16. To be scrupulously fair and just in all one's dealings with others

Copy of a Tibetan manuscript in the possession of Lobsang Lhalungpa and translated by him.

Appendix 4

The Charter of Hemis Monastery
(Kagyupa Order)

May peace prevail!
I prostrate myself before my root lama and the Three Jewels!

I pay my homage to the lama, who in his ultimate essence is the intrinsic nature of the universal phenomena.

This all-pervading state [of his supreme awareness] is endowed with the inherent bliss.

He is the spiritual guide and the source of all benefits and virtues.

I bow down to the Buddha, who has attained the illuminated state beyond samsara and Nirvana.

His innermost awareness is expansive and all-embracing.

His compassionate actions for sentient beings throughout the infinite cosmic universe are a never-ceasing stream.

He is the glorious master of all for he has attained the two supreme aspects of enlightenment.

The Sakyamuni Buddha is supreme among the thousand Buddhas of this noble cosmic clan.

He is the only Buddha who chose to appear in this age of crisis and conflicts.

I prostrate myself before this gods of gods.

May the Lotus Holder [Avalokitesvara] protect us.

Translation of the charter of Hemis monastery written by Rig-'dzin Tshe-dbang Norbu (1698–1755). This document is found in his Collected Works, vol. 5 (Dalhousie, India, 1977), pp. 661–681. Translated by Lobsang Lhalungpa.

He is the embodiment of the compassion of all Buddhas.
He stands out among all bodhisattvas.
Never closing the eye of compassion.
He appears as the Son of Buddha although he is the source of all Buddhas.

May the lineage of the Kagyupa order—who follows the great master Drogon Phakmo Drupa [fourteenth century]—protect us. This order attained the understanding and realization unsurpassed by other meditative orders.

May this disciplined assembly of monks be triumphant.
They bring forth fruit of higher realms.
They are the source of the ultimate goodness.
They are the support for the world.

[The text gives an historical outline of Buddhism in India and Tibet.]

The Hemis monastery in Ladhak was established under the guidance of the master yogi Ugyen Taktsang Raypa and the patronage of King Sunga Namgyal. This monastery is the main religious center representing the intellectual and spiritual tradition of the Drukpa Kagyupa order.

This charter is composed in order that the abbot, the monastic teacher, administrators of high and low ranks, as well as the monks may abide by and observe the code of conduct contained therein.

The doctrinal and meditative traditions of Buddhism are the source of well-being for the world. The cause of the Buddha's teachings rests in the assembly of monks, who in turn depend on the lay patrons such as the kings. The prince lama was entrusted with the running of Hemis monastery by Jetsun Drukpa Gyalwang [who was the head of this school; the headquarters were in Sangngak Chöling in southern Tibet]. However the prince was recalled to the palace to assume the role of the king. He assured the monastery of his continued guidance and support for its management.

The monks of Hemis shall henceforth abide by and observe the moral principles, holding them to be as precious as their eyes. In fulfilling their moral vows they shall resolve to work for the spiritual well-being of the assembly and the lay community.

Discipline is the most important condition not only for the preservation of Buddhism in general but also for promoting the standard of Buddhist study and meditative tradition known as the Drukpa Kagyupa order.

The first principle of the moral code of conduct is the undisputed observation of celibacy. Any monk whose celibacy has become the subject of criticism or doubt must be investigated to establish the truth. If he is found to have committed no major offense, he shall be allowed to reinforce his vow and continue his study and meditation. In case he is found guilty of breaking this primary vow, he shall be dealt with according to the degree of moral offense, either by simple expulsion or marking his forehead with a black cross.

Similarly offenders found guilty of stealing, lying, or any other major crimes shall be punished accordingly so as to set an example for the others.

No monk shall allow a woman to live in his cell at night.

Any monk wanting to travel must seek permission from the authority.

Since indulgence in intoxicating drinks is the custom of the land total abstinence may not be feasible. The monks must restrain themselves in this regard because intoxicating drinks are the basic cause of crime.

Monks shall not indulge in smoking tobacco. Further, they shall not make disturbing noises within the monastic precincts, nor shall they wear strange costumes and ornaments, nor shall they resort to violence of any kind. In short, they shall not do anything that might offend the society and set bad examples for others.

The monks shall memorize the collected texts on the liturgy, the treatises of tantra, and other obligatory texts.

They shall learn the chanting, the religious music, the drawing of the mandalas, the sacred dance, the dough-butter sculpturing of the ritual offering *torma* under the guidance of the responsible leaders.

Monks with special intellectual propensity shall learn grammar, etymology, rhetoric, prosody, astronomy, astrology, etc. [i.e., medicine, metaphysics, logic, psychology].

They shall receive by stages the three monastic ordinations—the primary [*barma rapjung*], the intermediate [*getsul*], and the full ordination [*nendzok*]—and shall observe the precepts of *vinaya* [the moral code of conduct].

They shall not discard the religious robes, consisting of three parts, and shall maintain an exemplary manner and behavior. Transforming their stream of consciousness through the application of the spirit of enlightenment [Jangchubkyi Sem; Sanskrit, *bodhicitta*], they shall endeavor to become serene, gentle, disciplined, worthy of being a spiritual guide.

They shall strive toward gaining insight into the unknown nature of the mind through the precept of wisdom, which finally leads to achieving the twin goals for themselves and all other sentient beings.

The leaders shall not only abide by the letter and the spirit of this charter but also enforce it without partiality, favor or disfavor, selfish or spiteful design.

In short, all the members of this monastery shall respect this charter in the spirit of harmony and service to His Holiness Kyabgon Drugchen Rinpoche, the great master and supreme head of the Drukpa Kagyupa order.

They shall devote themselves to the pursuit of happiness and well-being of all sentient beings by observing the moral precepts; studying the doctrine, subjecting everything to critical examination and meditation.

In order to enable the sacred community of monks to abide by and carry out the principles of this monastic charter, the management of this monastery has all along received the endowments comprised of land and fields on the mountains and in the valleys, properties from lay patrons of royal, aristocratic, and ordinary families. These endowments were received from the time of founding by Lama Tsaktsang Raypa. The title deeds issued by successive kings contain the detailed description of the endowments. In the water-bird year [1932], the pious ruler Gyalseg Rinpoche, upon assuming the royal authority, issued a new title deed bearing the new royal seal. This was done in order that everyone concerned may respect this document in the spirit of service to the teachings of Buddha.

His Highness Prince Tsewang Trinlay Tenzin Migyur Dorje, the nephew of His Highness the King Gyalseg Rinpoche, was installed as the supreme head of the monasteries of the Drukpa Kagyupa order in Ladhak by His Holiness Gyalwang Drukchen Rinpoche [the supreme head of the Drukpa Kagyupa monasteries in Tibet]. Everyone concerned in Ladhak shall recognize and respect him as the head of the Drukpa Kagyupa order in Ladhak. The managing director and other monastic functionaries shall administer the monastic affairs until the maturity of this prince lama. It is our desire to see the prince lama gradually attain his maturity and assume the role of the great teacher by attaining the perfect mastery of the three noble precepts [i.e., morality, contemplation, and meditation] and by adhering to the monastic tradition of attiring in orange robes.

All concerned in this monastery are expected to aspire to attain the standard of morality and attainment exemplified by the lives of the great saint Tsangpa Gyarey and his disciples. In doing so, they shall seek to practice the teaching of the Great Seal [Mahamudra], which is the heart of all Buddhist doctrine and meditation.

Furthermore I appeal to lay patrons to lead a virtuous and disciplined life and support the institution of the Buddhist teachings without any materialistic motivations. Those who respect the moral law and help monks and people according to their capacity will receive the blessings of the supreme refuge and the guardians of the dharma.

Those who violate the moral law and hold it in contempt will suffer the consequences of their deeds and retribution by the guardians of the teachings.

Appendix 5

Endowment of Funds for Namling Monastery in Western Tibet

[Register for the endowment given to Namling monastery in western Tibet by the chief commissioner Lhaijin Samdrup. The document begins with homage to the three refuges. The text is in verse.]

Tibet lies in the Himalayan mountain ranges north of Magadha [East Indian province, now part of Bihar]. Known as Bhot [Sanskrit], Tibet is illuminated by the Buddha's teachings and is considered as the realm of Bodhisattva Avalokitesvara. The territory of Tibet is comprised of three regions [i.e., Ü and Tsang, Dhotö, and Dhomay]. Western Tibet, known as Nari Korsum, is part of the Ü/Tsang region of central Tibet. The Namling monastery, belonging to the Sakyapa order is situated to the northwest of Khyungdzong Karpo [White Eagle Castle], the capital of the king of Guge [the descendant of the ancient Tibetan kings who ruled the western province from the ninth century to the eleventh century].

The chief commissioner Lhaijin Samdrup gave the following endowment to Namling monastery for conducting specific religious services every year on the dates mentioned hereafter. This pious act is motivated by the patron's wish for expanding the light of Buddha's teachings throughout the lands, far and near; for the long lives of the religious teachers; for the increased happiness of all sentient beings without discrimination; for the stable authority of the ruler; for the elimination of defilements of his father and mother; and for permanent peace for all human beings.

The terms of the endowment envisage the following obligations to be fulfilled by Namling monastery:

During the first lunar month, while commemorating the great miracles performed by Buddha, a group of twenty-five monks are required to perform

The text, written at the request of the donor by a well-known Nyingmapa lama, Rig-'dzin Tshe-dbang Norbu (1698–1755), is contained in his *Collected Works*, vol. 5 (Dalhousie, India, 1977), pp. 651–660. Translated by Lobsang Lhalungpa.

meditational rites, consecrating the inner realization deity Khachoema for three days. The other religious services these monks are required to conduct are specified as follows: Rites propitiating the religious guardians to be performed on the twenty-ninth or the last moon every month. These religious services are to be performed every year on the specified dates as long as the universe exists.

The endowment is comprised of one hundred and five Nepalese silver coins.

[In its final passage, the document dedicates the spiritual merits accruing from these religious services to the cause of Buddhism, to the fulfillment of the patron's spiritual aspirations in this life, and to the attainment of enlightenment at the time of his death. The dedication includes the spread of Buddhism, long lives of the religious teachers, peace for the world, and happiness for all sentient beings.]

Appendix 6

Selected Passages from the Charter of Sera Monastery

[The text begins with the usual homage to Buddha, the doctrine, and the holy community. It gives the historical background of Buddhism and a preamble to the formulation of rules and regulations governing the life of the monk community.

To emphasize the role and responsibility of each individual monk, the charter quotes the Buddha as having said:]

> I have shown to you the path for eliminating all existential miseries. O! monks, you should be your own guide, the supreme master Tathagatha ["one who has attained to the ultimate reality"].

Buddha has shown us the methods for destroying the root of all evils. It is of utmost importance for our own well-being to follow the precepts expounded in the *Tripitaka* in general and the *Vinaya Pitaka* [the canon of discipline] in particular.

This charter is based on the moral and ethical principles contained in the four parts of the *Vinaya* and the monastic regulations that are relevant to time and circumstances.

All branches of this monastery—the Jay, May, and Tantric colleges and their affiliated schools, Kavitsan and Mitsan—shall receive the three-part monastic ordination by stages. They shall use the three robes—lower and upper robes. The fully ordained monks shall use the *namjar* [the yellow robe made up from patches], and the begging bowl. Shirts with sleeves, fur dress, Chinese or Mongolian boots, ornaments, etc., are prohibited. The length of hair shall not exceed the traditional standard measurement.

The monks shall gather together in the assembly hall once the voice call is

Issued by the seventh Dalai Lama (1708–1757), the Tibetan text is found in his *Collected Works*, vol. 3 (1977), pp. 336–361. Translation is by Lobsang Lhalungpa.

made. They shall move gently while maintaining a good behavior. Running and entering through exits are not permitted. They must sit according to seniority. Leaning against the pillars or walls, spitting or blowing noses without covering their head with the gown, sleeping, chatting, playing, etc., are not allowed.

The monks shall perform the liturgy with pleasant voice and harmonized tone. They must not make noises while eating food or drinking tea and must not lick the bowls. The food must be consumed with the idea of sustaining the body.

[The text then specifies the liturgy to be performed.]

Community Feasts

As for the regulation for serving the congregation with tea and rice pudding as provided by patrons, this must be organized in such a way that it does not cause irritation on the part of the patrons. As regards the quantity of tea leaves each patron is expected to give to the monastery, the management may receive 60 nyag [approximately 60 kegs] of tea leaves and 180 nyag of butter for the total population of three thousand monks. The management must give patrons proper estimates for the supply. They shall not demand more than what patrons are willing to donate.

Concerning gifts [in cash or kind], the management must allow patrons to choose. Under no circumstance shall they demand anything from the patrons. In distributing gifts, the residence [of the abbot] shall receive four shares of whatever gift; the prefect, three; the kitchen staff, tea maker (*jama*), water carrier, and fireman one each. Instructors or other members who have to attend to lay patrons [and cannot attend the assembly] can receive gifts from patrons. The management shall receive the required quantity of butter from patrons for the butter lamps in the hall, the kitchen, and the torches of the corridors.

Kitchen Staff

The kitchen staff shall consist of one director (*jatsul dhodampa*), three tea makers (*jama*), two attendants for firewood, two for fetching water, and one inspector (*zhaltawa*). Patrons may send two observers to the kitchen.

Cash Gifts

The distribution of money shall be carried out according to the regulation for gift distribution: The members must be present in the hall to receive their gifts or come to listen to the prefect who will make announcements and convey the patron's request for congregational prayers. Except for the sick and for students in special retreat, monks who are absent at the gift-sharing occasion shall not receive their share. This restriction is applicable to those monks who left the monastery on their own for collecting donations in any areas of the country.

The used tea leaves must be collected for disposal. Skimming of the melting butter from the teapot by any kitchen aides is prohibited.

Any of the affiliated colleges who handle the gift of tea or money for the common assembly [*tshogehen*; "intercollege assembly"] as provided by patrons shall not divert such gifts, intended for the common assembly, to other colleges and vice versa. Such diversion of gifts is a serious act of deprivation, and the moral consequences will be unbearable.

The tea served by the management must be handled by the steward and the director jointly as usual.

Whenever the chief administrator of the endowment estates (*chiso*) distributes provisions [barley grain, flour, woolen cloth, salt, butter, etc.] to the common assembly, it must be done under the joint supervision of the chief steward (*canyer*), the prefect (*gekö*), and the representative of the management (*zhung*). Cases of absent recipients wishing to receive their share through representatives must be examined in all fairness. Deserving absentees must be given their shares.

Studies

Monks who wish to study must be encouraged. No monk student should study astrology, medicine, and other branches of arts and sciences until the completion of his doctrinal studies and of the dialectical system of metaphysics.

No healthy and intelligent monks should remain idle by merely absenting themselves from the sessions of congregational debates.

Monks should not engage in trade, profiteering, or money-lending business [on their own].

Monks who are studying elementary and advanced logic should be encouraged to go to the annual intermonastic debate at Rwawa Toe. Students who rely on learned instructors in the monastery do not join the intercollege debate. Premature shift from elementary knowledge to the superficial study of other subjects will prevent them from achieving the mastery of logic and other subjects.

Monks [who have completed the monastic studies] should be encouraged to join the tantric colleges in Lhasa.

Examination and Titles

No monks except those who have mastered central philosophy and metaphysics known as "wisdom gone beyond" (*uphar*) shall receive the degree of divinity [i.e., the title of geshe]. The title of kachu, i.e., the master of ten branches of metaphysics, should be conferred upon those who not only passed the congregational debate in central philosophy and "wisdom gone beyond" but achieved the mastery of the canon of discipline, the sublime doctrine, and logic. Those students—who passed the congregational debate on central philosophy, the "wisdom gone beyond," and the canon of discipline and who also passed textual explanation of the sublime doctrine and logic—should be allowed to contest their knowledge of the doctrine and their skill in debate at the intermonastic congregational debates during the great festival of Lhasa in order that successful candidates may receive appropriate titles.

Those successful candidates for the title of geshe who appear before the intercollege debaters should be treated with the same fairness in determining their mastery. Similarly, the minor and major dialectical debates at the respective colleges, the intercollege debate at the great assembly hall, as well as the debates during the retreat in the rainy season should be conducted according to well-established tradition.

Candidates for lingse geshehood[1] during the winter and summer must participate in the major intercollege debate (*rigchen*). No one shall repeat the same subject debated during the winter and summer examinations. The abbots and other functionaries should select in all fairness the best candidates for conferring the title of geshe (and other similar titles). Rumors that these titles can be obtained by way of bribery are very damaging to the monastic colleges and to Buddhist scholarship.

Concerning the appointment of the abbot, all monks should select by common agreement candidates who distinguished themselves in their learning. Affiliated colleges and branches must not show special favor in selecting candidates.

The selection of the grand prefect (for the common assembly hall) shall be carried out according to existing procedures.

The chief steward (*chinyer*) and the master of liturgy (*udzey*) at the great assembly hall shall be appointed from deserving candidates of the two main colleges (Jay and May) according to established procedures.

Monk students who have not achieved good scholarship should not be allowed to take part in the intercollege debate at Namning Chode monastery (in western Tibet) lest they harm the reputation of this monastery.

Students wishing to join in the summer intermonastic debate at Sangphu [summer country resort situated southwest of Lhasa] may do so after completing the dialectical debate on the "wisdom gone beyond" [at their original college].

Entertaining Lay Patrons

During the Zhoton festival [two days in August or September], women who are relatives, friends, or visitors should be allowed to stay with monk hosts only during the day. [During this celebration some colleges invite lay patrons to witness dance dramas performed by professional minstrels, and monks entertain their patrons, families, and friends with food and tea.] Under no circumstances may anyone indulge in intoxicating drinks; singing and similar behavior shall not be permitted.

Monks are allowed to receive religious discourses from teachers of other colleges or monasteries [of the same order]. Similarly they are free to receive privately any initiation into esoteric tantric meditation.

Criminal Justice

A thorough investigation should be conducted in cases of any monk who is seen or suspected of having violated the four fundamental precepts and the principle of nonindulgence in any intoxicating drinks. Upon guilt being established, the offender should be expelled from the monastery.

Any monk who verbally and physically attacks the grand prefect should be expelled. Brandishing knives or swords against others, wounding or attacking, and any other offenses should be dealt with firmly and fairly by the two grand prefects. They have the responsibility of maintaining law and order within the boundry of the monastic complex. Monk criminals who commit crimes outside the boundaries should be tried and punished suitably under the supervision of the steward and the *zimkhang* [the general manager].

Any gambling with dice [*migurang*], archery, stone throwing, or jumping is not permitted inside and outside the monastery.

Undertaking pilgrimage by monk students is likely to distract them from their study. They should refrain from it. Gifts received by monks which are not sufficient for distribution should be stored in the common treasury.

Begging for sustenance is permitted by the sacred canon. Monks may do so in Tibet. No monks should beg in other countries such as Mongolia and China except to collect contributions for the monastery.

The four gates of the walls and the giant prayer flag and the residences of the three abbots are the charge of the zimkhang. They should arrange for whitewashing the walls.

Only the abbots and the zimkhang shall keep horses and mules at their residences. The two stewards shall be allowed to keep three; and the two tea supervisors, two.

Congregational Ceremonies

Novices and fully ordained monks shall attend the Sojong ceremony [the process of spiritual regeneration] upon hearing the sound of the gong. Similarly they shall attend the congregational ceremony of Gakyay [the end of restriction on movement enforced during the summer retreat]; the day of visiting the town (*jonggyu*) shall be used for beneficial activities.

All the monks should be conscious of the major and minor precepts and shall observe them.

1. Lingse geshe is a geshe degree of the monastic complex.

Notes

Chapter 1

1. For the treaty of 1842 between Tibet and Ladakh, see H. E. Richardson, *A Short History of Tibet* (New York, 1962), pp. 246–247.

2. See map on p. iv.

3. See Richardson, op. cit., p. 3.

4. Ibid., p. 6.

5. See Tsepon W. D. Shakabpa, *Tibet: A Political History* (New Haven, 1967), p. 6.

6. See R. A. Stein, *Tibetan Civilization*, trans. S. Driver (Stanford, 1972), p. 28; see Shakabpa, op. cit., p. 5.

7. A tara is a female bodhisattva, the counterpart to a male incarnation.

8. See Shakabpa, op. cit., p. 5.

9. See Richardson, op. cit., p. 5.

10. Ibid., pp. 5–6.

11. See Stein, op. cit., p. 248.

12. See Roy A. Miller, "Thon-mi Sambhota and His Grammatical Treatises," and "Once More on Thon-mi Sambhota and His Grammatical Treatises," in *Studies in the History of Linguistics*, Amsterdam Studies in the Theory and History of the Linguistic Science III, vol. 6 (Amsterdam, 1976), pp. 485–502, and pp. 85–101. See also Chapter 2, note 9.

13. See Adriane MacDonald, "Essai sur la formation et l'emploi des mythes politiques dans la religion royale de Sronbcan Sgam-po," in *Etudes Tibetaines*, Dédiées a la memoire de Marcelle Lallu, Librairie d'Amerique et d'Orient (Paris, 1971), pp. 190–391.

14. An intriguing parallel could be drawn between this royal cult of the early Tibetan kings and their use of diviners and the magic cult and use of divination by the rulers of the Chinese Shang dynasty (1766–1112 B.C.). As in the case of the Shang, the magic cult of the early Tibetan kings was replaced by a rational sanction of rule and organization of government.

15. For a fuller account of Buddhist religion and schools, see R. C. Zaehner, ed., *The Concise Encyclopedia of Living Faiths* (Boston, 1957), Chapters 7a and 7b, by L. B. Horner and Edward Conze ("Buddhism, the Theravada" and "Buddhism, the Mahayana"). On Tibet, see David Snellgrove and Hugh Richardson, *A Cultural History of Tibet* (London, 1968), pp. 62 ff.

16. For a study of the Theravada monk community in Burma and its relationship to the Burmese state, see E. Michael Mendelson, *Sangha and State in Burma: A Study of*

Monastic Sectarianism and Its Leadership (Ithaca and London, 1975).

17. See Zaehner, op. cit., Chapter 7b.

18. A. L. Basham, *The Wonder That Was India: A Survey of the History and Culture of the Indian Sub-Continent Before the Coming of the Muslims* (London, 1954), p. 275.

19. A popular, frequent Western rendition of Vajrayana as the "vehicle of the thunderbolt" probably came from an earlier, non-Buddhist mythology relating to the concept of magic power.

20. The well-known formula *Om mani padme hum* in praise of Avalokitesvara was the most common of the Tibetan ritual mantras.

21. See Stein, op. cit., pp. 229–236. According to uncertain traditional accounts, Bon rituals had also been affected, or even introduced, by practitioners from Iran who were brought in by early chieftains. Whatever this influence may have been, Bon was a native practice before the acceptance of Buddhism. As said earlier, it does not appear that Bon was an organized religion before the advent of Buddhism (see note 13). Its practice by sorcerers, magicians, and diviners was rather part of a folk religion, linked to legends of spirits and deities that were believed to exist in nature and in the realm of the universe. These beliefs also dealt with the relationship among humans, damtsik, which meant a vow of loyalty to superiors, that was characteristic of a clan society and was later used for the student-teacher and student-student relationship in Buddhism. See also Helmut Hoffmann, *The Religions of Tibet*, trans. Edward Fitzgerald (London, 1961), pp. 24 ff.

22. See Hoffmann, op. cit., pp. 66 ff. Hoffmann outlines the political basis of the struggle over the religious ideologies. See also Turrell Wylie, "Some Political Factors in the Early History of Tibetan Buddhism" (Paper read at the University of Wisconsin, Madison, August 1976), in which Wylie also comes to the conclusion that the religious conflict between Bon and Buddhism was but "an expression of the covert competition for political and economic power" and adds that it "undermined and finally destroyed the monarchy."

23. See Hoffmann, op. cit., p. 43.

24. For a quotation from the later literature on Padmasambhava, which stresses his magic powers and self-assurance, see Snellgrove and Richardson, op. cit., pp. 97–98. Hoffmann (op. cit., pp. 50–65) takes a whole chapter to deal with what he regards as Padmasambhava's attempt to establish a religion of his own.

25. Gampopa had studied also with followers of Atisha.

26. See Chapter 2, section on "The Making of a Religious Government."

27. For a short introduction to Max Weber's theories and his extensive writings, see Reinhard Bendix, *Max Weber, an Intellectual Portrait* (New York, 1962).

28. Max Weber, *Essays in Sociology* (New York, 1946), pp. 196–204.

29. Ibid., p. 78.

Chapter 2

1. Namri Songtsen, the thirty-second king of Tibet according to *rGyal-rabs gSal-ba'i me-long* by Sa-skya bSod-nam rGyal-mtshan (later cited as *Me-long*), was the father of the well-known king Songtsen Gampo.

2. Songtsen Gampo, known to the Chinese as Ch'i-tsung Lung-tsan, is one of the first Tibetan kings mentioned in the Tungkuang documents. He married a Chinese princess as well as a Nepalese princess and established friendly relations with both countries. Under his rule, the military prowess and prestige of Tibet were placed on a firm basis, and that led to two hundred years of stability—and almost imperial greatness. Buddhism began to appear, and for the first time a Tibetan king began to take interest in it. For details, see David Snellgrove and Hugh Richardson, *A Cultural History of Tibet* (London, 1968), pp. 27–31, and Tsepon W. D. Shakabpa, *A Political History of Tibet* (New York, 1970), pp. 25–30. Also see *Mani 'Ka'-'bum* (later cited as *Dga-ston*).

3. See map on p. iv.

4. For the limitations of Bon magical practitioners and of the royal cult of Tsug and the religion of the mountain gods (*kulha*), see Chapter 1, section on "Tibetan Buddhism," and note 13, which refers to the article by Adriane MacDonald on the royal cult of Tsug. For Bon, see the article by Lobsang Lhalungpa in *Religious Culture of Tibet*, 1:3 and 4 (Autumn 1976), and David Snellgrove, *The Nine Ways of Bön* (Boulder, 1980).

5. See Chapter 1, section on "Tibetan Buddhism," for the schools of Buddhism that contributed to the Tibetan form of the Buddhist religion.

6. The Chinese consort of King Songtsen Gampo was Princess Wen-ch'eng Kung-chu, a daughter of the Chinese emperor T'ai-tsung (see Shakabpa, op. cit., p. 32, *Me-long*, and *Dga-ston*). The Chinese princess is also mentioned in Tungkuang documents of the time (see R.A. Stein, *Tibetan Civilization*, trans. S. Driver [Stanford, 1972], p. 58 footnote).

7. The Nepalese consort of King Songtsen Gampo was Princess Brikuti Devi, the daughter of the Nepalese king Amshurarman (see Shakabpa, op. cit., p. 34; Snellgrove and Richardson, op. cit., pp. 32–36; *Me-long*; and *Dga-ston*). Turrell Wylie has questioned the historicity of the Nepalese princess (see "Some Political Factors in the Early History of Tibetan Buddhism" [Paper read at the University of Wisconsin, Madison, August 1976]). Wylie mainly bases his argument on the fact that the Nepalese princess was not mentioned in the Tungkuang annals, nor does the term *Balpo* appear there, the Tibetan name for Nepal, which Wylie regards as the summer residence of the kings. It appears to us that the authors of the Tungkuang annals were concerned with the Chinese role in Tibet and obviously had little interest in the Nepalese aspect of Tibetan policy. Therefore the omission of any mention of the princess or the country in the Tungkuang accounts is not a convincing argument against this Nepalese aspect of the king's policy or the role of the princess, whose father (or uncle) is a figure in Nepalese history.

8. Jokhang, which literally means "the Lord's abode," was built by the princess of Nepal to house the image of Buddha that she had brought with her. The temple was built by filling a lake with logs and earth, which were carried there by a large number of goats. At the completion of the temple, the figure of a goat was placed in one of the shrines to honor the animal. The temple's official name, Rasa Trulnang Tsukla-khang, literally means "goat-earth miraculous appearance temple." Popularly known as Jokhang, it still stands in Lhasa today. Ramoche temple, literally "great she-goat temple," built by the Chinese consort of the king for her Buddha image, is also still

standing in Lhasa. See Snellgrove and Richardson, op. cit., pp. 73–74; Shakabpa, op. cit., pp. 25–30; and *Dga-ston*.

9. Thonmi Sambhota is believed to have been the only survivor of a group of students sent by King Songtsen Gampo to Kashmir and India to study with Indian Buddhist pandits Devavidhya Sinha and Dramze Libikara (as mentioned in the commentary of Thonmi Sambhota's grammar). The historicity of Thonmi Sambhota has been doubted (see Roy A. Miller, "Thon-mi Sambhota and His Grammatical Treatises," and "Once More on Thon-mi Sambhota and His Grammatical Treatises," in *Studies in the History of Linguistics*, Amsterdam Studies in the Theory and History of the Linguistic Science III, vol. 6 [Amsterdam, 1976], pp. 485–502, and pp. 85–101).

Without entering into the argument between Miller and the Japanese scholar Inaba Shoju about the age of the grammatical texts ascribed to Thonmi Sambhota and the question of the man's historicity, it seems clear that grammatical scholarship in Tibet may well be traced back to the time of Thonmi Sambhota. To doubt his authorship of extant texts or his role in the introduction of writing and grammatical scholarship without being able to replace this allegedly legendary figure with an approved historical one appears to be an excessive disregard of the oral tradition in non-Western societies. One should remember that Western scholarship claimed that the Chinese account of the Shang dynasty was pure legend but the finding of the oracle bones not only proved the existence of the dynasty but verified many of the names of emperors and dates of events transmitted by the oral tradition.

10. A script developed during the reign of the Gupta dynasty in India in the fourth and fifth centuries A.D. This was the era when Buddhism was flourishing in India, a period often referred to as the "golden age" of India. For details, see *A Wonder That Was India* by A. L. Basham (New York, 1954).

11. The Tibetan language is believed by most linguists to belong to a major linguistic subgroup of the Sino-Tibetan linguistic stock or family, Tibeto-Burman. For details, see Chapter 1, section on "Land and People."

12. The Tang dynasty (A.D. 618–907) has been regarded as the most glorious period of Chinese history. The Tang capital, Changan (now Sian), was the largest metropolis on the globe and a cosmopolitan center of culture and religious tolerance. It appears all the more important that Tibet turned to India for its literary culture.

13. King Trisong Detsen was the second of the great religious kings of Tibet. To him is attributed the actual establishment of Buddhism in Tibet, and he invited the Indian Buddhist teachers Santaraksita, Kamalashila and Padmasambhava to Tibet. For details, see Shakabpa, op. cit., pp. 36–40 and pp. 43–47; Charles Bell, *Tibet, Past and Present* (Oxford, 1924), pp. 26–29; Tshal-pa Kun-dga rDor-rje, *Deb-Ther dMar-po* (later cited as *Deb-dMar*); and *Dga-ston*.

14. The first Buddhist teacher historically known to have been invited to Tibet was the learned Indian pandit Santaraksita, and he was held in great esteem by the king and the court. Together with Padmasambhava, he is believed to have been the founder of the monastery of Samye. See Bell, op. cit., pp. 34–35; Shakabpa, op. cit., pp. 36–37; Richardson, op. cit., p. 31; *Dga-ston*; and *Deb-dMar*.

15. Padmasambhava is regarded as the first Buddhist teacher who planted the firm roots of tantric Buddhism in Tibet. Through the introduction of tantric rituals, he

was believed to have subdued the Bon spirits, which were supposedly hostile to Buddhism, and to have incorporated them into the Buddhist pantheon after the spirits allegedly had taken an oath to defend Buddhism (see Charles Bell, *The Religion of Tibet* [Oxford, 1931], pp. 36–37; Stein, op. cit., pp. 73–74; Padmasambhava, *Pad-ma bka'-thang* [An account of Padmasambhava and the Samye monastery]; Snellgrove and Richardson, op. cit., pp. 96–98; and Chapter 1, section on "Tibetan Buddhism").

16. See *Dga-ston.*

17. Kamalashila, a disciple of Santaraksita, was invited to Tibet during the reign of King Trisong Detsen. He was the Indian teacher who opposed the Chinese monk Makotse in the Great Debate. As the Chinese monk was said to have taught that salvation was gained not by meritorious action but by a state of quiescence (related to the Taoist *wu wei*), he was accused of having misled many Tibetans into lethargy and laziness to the detriment of the economy and society of the country. The accusation was used to bring about the debate and the defeat of the Chinese monk, probably not only for domestic reasons but also for international political reasons. Kamalashila and other Indian teachers of the time continued to teach the "middle doctrine" (*Madhyamika*) as propagated by the Indian Mahayana teacher Nagarjuna. Kamalashila had many notable students among the Tibetan Buddhist scholars. See Bell, *Religion of Tibet*, pp. 40–41; Shakabpa, op. cit., pp. 37–38; Stein, op. cit., pp. 67–69; and Bu-ston Rinchen-grub, *Gsung-rab rinpoche'i dzod*, ff. 1440–1480.

18. See Snellgrove and Richardson, op. cit., p. 79.

19. See Stein, op. cit., p. 67.

20. According to Sumpa mKhan-po Yeshes dPal-'jor in his book *Gangs-chan bod-yul-du dam-chos rin-chen byung-tshul Dpag-bsam Ljon-bzang* (Varanasi, India, 1963), the Chinese monk acknowledged his defeat by offering a flower garland to the Indian victor but then left for China, presumably in a hurry as he left one of his shoes behind. This was interpreted as a sign that he believed that his teaching would survive in Tibet (an obviously legendary account). According to Shakabpa, the Indian monk was later assassinated at the instigation of Makotse's partisans.

21. See M. Demiéville, "Concile de Lhasa," and Yoshiro Imaeda, "Documents Tibétains de Touen-Houang concernant le Concile du Tibet," *Journal Asiatique* (1975), pp. 125–146.

22. See Snellgrove and Richardson, op. cit., p. 79.

23. The third and last religious king, Ralpachen, was a very devoted Buddhist who decreed that the position of the monks was to be elevated and that they should be held in great esteem, thus generating the special place that the monks came to hold in Tibetan society. During his rule, the translation of the major Buddhist canons from Sanskrit into Tibetan was begun. With him ended the first phase of the introduction of Buddhism into Tibet (see Shakabpa, op. cit., pp. 38–42; Bell, *Religion of Tibet*, pp. 26–29; *Dga-ston; and Deb-dMar*).

24. Prior to the monastic endowment established by Ralpachen, King Trisong Detsen—who built Samye—decreed that the monastery should be supported by a grant of land along with three families of tenants for each individual monk (see Chapter 7 (*ja*) of *Dga-ston*, f. 113). Ralpachen extended the number to seven.

25. See Shakabpa, op. cit., pp. 52 ff.

26. With Atisha, who was a famous teacher of Nalanda University, there began the second phase of Buddhist regeneration in Tibet. For details, see Snellgrove and Richardson, op. cit., pp. 129–131; 'Gos Lo-tsa-ba gZhon-nu-dpal, Deb-Ther sngon-po; and Chapter 1, section on "Tibetan Buddhism."

27. See Shakabpa, op. cit., pp. 56–60.

28. During his visit to central Tibet, the Indian teacher Atisha had prophesied that an important monastery would be built at this favorable location, marked by whitish earth (sakya).

29. See Giuseppe Tucci, Tibetan Painted Scrolls (Rome, 1949).

30. Sakya Pandita, though not actually the founder of the Sakyapa sect, was the true organizer of the sect who diversified and advanced the standard of teaching and study and founded leading Sakya monasteries (see A-myes-zhabs Kun-dga' bsod-nam, Sa-sKya'i gdung-rabs chen-po rin-chen bang-mdzod (later cited as Sa-skya gdung-rab).

31. 'Gro-mgon Chos-rgyal 'phags-pa Blo-gros rgyal-matshan, known as Phagpa, the first monk to rule Tibet, was responsible for instituting the basic religiopolitical administrative structure that became the pattern for the Tibetan system under rule by incarnation. In 1268, at the request of Godan Khan, Phagpa created a square-style script that could be used by all the languages of the Mongols' vast empire. Although short-lived as a functional system of writing, it is still known today as Phagpa script (see Sa-skya gdung-rab).

32. After the breakdown of central unity, the principalities each had established some form of administration, all of which were unified and systematized by the Sakya.

33. For this and the following account, see Shakabpa, op. cit., p. 61.

34. See Chapter 4, note 7.

35. Karmapa, a disciple of Gampopa who founded the Kagyupa sect, founded a subsect known as Karma Kagyupa. When his death approached, he prophesied his reincarnation, thereby initiating the institutional system of incarnation in Tibet. For details, see Lobsang Lhalungpa, "The Child Incarnate," Parabola 4:3 (1980), p. 72. See also Karmapa: The Black Hat Lama of Tibet, comp. Nik Douglas and Meryl White (London, 1976).

36. See Snellgrove and Richardson, op. cit., pp. 180–183; DKa-chen ye-shes rGyal-mtshan, Lam-rim bla-ma brgyud-pai' rnam-Thar; and mKhas-grub dGe-legs dPal-bzang, Dad-pa'i 'jug-ngogs.

37. See Shakabpa, op. cit., pp. 92–96.

38. The Dalai Lamas:

First	Gedun Drubpa	1391–1475
Second	Gedun Gyatso	1475–1542
Third	Sonam Gyatso	1543–1588
Fourth	Yontan Gyatso	1589–1617
Fifth	Nawang Lobsang Gyatso	1617–1682
Sixth	Tsangyang Gyatso	1683–1706
Seventh	Kalzang Gyatso	1708–1757
Eighth	Jampal Gyatso	1758–1804
Ninth	Lungtok Gyatso	1806–1815

Tenth	Tsultrim Gyatso	1816–1837
Eleventh	Khedrup Gyatso	1838–1856
Twelfth	Trinlay Gyatso	1856–1875
Thirteenth	Thuptin Gyatso	1876–1933
Fourteenth	Tenzin Gyatso	1935–

The Gyalwa Karmapas:

First	Karma Dusum Khenpa	1110–1193
Second	Karma Pakshi	1204–1283
Third	Karma Rangjung Dorje	1284–1339
Fourth	Karma Rolpai Dorje	1340–1383
Fifth	Karma Dezhin Shekpa	1384–1415
Sixth	Karma Thongwa Dondan	1416–1453
Seventh	Karma Chodrak Gyatso	1454–1506
Eighth	Karma Mikyo Dorje	1507–1554
Ninth	Karma Wangchuk Dorje	1556–1603
Tenth	Karma Choying Dorje	1604–1674
Eleventh	Karma Yeshe Dorje	1676–1702
Twelfth	Karma Jangchub Dorje	1703–1732
Thirteenth	Karma Dudul Dorje	1733–1797
Fourteenth	Karma Thekchog Dorje	1798–1868
Fifteenth	Karma Khakhyab Dorje	1871–1922
Sixteenth	Karma Rangjung Rigpai Dorje	1924–1981

39. See Chapter 1, section on "Tibetan Buddhism."

40. For Nyingmapa, see Bdud-'jom 'jig-dral Ye-shes rDor-rje, *Gsang-chen rnying-ma'i chos-'byung*.

41. Ibid.

42. In contrast to Nyingmapa, the later schools were based on new translations of tantras and were called *sang-ngak sarma*.

43. See Chapter 1, section on "Tibetan Buddhism."

44. The four major subsects are Karma, Phagdru, Tsalpa, and Bahram. The eight minor subsects are Drigung, Taglung, Trophu, Drukpa, Yamzang, Shugseb, Martsang, and Yerpa. They are all derived from a lineage of the five great masters: Tilopa, Naropa, Marpa, Milarepa, and Gampopa, the last being the founder of Kagyupa, from which all the branches derived.

45. The "five ling" are Kundeling, Tshechogling, Dedruk, Tengyeling, and Rading.

46. This monastery was founded in A.D. 1708. For a full account of this monastery, see Joseph F. Rock, *The Na-khi Naga Cult and Related Ceremonies*, Serie Orientala, IV (Rome, 1952).

47. Lobsang Lhalungpa; also comments by Sonam Paljor Denjongpa and many others.

48. The Panchen Lama was believed to be an incarnation of Amitabha, first recognized in Panchen Lobsang Chogyen, who was a teacher of the fifth Dalai Lama.

The following is a list of the Panchen Lamas:

First	Panchen Lobsang Chogyen	1560–1662
Second	Panchen Lobsang Yeshe	1663–1737
Third	Panchen Palden Yeshe	1738–1780
Fourth	Panchen Tenpai Nyima	1782–1853
Fifth	Panchen Tenpai Aungchuk	1855–1882
Sixth	Panchen Chokyi Nyima	1883–1937
Seventh	Panchen Trinlae Lhundrup	1938–

49. An indication of the ranking of the highest incarnations has been given by Drukpa Thuksae Rinpoche, at Hemis monastery in Ladakh, who observed, on several ceremonial occasions, the seating arrangements in Lhasa in the following official order: (1) His Holiness the Dalai Lama, (2) His Holiness the Sakya Trizin, (3) the senior tutor of H.H. the Dalai Lama, (4) the junior tutor of H.H. the Dalai Lama, (5) His Holiness the Gyalwa Karmapa.

50. According to Lobsang Lhalungpa and Tashi Densapa (Barmiok Rinpoche), two such incarnations, interviewed at Rumtek, had been found in exile – from scholarly and business families – and confirmed by the Gyalwa Karmapa.

51. In the view of several informants, it was the very fusion of the two aspects of the Tibetan order that was its great strength. W. G. Kundeling, a man of great experience in government and monastic administration, felt "happy" in retrospect that he had governed on "the background of religion and religious culture." A distinguished geshe in Dharamsala held that the "union of religion with politics had been a happy one" and that even those without full religious knowledge had gained "peace and happiness because of their innate faith."

52. The majority of them were novices who had taken only the basic vows.

53. Information from Kungo Tsatora who remembered a list of 240 dzongs posted at the gate of the Kashag in Lhasa.

54. Interviews with Kungo Thubten Sangye, Kungo Thubten Nyingee, Wangdu Dorje, Kalon Liushar, Kungo Dennyertsang, Kungo Tsatora, Kalon Kundeling, and others.

55. Interviews with Kungo D. N. Tsarong, Kungo Tashi Palrae, Kungo Nawang Norbu Nornang, and others.

56. Ibid.

57. Stein, op. cit., p. 290, quotes R. Colbourn for five criteria of feudalism: "The essential relationship is that between lord and vassal; political action depends on personal agreements between a limited number of individuals, with political authority treated as a private possession; distinctions of office (military, judiciary, etc.) are relatively few; there is a pronounced hierarchical structure within the aristocracy; and land – the fief – is usually given by the lord in return for certain services." Stein believes that "by and large these criteria do hold for Tibet." We totally disagree; indeed it is clear that none of them do.

58. A further misuse of the term *feudal* derives from the unilinear Marxist-Leninist doctrinal interpretation of history, according to which all human development moves through primitive, slavery, feudal, and capitalist stages to the socialist and communist

millenium. This misuse has created a good deal of mischief in popular and pseudo-scientific writing.

59. For details see Chapter 6, section on "Local Community Leadership and Participation in Government."

60. This important issue, which has not been given much attention in previous studies, has been systematically explored in the excellent book by Barbara Nimri Aziz, *Tibetan Frontier Families* (New Delhi, 1978). Using information the author gained from the study of a cohesive group of refugees, it is a detailed anthropological study of the Tibetan frontier area of D'ing-ri as it functioned before the Chinese takeover. In the area that Aziz studied, the local term for the taxpaying group of village mi-ser was *dr'ong-pa*.

61. For details, see Chapter 6, section on "Local Community Leadership and Participation in Government." Also, some information was provided by D. N. Tsarong.

62. Interviews with Damcho Yongdu, chief steward of the Gyalwa Karmapa; Mr. Dennyertsang; W. G. Kundeling; and others.

63. A case in point was the monastery of Rudo in western Tibet, whose abbot was a high lama (not incarnated) sent from Sera. That the labrang in this case was linked to the office and not the respective lama could be seen from the fact that on the abbot's recall and replacement, the labrang was transferred to the new abbot (interview with Losang Degor).

64. See note 62; also interviews with Thubten Nyingee and Losang Degor.

Chapter 3

1. A list of the high lamas who acted as regents follows: Demo Ngawang Jampal Delek Gyatsho (1757–1777); Samati Pakshi Ngawang Tsultrim (1777–1781); Tatshag Yeshe Tenpai Gonpo (1789–1790); Samati Pakshi Ngawang Tsultrim (1790–1791); Tatshag Yeshe Tenpai Gonpo, second term (1791–1810); Demo Lobsang Thubtan Jigme Gyatsho (1811–1819); Tshemon Ling Ngawang Jampal Tsultrim (1819–1844); the Fourth Panchen Tenpai Nyima (1844–1845); Rading Ngawang Yeshe Tsultrim Gyaltshan (1845–1855); Rading Ngawang, second term (1856–1862); Shedra Wangchuk Gyalpo, a lay aristocrat (1862–1864); Dedruk Lobsang Khenrab Wangchuk (1864–1872); Tatsak Ngawang Palden Chokyi Gyaltshan (1875–1886); Demo Ngawang Lobsang Trinlae Rabgye (1886–1895); Tri Rinpoche Lobsang Gyaltshan (1904–1909); Tri Rinpoche Ngawang Lobsang Tenpa (1910–1912); Rading Thubtan Jampal Yeshe Gyaltshan (1934–1941); Takdrag Ngawang Sungrab Thutob Tenpai Gyaltshan (1941–1950).

2. See "Chart of Tibetan Polity", pp. 54–55.

3. Information about the Tseyigtsang comes from interviews with Kungo Ngawang Chozang, Kungo Dragpa Tendar, Kungo Thubten Nyingee, and Kungo Lobsang Lhalungpa.

4. See Barbara Nimri Aziz, *Tibetan Frontier Families* (New Delhi, 1978), Appendix IV. In the border area of D'ing-ri, the proportion was seventeen army recruits to sixty monk draftees. Further information from Kalon Liushar.

5. Interview with Kungo Thubten Sangye and others.

6. In the case of double appointments of monks and secular officials, the monks always held the senior rank, according to Lobsang Lhalungpa and others.

7. Rapjung denotes the first monastic ordination to embrace the dharma as a profession for life. Getsul is the first order of monkhood and is still a novice category. The vows of final ordination cannot be administered until the candidate reaches the age of twenty-one. See the Vinaya chapters of the *Kanjur*.

8. Interview with Kungo Thubten Sangye and others.

9. Interview with monk-painter Jamyang.

10. Interview with Kungo Thubten Sangye.

11. Lobsang Lhalungpa and others.

12. It is of interest to compare and contrast this role of the monk bureaucracy in Tibetan society and state with that of the Chinese gentry in imperial China. In China, the status of the scholar-gentry was obtained by passing examinations and gaining the degrees of *sheng-yuam*, *chu-jen*, and *chin-shih*, which led to lower and higher gentry status. This elite status system and its gradations may be compared with the status of novice and that of fully ordained monk, depending on the vows taken by the Tibetan monks. On all levels, monk status in Tibet, like gentry status in China, opened the door to government service. However only forty thousand of the one million to one and a half million academic degree holders in China held official offices; the large majority functioned as leaders in society. In Tibet, the disproportion was even more extreme. The limited number of only a few hundred monk officials, supplemented by a smaller number of secular officials, contrasted with the large number of perhaps half a million monks. This disproportion indicates the limitation of state control, the large area of social autonomy, and the important role played by the monk elite in the social order. The differences existing between "this-worldly" Confucianism and "other-worldly" Buddhism—and between the philosophy, attitude, and concepts of service of the monk and those of the scholar-gentry—are perhaps more obvious. For China, see Chang Chung-li, *The Chinese Gentry: Studies on Their Role in Nineteenth-Century Chinese Society* (Seattle, 1955), "Introduction" by Franz Michael.

13. Most of this information was provided by Lobsang Lhalungpa, who had extensive experience in the service of these government institutions.

14. During the rule of the last Dalai Lama, one of the Cabinet ministers was also governor of Kham in eastern Tibet, the most populous region. Kham is located on the Chinese border, and therefore it was of greatest strategic importance (interview with Kalon T. D. Yuthok; see also Chapter 4, section on "The Military").

15. In retrospect it may appear that the dominance of the serdegasum, as expressed by the voice of those monastic leaders and the occasional protest demonstrations by the monk populations, was at times a serious restraint to the Dalai Lama's authority.

Chapter 4

Much of the information in this chapter was provided by Lobsang Lhalungpa, who held many positions in this administrative system.

1. Information from Kungo Nawang Norbu Nornang. During the time of his service in the department, there were fifteen such candidates.

2. Information from Kungo Tashi Palrae.

3. Information from Kungo D. N. Tsarong.

4. See Chapter 8, section on "Reforms."

5. Regardless of sect.

6. For the sixteen-article code, see Appendix 3.

7. For a detailed analysis of the original text and the later changes of the sixteen-article code, see Gera Uray, "The Narrative of the Legislation and Organization of the Mkhas-pa'i Dga'-ston; The Origins of the Traditions Concerning Sron-brcan Sgam-po as First Legislator and Organizer of Tibet," in *Acta Orientalia Academiae Scientiarum Hungaricae*, bk. 26 (1) (Budapest, 1972). In Uray's view, "In spite of the deliberate forgeries and errors, the traditions are not far of the historical truth, as the administrative organization and codification executed shortly after Songtsan-Gampo's death and later attributed to him are but the last stages of the development during his reign" (p. 68).

8. Under the thirteenth Dalai Lama, capital punishment and mutilation were officially abolished.

9. In one case, that of Lungshar (see also Chapter 8, section on "Reforms"), the punishment of blinding was still applied for the crime of high treason. The decision was recommended by a special commission and approved by the regent Rading.

10. See Chapter 8, section on "Reforms."

11. See rNam-rgyal-dbang-'dus rGyal-rtse, *Bod-ljangs dMag-gi Lö-rgyus* [Military history of Tibet] (1977).

12. See Uray, op. cit.

13. Information from Lobsang Lhalungpa.

14. See Chapter 8, section on "Reforms."

15. Information by Lobsang Lhalungpa.

16. Ibid.

17. Of similar importance was astrology, a field in which some monks received special training. The role of the astrologer was to determine lucky and unlucky days for government activities, for journeys of high leaders, and for private occasions such as marriages, pilgrimages, etc. The astrologer was also consulted on the preparation of the calendar, a tradition still carried on in exile by Tibetan monk emigrants. Information from Gen Lodro Gyatso, monk astrologer, who stemmed from a farmer mi-ser family in Amdo. His special monastic training was based on a discourse on astrology, ascribed to the Lord Buddha, which was translated from Sanskrit into Tibetan.

Chapter 5

1. See Ram Rahul, *The Government and Politics of Tibet* (New Delhi, 1969), p. 43.

2. See David Snellgrove and Hugh Richardson, *A Cultural History of Tibet* (London, 1968), p. 295.

3. See Chapter 1, section on "Land and People."

4. In 1931–1932, the Chinese annexed the part of Derge east of the river Drichu, making use of the armed conflict between two monasteries—Dargye monastery and Beri monastery—and supporting the latter. For Muli, see Joseph F. Rock, *The Muli Kingdom* (Rome, 1956).

5. Information from Ponkha Phomatsang.

6. The other informants were Tshering Dramdul, Kunga Yonten, and others.

7. See note 6.

8. Information from Dodrupchen Rinpoche. The fierce and fanatical character ascribed to the Golokpa may be deduced from the following anecdote about the introduction of the teachings of the Drigung Kagyupa order into Golok country. Gelong Yontshang Choeden was a disciple of the Fourth Chetshang Rinpoche of Drigung Tenzin Padma Gyaltsen (b. 1770). Once Choeden was traveling in Kham, having been named lama of an establishment in Dzachukha. On the road, he met a wild and crafty Golok who was just about to do him in. The Golok asked impolitely, "Who are you?" Choeden said, "I am a student of Drigung Chamgon Padma Gyaltsen." Thereupon the Golok said, "I want a relic of this lama." Choeden then gave the Golok a piece of his master's robe. The Golok said, "I shall see whether it's a true relic or not." He tied the piece of cloth to the neck of a dog, drew his gun, and shot. The dog's skin was undamaged. As a result, the Golok became filled with great faith and made many presents to Choeden, whose reputation spread widely. (This story is found on page 18B of the history of the tantric masters [Vajracarya] of the Hermitage of Yangrigar, "Grub pa'i bsti gnas Byang gling dpal gyi Yang rir rdo rje slob dpon rim par byon pa'i rtogs brjod nor bu'i ljon shing" by Ngesdon-rgyamtsho.)

9. Information from Kalon T. D. Yuthok, Kungo Thubten Sangye, and others. This information from former officials is probably more accurate than the more theoretical figures in the table in Chapter 4, section on "The Military."

10. Information from Kungo Dennyertsang.

11. Ibid.

12. Ibid.

13. The authors used a Tibetan list of the dzongs of Kham provided by Lobsang Lhalungpa.

14. A partial list of the dzongs of Ngari follows: (1) Rutok Dzong, (2) Zhokha Dzong, (3) Tingkye Dzong, (4) Nyanang Dzong, (5) Kyedrong Dzong, (6) Purang Dzong, (7) Tsareng Dzong, (8) Dzongga Dzong, (9) Dingri Dzong, (10) Dzonga Dzong, (11) Shelkar Dzong, (12) Dzoga Dzong, (13) Zang Dzong, (14) Rintse Dzong, (15) Rongshar Dzong, (16) Dakhar Dzong, (17) Jodzong, (18) Yarto Dzong, (19) Dapa Dzong, and (20) Saga Dzong.

15. The following is a list of units located by the authors: Lhakhang Dzong, monk official; Tshona Dzong, one monk and one lay official; Digu Dzong, monk official; Nedong Dzong, one monk and one lay official; Chonggye Dzong, one monk and one lay official; Tsedon Dzong; Gongkar Dzong; Sengdzong; Lingkar Dzong; Darma Dzong; Ondzong; On Drakha Dzong; Tsethang Dzong; Phari Dzong; Lhuntse Dzong, one monk and one lay official; Sangdzong; Tsegang Dzong; Olga Dzong; Dho Dzong; Lhasol Dzong; Nangkatse Dzong; Sangngak Ch Dzong; Gyam Dzong; Tsepla Dzong; Zhoga Dzong; Jomo Dzong; Byamagang Dzong; Jayul Dzong, one monk official; Gyatsa Dzong; Chökhorgyal Zhika, one lay official; Drach Zhika, one lay official; Dranang Zhika; Dol Zhika, lay official; Phodrang, lay official; Draktrend Zhika, lay official; Samye Dzong, monk official; Zhae Zhika, lay official; Chokhorgyal Zhika, lay official. In addition, there were several dzongs along the southern border, administered by monk officials, that have not yet been located.

16. See Chapter 1, section on "Land and People."

17. See R. A. Stein, *Tibetan Civilization*, trans. S. Driver (Stanford, 1972), p. 28; Snellgrove and Richardson, op. cit., p. 23.

18. A British military campaign, to enforce British relations with Tibet (see H. E. Richardson, *A Short History of Tibet* [New York, 1962], pp. 84–89).

19. Information from Matrul Rinpoche.

20. See Chapter 1, section on "Tibetan Buddhism."

21. Many copies of the prints from these woodblocks were sent by the fourteenth Dalai Lama to Sikkim shortly before the Chinese invasion and the destruction of this and most other monasteries.

22. Its abbot and many monks escaped to India and have established there, along with other Bon priests and laymen, a Bon religious and educational center near Simla.

23. Information from Lobsang Lhalungpa.

24. Comment by Ngakcho Ngawang Jigme.

Chapter 6

1. Interviews with Kungo Thubten Nyingee, Kungo Ngakcho Ngawang Jigme, and Kungo Ngawang Chozang. Kungo Nyingee was sent by the Tseyigtsang to Daklha Gampo, the monastery of Gampopa, the founder of the Kagyupa order, in Dakpo Province, to repair the monastery. Later he supervised sixteen monasteries of all sects in Gyantse, appointing managers from elected candidates, settling intermonastic conflicts, and checking on questions of corruption. Kungo Ngakcho Ngawang Jigme worked in the Tseyigtsang and confirmed that that office was indeed responsible for all sects. Kungo Ngawang Chozang detailed the support given by the Tseyigtsang to all sects.

2. The abbot may or may not have been an incarnation.

3. Information by Kungo Ngawang Chozang, who explained that in some monasteries in Lhasa the four treasurers were selected from monks coming from Mongolia, Kham, Chamdo, and Changtang because it was believed that they would be able to handle local economic affairs more objectively and that they would also be more attuned to monks who stemmed from those areas.

4. This fact, often related, was asserted also by H.H. the Sakya Trizin.

5. According to information by H.H. the Sakya Trizin and a Sakya abbot, Khenpo Abey, fifty aristocratic families provided secular officials, who were trained in a special school. The administration consisted of one minister, four secretaries, and a staff of about thirty people. Lhasa was recognized as the central government, and Sakya administered only local disputes. A percentage of the tax was sent to Lhasa, which also controlled the local militia.

6. These well-known families were Sampho, Lhalu, Phunkhang, Yuthok, Langdun, and Taglha.

7. This caste, which has been described in Barbara Nimri Aziz, *Tibetan Frontier Families* (New Delhi, 1978), pp. 56–66, appears to have been recognized as a special social stratum only in the South Tibetan area of D'ing-ri, the location of Aziz's study.

The stratum consisted chiefly of butchers, beggars, and a potential criminal element. Although the beggars were obviously an established group in Buddhist society, we have found no such social categorization for other parts of Tibet.

8. Ibid., see table on p. 68.

9. See cases by Dieter Schuh in *Urkunden und Sendschreiben aus Zentraltibet, Ladakh, and Zanskar* (St.Augustin, 1976).

10. Kungo George Taring, in commenting on the relationship between landlord and the tral-pa farmer, stated simply that "if the treatment was not proper, the farmer would leave."

11. See Schuh, op. cit.

12. Information from Kungo D. N. Tsarong and others.

13. For the position of tral-pa and mi-ser in general, their freedom of economic action, and their accumulation of wealth, information is from interviews with Angi, Kungo George Taring, Angam from Kham, Mrs. Thachoe Nayang, Mrs. Dennyertsang, Mrs. Dolma Chozom Shatsang from Kham, Phomatsang from Derge, Tshering Dramdul from Derge, Kalon W. G. Kundeling, and others. See also Tashi Andrugtsang, *Four Rivers, Six Ranges* (Delhi, 1973), pp. 28–29.

14. See note 13.

15. With few exceptions, all monk officials interviewed came from mi-ser families. Kalon W. G. Kundeling, one of the most influential administrators, was, for instance, of dü-chung origin. See also Aziz, op. cit., p. 71.

16. See Aziz, op. cit.

17. Kungo Thubten Sangye made the point that trade flourished because "in Tibet, the merchants felt very secure."

18. For the chief town of Gang-gar in D'ing-ri, Aziz gives a breakdown of 40 percent tsong-pa, 40 percent dü-chung, 8 percent Nepali traders, 1 percent monks, 1 percent aristocrats, and a (high) 10 percent of yawa. In her words (op. cit., p. 35), "The town attracted people of all classes: wealthy independent traders and administrators, retired military and government officers, other officials on business, artisans, thieves, run-away servants and debtors" as well as temporary pilgrims and other visitors.

19. How ingrained the Western interpretation of this system as serfdom has become can be seen in Schuh's study of documents of mi-bog obtained from refugee families in India (Schuh, op. cit.). The documents relating to mi-bog payments for various occasions do not even contain the terms mi-ser or tral-pa in their Tibetan originals, but in the German version, Schuh inserted the word *Leibeigener* in each case, obviously assuming that this expressed properly the status of the tenant family member given permission to leave in exchange for paying the mi-bog.

20. Wangdu Dorje mentioned sixteen *thongken* (another term for genpo), who were partly elected and partly appointed by the manager of the Surkhang estates and formed "the link between the staff and the people." They oversaw land distribution, irrigation, and other common tasks.

21. All former dzongpon and estate managers commented on these meetings, which were called by them or sometimes by the representatives themselves, usually once a year and also on special occasions. These yearly meetings were held throughout the regular Lhasa administrative areas and also in eastern Kham and the Golok area. In Sakya, these meetings were called *thume* (information from Khenpo Abey).

22. Information from Wangdu Dorje and Kungo Thubten Nyingee.

23. Information from Kalon Liushar and others.

24. Information from Kungo George Taring.

25. Information from Kungo Tashi Palrae, Kungo Thubten Nyingee, and others.

26. According to Mr. and Mrs. Tshellog, the people of Kham contributed at least 40 percent of their yearly income to the monasteries. According to Kungo George Taring and Kungo D. N. Tsarong, up to one-half of estate or trade income was given to the church.

27. See Aziz, op. cit., for a description of the relationship between ser-kyim villages and lay villages on a regular interdependent basis in the D'ing-ri region. According to her, 20 percent of the rural population in the region formed such religious village communities. The religious practitioners could be either the men or the women in the ser-kyim families. Training and tradition were carried on by each generation. Marriage was largely within the ser-kyim villages (pp. 76 ff.; chart on p. 77).

28. The other two were the *Abhidharma Pitaka*—doctrine of metaphysics—and the *Sutra Pitaka*—doctrine of methods of liberation, meditation, etc.

29. See interesting data in Aziz, op. cit., pp. 132–161.

30. See R. A. Stein, *Tibetan Civilization*, trans. S. Driver (Stanford, 1971), pp. 101 ff., for such court intrigues. Many such stories appear also in the romantic tales of Tibetan folklore.

31. Interview with Kungo D. N. Tsarong.

32. In some Black Forest farmer families in Germany, the system was one of ultimogenitur.

33. The importance of the uncle-nephew relationship was much broader than in the limited cases of polyandry. As many accounts indicate, the uncle's support of the nephew in his career, particularly if the uncle or the nephew or both were monks, was generally practiced and expected.

34. Pholha, a male deity; Dralha, a deity of war; Soklha, a deity of life; Molha and Zhanglha, deities of kinsmen. The collective name for the five deities is *ghowai lhanga* (the "five indwelling deities").

35. Among many assertions of the importance of the shrines and the strength of religious belief was a vigorous comment by Mrs. Dolma Chozom Shatsang, for whom any question about her faith was incomprehensible. The strong faith of the Lhasa aristocracy in the importance of the shrines was indicated by the accounts of D. N. Tsarong, his wife, and many others.

36. See Chapter 1, section on "Tibetan Buddhism."

37. It is here where the ser-kyim practitioners, referred to earlier, had their chief role.

Chapter 7

1. See Chapter 1, section on "Land and People."

2. The figures vary greatly. Among the serious authors, H. E. Richardson, *A Short History of Tibet* (New York, 1962), p. 14, estimates one-eighth of the population, presumably 25 percent of the male population, entered monasteries. Tsepon W. D. Shakabpa, *Tibetan Political History* (New Haven, 1967), writes of 18 percent of the whole population, presumably 36 percent of the male population. Sir Charles Bell, *The People of Tibet* (Oxford, 1928), estimates a broad range of two hundred thousand

to five hundred thousand monks in all of Tibet, which is at best a very sweeping and vague figure. The only actual counting was done by a Chinese anthropologist in pre-Communist time in the Chinese region of Derge. His figure is a rather high 33.5 percent of the population of that region (see Li An-che, "Derge: A Study of Tibetan Population," *Southwestern Journal of Anthropology*, 3:4 [Winter 1947]).

3. Information by Kungo D. N. Tsarong and Kalon Tashi Dondrup Yuthok. See also Richardson, op. cit., p. 14.

4. Although varying in detail, all of our informants were uniformly of the opinion that literacy was high: that all monks and nuns were literate; for the secular rural population, the average estimate was that 20 percent of the people were literate; for the urban population, the average estimate was that 66 percent were literate (information from Kungo Thubten Sangye, Kungo Ngakcho Ngawang Jigme, Wangdu Dorje, Kalon Liushar, and Kungo Tashi Palrae). Kungo George Taring assumed a two-thirds literacy of his estates at Gyantse, and a similar estimate of two-thirds was given by Tshering Dramdul for Derge, with its high population of craftsmen.

5. Information on private teachers was given by Kungo Lobsang Lhalungpa, Kungo Thubten Sangye, Kungo Ngawang Chozang, Wangdu Dorje, Kalon Liushar, Mrs. Tsarong, Kungo Jampa Tsondru, and others.

6. Same informants as in note 5.

7. According to Rabden Chazotsang, in the past, the religious texts were simply memorized and chanted. At the modern school in Mussoorie, there is a new emphasis on explaining the meaning of religous texts at an early stage.

8. It was a prayer of protection from the "eight fears," which included protection from physical harm—such as done by robbers or fire—and also from spiritual harm—such as done by the vices of envy (symbolized by the snake), of aggressiveness (symbolized by the lion), of narrow-minded ignorance (symbolized by the bull), of miserliness, or of clinging to objects and people of the physical world—and lastly for protection from internal conflicts, symbolized by the image of "demons out to devour people."

9. An English translation of the *Dolmai Topa* has been provided by Stephen Byer in *The Cult of Tara* (Berkeley, 1973).

10. See Appendix 2.

11. All of our monk informants were in agreement on such prior learning in early childhood.

12. Information from Kalon Liushar, Kungo D. N. Tsarong, and others.

13. Estimated by Kungo Thubten Sangye and confirmed by others.

14. A classic case is that of Kalon W. G. Kundeling.

15. For the monk, the performance of these sacred dances was a religious rite that served to provide enlightenment and drive out evil. The chief ritual dancer represented one tantric deity accompanied by surrounding deities. The performing monks were so attuned to their parts that no special preparation (such as going into trance) was required as conditioning for each occasion. As one former ritual monk dancer, Juchen Thubten (presently minister of education in Dharamsala), explained it, "I felt that by following the rituals and performing them as taught to me, living each role as well as I could, I would subconsciously affect the people and contribute to enlightenment."

Chapter 8

1. See E. Michael Mendelson, *Sangha and State in Burma: A Study of Monastic Sectarianism and Its Leadership* (Ithaca and London, 1975), p. 13.

2. Information from Kungo D. N. Tsarong, Kalon Tashi Dondrup Yuthok, and others.

3. Information on the life of Dasang Damdul Tsarong from Kungo D. N. Tsarong and Kungo Thubten Sangye; also from an interview with Kalon Tashi Dondrup Yuthok. See also Rinchen Dolma Taring, *Daughter of Tibet* (London, 1970), which contains a family tree of the Tsarong family. For the role of Tsarong, see Tsepon W. D. Shakabpa, *Tibet: A Political History* (New Haven, 1967), pp. 241, 264–265, 274–275; Ram Rahul, *The Government and Politics of Tibet* (New Delhi, 1969), pp. 58–59, 64–65, 69–70. For the problem of the conflict between monastic leaders and reformers, between "monk and noble," see H. E. Richardson, *A Short History of Tibet* (New York, 1962), pp. 130–131.

4. See Shakabpa, op. cit., p. 229.

5. Ibid., p. 239.

6. Tsarong eventually married another, younger daughter of the former Tsarong. See the Tsarong family tree in Taring, op. cit.

7. See Shakabpa, op. cit., p. 259.

8. Ibid., p. 264.

9. The same reaction occurred in the 1940s against a new attempt to establish an English school in Lhasa. But there was no objection to the training of Tibetan students in English schools in India under a program administered by Lobsang Lhalungpa.

10. Shakabpa, op. cit., p. 264.

11. Information from Kalon Tashi Dondrup Yuthok.

12. Shakabpa, op. cit., p. 264.

13. See reference to this incident in Richardson, op. cit., p. 130.

14. In the words of a Tibetan military historian: "due to the demand by the military leaders for a large increase in their representation in the Great Assembly, His Holiness advised and cautioned them." The removal of a cabinet minister (Khemey) and two colonels (generals according to other information) and the demotion of Tsarong were punishment for "their unrestrained demands" (see rNam-rgyal-dbang-'dus rGyal-rtse, *Bod-ljongs dMag-gi Lö-rgyus* [Military history of Tibet] [1977]).

15. See Shakabpa, op. cit., pp. 264–265.

16. Ibid.

17. See Richardson, op. cit., p. 130.

18. Information from Kalon Tashi Dondrup Yuthok.

19. For the reason why the Dalai Lama felt that he had to draw back from outside influence, see Richardson, op. cit., p. 131.

20. Comment by Lobsang Lhalungpa.

21. Information from Kalon Tashi Dundrup Yuthok.

22. Comment by Kungo Ngawang Chozang.

23. See Richardson, op. cit., p. 130.

24. Ibid. That there was, in principle, no objection to modernization, including the military strengthening, was indicated by all testimony and was also pointed out by the rather conservative Geshe Gomo Rimpoche. It was especially stressed by Kalon Tashi Dondrup Yuthok.

25. See Shakabpa, op. cit., p. 274.

26. Information from Kungo D. N. Tsarong.

27. See Appendix 1 for the thirteenth Dalai Lama's last testament.

28. See Richardson, op. cit., p. 130.

29. See Ram Rahul, op. cit., p. 72. For a full translation of the thirteenth Dalai Lama's last testament, see Appendix 1.

30. See Appendix 1.

31. Information from and translation by Lobsang Lhalungpa.

32. What form this could have taken is entirely a matter of speculation. What comes to mind might have been the establishment of a "department of defense" under the Kashag, similar to the other most important secular department, the Tsikhang. Such a department could have been headed by a high monk official who, like the governor of Kham, could have been a member of the Kashag. Under such a department, professional military commanders, headed by a chief of staff could have provided the military expertise. Such an arrangement, fitting the professional military into the political system, could also have served to combine the professional military with the militia and volunteer forces. It might not have prevented conflicts of views, but it could at least have overcome the lack of communication between the domestically oriented monk bureaucracy and the Dalai Lama's views of the strategic necessities.

33. The lack of cooperation was commented upon, among others, by the Gyalwa Karmapa.

34. See Melvyn C. Goldstein, "Ethnogenesis and Resource Competition Among Tibetan Refugees in South India: A New Face to the Indo-Tibetan Interface," in *Himalayan Anthropology: The Indo-Tibetan Interface*, ed. James F. Fisher (The Hague and Paris, 1978), pp. 395–420. See also Melvyn Goldstein's thesis on the same settlements.

35. Ibid., p. 404.

36. Ibid.

37. Ibid.

38. The Dharamsala government financially supports some Nyingmapa and even Bon monasteries.

Selected Bibliography

Western Texts

Books

Andrugtsang, Tashi. *Four Rivers, Six Ranges*. Delhi, 1973.

Aziz, Barbara Nimri. *Tibetan Frontier Families*. New Delhi, 1978.

Basham, A. L. *The Wonder That Was India*. New York, 1954.

Bell, Charles. *Tibet, Past and Present*. Oxford, 1924.

———. *The People of Tibet*. Oxford, 1928.

———. *The Religion of Tibet*. Oxford, 1937.

———. *The Portrait of the Dalai Lama*. Oxford, 1968.

Bendix, Reinhard. *Max Weber: An Intellectual Portrait*. New York, 1962.

Carasco, Pedro. *Land and Policy of Tibet*. Seattle, 1959.

Chang, Chung-li. *The Chinese Gentry: Studies on Their Role in Nineteenth-Century Chinese Society*. Introduction by Franz Michael. Seattle, 1955.

Dalai Lama, fourteenth. *My Land and My People*. New York, 1962.

———. *The Buddhism of Tibet and the Key to the Middle Way*. New York, 1974.

Das, Sarat Chandra. *Contributions on the Religious History of Tibet*. New Delhi, 1970.

Harrer, Heinrich. *Seven Years in Tibet*. London, 1953.

Hoffman, Helmut. *The Religions of Tibet*. Translated by Edward Fitzgerald. London, 1961.

Karmapa: The Black Hat of Tibet. Compiled by Nik Douglas and Meryl White. London, 1976.

Lhalungpa, Lobsang. *Life of Milarepa*. New York, 1977.

Norbu, Thubten Jigme, and Colin Turnbull. *Tibet: Its History, Religion, and People*. London, 1969.

Rahul, Ram. *The Government and Politics of Tibet*. New Delhi, 1969.

Richardson, Hugh E. *A Short History of Tibet*. New York, 1962.

———. *Tibet and Its History*. London, 1962.

Rock, Joseph F. *The Ancient Na-khi Kingdom of Southwest China*. 2 vols. Cambridge, 1947.

———. *The Na-khi Naga Cult and Related Ceremonies*. Rome, 1952.

———. *The Muli Kingdom*. Rome, 1956.

Rockhill, W. W. *Diary of a Journey Through Mongolia and Tibet in 1891–2*. Washington, D.C., 1894.

_____ . *Notes on the Ethnology of Tibet*. Washington, D.C., 1895.

Schuh, Dieter. *Urkunden und Sendschreiben aus Zentraltibet, Ladakh, und Zanskar*. St. Augustin, Germany, 1976.

Shakabpa, Tsepon W. D. *Tibet: A Political History*. New Haven and London, 1967.

Shen, Tsing-lien and Liu Shen-chi. *Tibet and the Tibetans*. Stanford, Calif., 1953.

Snellgrove, David. *The Nine Ways of Bön*. Boulder, 1980.

Snellgrove, David and Hugh Richardson. *A Cultural History of Tibet*. London, 1968.

Stein, R. A. *Tibetan Civilization*. Translated by S. Driver. Stanford, 1972.

Taring, Rinchen Dolma. *Daughter of Tibet*. London and New Delhi, 1970.

Tucci, Giuseppe. *Tibetan Painted Scrolls*. Rome, 1949.

Waddell, L. Austine. *Buddhism and Lamaism of Tibet*. Cambridge, 1894; London, 1895; reprinted New Delhi, 1979.

Weber, Max. *The Religion of India: The Sociology of Hinduism and Buddhism*. Translated by Hans Gerth and Don Martindale. Glencoe, Ill., 1958. Volume 2 of *Gesammelte Aufsaetze zur Religionssoziologie*. Tübingen, 1922–1923.

_____ . *The Theory of Social and Economic Organization*. Translated by A. M. Henderson and Talcott Parsons. Glencoe, Ill., 1964.

_____ . *Economy and Society: An Outline of Interpretive Sociology*. Edited by Guenther Roth and Claus Wittich. New York, 1968.

Zaehner, R. C., ed. *The Concise Encyclopedia of Living Faiths*. Chapters 7a and 7b by L. B. Horner and Edward Conze. Boston, 1957.

Articles

Demiéville, M. "Concile de Lhasa." *Journal Asiatique* (1975).

Goldstein, Melvyn C. "Ethnogenesis and Resource Competition Among Tibetan Refugees in South India: A New Face to the Indo-Tibetan Interface." In *Himalayan Anthropology: The Indo-Tibetan Interface*. Edited by James F. Fisher. The Hague and Paris, 1978.

Imaeda, Yoshiro. "Documents Tibétains de Touen-Houang concernant le Concile du Tibet." *Journal Asiatique* (1975).

Lhalungpa, Lobsang. "The Mandala: An Introduction." Burnaby Art Gallery with Talon Books. Vancouver, 1973.

_____ . "Bön." *Religious Culture of Tibet* 1:3–4 (Autumn 1976).

_____ . "The Child Incarnate." *Parabola* 4:3 (1980).

_____ . "Tibetan Music, Sacred and Secular." *Journal of Religions* (London).

Li An-che. "Derge: A Study of Tibetan Population." *Southwestern Journal of Anthropology* 3:4 (Winter 1947).

MacDonald, Adriane. "Essai sur la formation et l'emploi des mythes politiques dans la religion royale de Scronbcan Sgam-po." In *Etudes Tibetaines*. Dediées a la memoire de Marcelle Lallu. Paris, 1971.

Miller, Roy A. "Thon-mi Sambhota and His Grammatical Treatises" and "Once More on Thon-mi Sambhota and His Grammatical Treatises." In *Studies in the*

History of Linguistics. Amsterdam Studies in the Theory and History of the Linguistic Science III. Vol. 6. Amsterdam, 1976.

Uray, Gera. "The Narrative of the Legislation and Organization of the Mkhas-pa'i Dga'-ston: The Origins of the Traditions Concerning Sron-brcan Scam-po as First Legislator and Organizer of Tibet." In *Acta Orientalia Academiae Scientiarum Hungaricae*, bk. 26 (1). Budapest, 1972.

Wylie, Turrell. "Some Political Factors in the Early History of Tibetan Buddhism." Paper read at the University of Wisconsin, Madison, August 1976.

Tibetan Texts

(Each name and title is first transliterated and then spelled phonetically.)

A-myes-zhabs Kun-dga' bsod-nam (Amezhab Kunga Sonam). *Sa-sKya'i gdung-rabs chen-po rin-chen bang-mdzod (Sakyai dungrab chenpo rinchen bangzö)* [The treasure house: genealogy of the ruling Sakya families].

Bdud-'jom 'jig-dral Ye-shes rDor-rje (Dujom Jigdral Yeshe Dorje). *Gsang-chen rnying-ma'i chos-byung (Sangchen nyingmai chöjung)* [History of the ancient mystic order].

Bskal-bzang rGya-mtsho (Kalzang Gyatsho). *Gsung-'bum (Sungbum)* [Collected works of the seventh Dalai Lama]. 1975.

Bu-ston Rinchen-grub (Buton Rinchen-drub). *Gsung-rab rinpoche'i dzod (Sungrab rinpochei-dzö)* [The treasure of scriptures: history of Buddhism in India].

DKa-chen ye-shes rGyal-mtshan (Kachen Yeshe Gyaltshen). *Lam-rim bla-ma brgyud-pa'i rnam-Thar (Lamrim lama gyupai namThar)* [The hagiography of the Lamrim lineage (Lamrim-stages to enlightenment)].

'Gos Lo-tsa-ba gZhon-nu-dpal (Gö Lotsawa Zhonnupal). *Deb-Ther sngon-po (DebTher ngonpo)* [History of Tibetan Buddhism (the Blue Annal)].

mKhas-grub dGe-legs dPal-bzang (Khedrub Gelek Palzang). *Dad-pa'i 'jug-ngogs (Depai jukngok)*. [The entrance to faith: life and liberation of Tsongkapa].

Nga-dbang bLo-bzang rGya-mtsho (Ngawang Lozang Gyatsho, the fifth Dalai Lama). *Du-Ku-La'i gos-bzang (DuKulei gözang)* [The collected works of the fifth Dalai Lama]. Xylograph, 4 vols.

Nges-don rGya-mtsho (Ngedon Gyatsho). *Grub-pa'i bsti-gnas byang-Ling dpal-gyi yang-rir rdo-rje slob-dpon rim-par byon-pa'i rtogs-bjod nor-bu'i ljon-shing (Drubpai Tiney jangling palgyi yangrir dorje lobpon rimpar jonpai togjo norbui jongshing)* [The hagiography of the abbots of Jangling Palgyi Yangri].

Padmasambhava. *Pad-ma bKa'-thang (Pema Kathang)* [An account of Padmasambhava and the Samye monastery].

Rig-'dzin Tshe-dbang Norbu (Rigzin Tshewang Norbu). *Gsung-'bum (Sungbum)* [Collected works].

rNam-rgyal dbang-'dus rGyal-rtse (Namgyal Wangdu Gyaltse). *Bod'ljongs dMag-gi Lö-rgyus (Böjong Makgyi Logyu)* [Military history of Tibet]. 1977.

Sa-skya bSod-nam rGyal-mtshan (Sakya Sonam Gyatshen). *rGyal-rabs gSal-ba'i me-*

long (Gyalrab salwai melong) [The history of the Tibetan kings].

Srong-btsan sgam-po (Songtsen Gampo). *Mani 'Ka'-'bum (Mani Kabum)* [The mystic teachings of the mani-mantra (whose original source was attributed to Songtsen Gampo)]. Quoted in Dpa-bo gtsug-lag (Pawo Tsuglak). *Dga-ston (Gaton)* [A history of the Tibetan Buddhism].

Sumpa mKhan-po Yeshes dPal-'jor (Sumpa Khenpo Yeshe Paljor). *Gangs-chan bod-yul-du dam-chos rin-chen byung-tshul Dpag-bsam Ljon-bzang (Jangchan Boyul-du dam-cho rinchen jungTshul Pagsam Jonzang)* [How Buddhism was established in Tibet]. Varanasi, India, 1963.

Tham-deb Long-ba'i dmigs-bu (Thamdeb Longwai Migbu) [The record of the seals of the Dalai Lamas and regents]. A manuscript in the Tseyigtsang, Potala Palace.

Tshal-pa Kun-dga rDor-rje (Tshalpa Kungo Dorje). *Deb-Ther dMar-po (DebTher Marpo)* [History of Tibet (the Red Annal)].

Principal Informants

In Dharamsala

Kungo Ngawang Chozang: monk official from farmer mi-ser family; former staff member of Tseyigtsang

Wangdu Dorje: former administrator of Surkhang estates from farmer mi-ser family; now Cabinet minister of the exile government in Dharamsala

Geshe Gomo Rinpoche: monastic teacher from mi-ser family

Kungo Ngakcho Ngawang Jigme: monk official from farmer mi-ser family; former staff member of Tseyigtsang and the reform commission

Kalon Liushar: monk official from farmer mi-ser family; former dzongpon and Cabinet minister

Kungo Thubten Nyingee: monk official from farmer mi-ser family; formerly monastic administrator and dzongpon, now Cabinet minister

Kungo Tashi Palrae: aristocrat; former mayor of Lhasa

Kungo Thubten Sangye: monk official from well-to-do mi-ser family of Gongardzong, south of Lhasa; former dzongpon in Kham and tax collector in Phagri

Kungo Dragpa Tendar: monk official from mi-ser family; former staff member of Tseyigtsang

In Mussoorie

Mr. Rabden Chazotsang: principal of the Central Tibetan School, Happy Valley, Mussoorie

Mrs. Khando Chazotsang: wife of the above and niece of H.H. the Dalai Lama; secretary of the Tibetan Homes Foundation, Happy Valley, Mussoorie

Kungo Dennyertsang: monk official from well-to-do mi-ser family; formerly monastic administrator and dzongpon

Mrs. Dennyertsang: wife of the above (second marriage) from well-to-do mi-ser family; housewife and businesswoman

Gen Lodro Gyatso: monk astrologer from mi-ser family

Jamyang: monk and painting master from professional middle-class painter's family of ten generations of artists

Mrs. Thachoe Nayang: from well-to-do mi-ser family; married to an aristocrat, housewife

Mrs. Dolma Chozom Shatsang: from eastern Tibetan (Khampa) farmer family; housewife and businesswoman

Kungo Tsatora: monk official from middle-class family in Lhasa; formerly provincial tax collector and dzongpon

Mr. Tshellog: nomad gopa from Amdo Tashi Gomang; trader

Mrs. Tshellog: housewife

In Rajpur

Khenpo Abey: abbot of Sakya monastery

Kalon W. G. Kundeling: monk official from dü-chung family; former administrator of Kundeling labrang and estates

Kungo Nawang Norbu Nornang: Lhasa aristocrat; former salt tax collector and dzongpon

Kungo Jigme Taring: Lhasa aristocrat; former head of the Treasury of Labrang at Lhasa, for many years principal of the Central Tibetan School, Happy Valley, Mussoorie

Rinchen Dolma Taring: Lhasa aristocrat and daughter of Tsarong family; once married to Kalon D. D. Tsarong, later married the above Kungo Jigme Taring, author of *Daughter of Tibet* and for many years secretary of the Tibetan Homes Foundation, Happy Valley, Mussoorie

Kalon Juchen Thubten: from aristocratic family in Derge; monk official, ritual dancer, now Cabinet minister

His Holiness Sakya Trizin: head of the Sakya sect and high incarnation

In Gangtok

Angam: Khampa nomad and former ponka; former Khampa resistance leader

Angi: Khampa farmer from well-to-do landowner family; hotel owner in Gangtok

Ponkha Phomatsang: Khampa refugee leader

Dodrupchen Rinpoche: from well-to-do farmer family in eastern Tibet; former head of monastery in Golok

Kungo George Taring: Lhasa aristocrat; former Gyantse estate manager

Kungo Phuntsok Tashi: brother-in-law of H.H. the Dalai Lama; former commander of the bodyguard

Kungo Yonten: from Derge mi-ser family; former monk administrator and monastic trader

In Rumtek

His Holiness Gyalwa Karmapa: highest incarnation of and head of the Kagyupa sect

Jamgon Kongtrul Rinpoche: high incarnation of Kagyupa sect from well-to-do Khampa family

Damcho Yongdu: *chakdzo* ("steward") of Gyalwa Karmapa

In Ladakh

Losang Degor: from mi-ser family; former monk administrator

Tshering Dramdul: farmer from Derge

Kungo Jampa Tsondru: monk official from government mi-ser family; former salt tax collector, now manager of a Tibetan refugee camp

In United States

Kungo D. N. Tsarong: Lhasa aristocrat and son of Kalon D. D. Tsarong; businessman

Mrs. Dorje Yuthok: daughter of aristocratic Surkhang family; former wife of Kalon T. D. Yuthok

Kalon Tashi Dondrup Yuthok: Lhasa aristocrat; former governor of Kham

Index

LOOK FOR BARCODE

←